SOUTHPORT

in the age of the tram

A lovely animated shot at the Smedley terminus on Trafalgar Road, Birkdale, in the evening sunshine in about 1930. Car 9 has just arrived on route 8 from the Botanic Gardens and two intending passengers approach it as others are alighting. This ex-Company open-top car has been rebuilt by the Corporation, totally enclosed and mounted on Brill bogies. It has run right to the end of the track at the corner of Grosvenor Road. *E. N. Osborne, courtesy of Online Transport Archive*

SOUTHPORT
in the age of the tram

James Dean & Cedric Greenwood

·THE NOSTALGIA OF BRITAIN·
from
The NOSTALGIA Collection

First published in 2008
British Library Cataloguing in
Publication Data
A catalogue record for this book is
available from the British Library.
ISBN 978 1 85794 304 7

Silver Link Publishing Ltd
The Trundle
Ringstead Road
Great Addington
Kettering
Northants NN14 4BW

Tel/Fax: 01536 330588
email: sales@nostalgiacollection.com
Website: www.nostalgiacollection.com

Printed and bound in the
Czech Republic

A Silver Link book
from
The NOSTALGIA *Collection*

BIBLIOGRAPHY

The following is a list of publications consulted
for information:

Southport Town Council minutes of
  proceedings
Southport Visiter and *Southport Guardian*
  newspapers

Bailey, Francis *A History of Southport* (1955)
Barlow, A. *The Southport Gasworks Railway*
Bland, E. *Annals of Southport* (1903)
Brough, Harold *What the Butler Saw – and
  All That: a Pictorial History of Southport's
  Historic Pier* (2006)
Duncan, W. W. *Duncan's Manual of British
  and Foreign Tramway Companies, 1886-
  1899*
Garcke, Emile *Manual of Electrical
  Undertakings, 1900-1902*
Greenwood, Cedric *Thatch, Towers and
  Colonnades: the Story of Architecture in
  Southport* (1971, revised 1990)
Randall, D. *Fifty Years a Busman* (1970)
Rider, John Hall *Electric Traction* (1903)
Tarbuck, Joan *Southport As It Was* (1971)
Turner, Brian *Circular Tour: Seaside Pleasure
  Riding by Tram* (includes chapter on
  Southport's toastrack tours) (1999)

Turner, K. *Pier Railways* (1972)

BET Monthly Gazette, October 1903: report
  on the new demi-car
The Electrical Review, 8 August 1902: report
  of the opening of the Birkdale District
  Electric Supply Company
Modern Tramway magazine, April and May
  1941: 'Electric Tramways In Southport',
  article by Henry B. Priestley
  April, 1969: letter about Blowick coal
  tramway by J. B. Horne
  July 1969: 'Crossing the Ribble', article by
  A. Winstan Bond
  November, 1970: 'Southport Pier
  Tramway', article by A. Winstan Bond
The Short Axle, magazine of the West
  Lancashire Light Railway Association,
  Spring 1988
Tramway & Railway World magazine,
  August and September 1901: reports of the
  opening of the Southport Tramways
  Company
Tramway Review magazine, Nos 124 and
  125, 1985: 'The Tramways of Southport',
  article by Henry B. Priestley

CONTENTS

ACKNOWLEDGEMENTS

James Dean's unfinished manuscript has been edited and completed by Cedric Greenwood, of Holt, Norfolk, formerly of the *Southport Visiter*, with contributions from Graham Fairhurst, of Telford, formerly of Southport Borough Engineer's Department, and two north-west transport historians and authors, T. B. Maund, of Oxton, and Ron Phillips, of Grappenhall.

Thanks are due to the Local History Librarian, Matthew Tinker, and other reference library staff at the Atkinson Library, Southport, for patiently plying the researchers with Council minutes, newspaper files and Southport directories and guide books contemporary with the tramways. Thanks are also due to Roger Benton and Chris Gent at the library of the National Tramway Museum, Crich, for supplying photocopies of relevant reports in the tramway trade press of the period 1886-1903 and copies of pictures in the library collection. Extracts from the *Southport Visiter* in Appendix 3 are reproduced by kind permission of Trinity Mirror North West & North Wales Ltd.

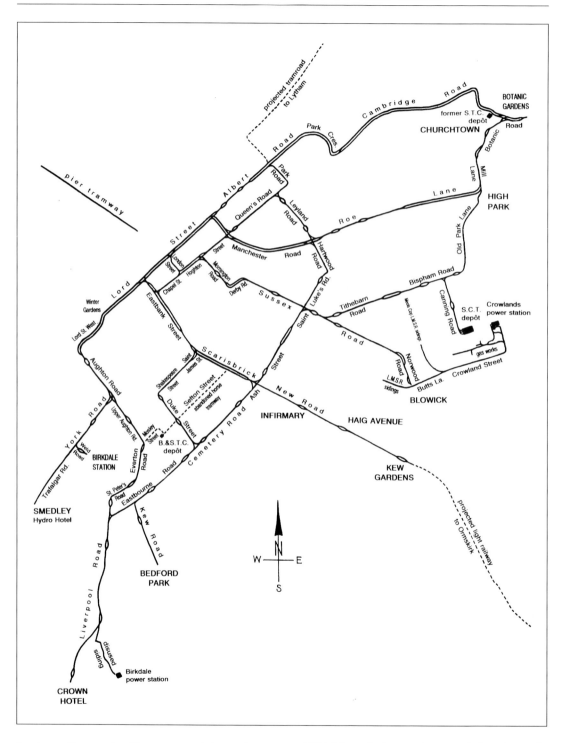

Southport Corporation Tramways at their maximum extent, 1928. The single track shown in Eastbank Street and Albert Road was interlaced double track, effectively single. The local authority boundary between Southport and Birkdale until 1912 ran in a straight line diagonally across the map from Lord Street West through Mosley Street and the point where Cemetery Road meets Eastbourne Road. *Cedric Greenwood*

INTRODUCTION

Southport was founded as a sea-bathing resort on the dune-fringed coast of the rural south-west Lancashire plain in 1798. At first it catered mainly for visitors who came by canal from Liverpool and Manchester, changing at Scarisbrick to horse-drawn coaches operated by Southport hotels 'only in the bathing season'. With the opening of the railways from Liverpool in 1848 and Manchester in 1854, Southport became a dormitory town and a place of retirement for businessmen from those cities. As many as five railway routes converged on Southport between 1848 and 1887 and put the town on the map as one of Britain's premier seaside resorts.

Southport and Birkdale were planned by the lords of three manors that met here: Charles Scarisbrick, Charles Hesketh and Thomas Weld-Blundell. They laid out wide, straight streets intersecting at right angles, privately developed with fine villas and commercial and public buildings, many of which are gems of the Regency, Victorian and Edwardian periods. The wide, level, tree-lined streets made Southport an ideal place for retirement and convalescence and facilitated the spread of street railways, or tramways, from 1873 onward, which helped to develop the town by giving mobility to the majority of residents and visitors who did not own a horse and carriage.

The tramways were an important part of local history that has been virtually ignored by existing local history books, so I have tried to compile a book to interest readers of local history and social history as well as transport history. The tram helped to develop our towns by providing smooth travel on rough, dusty roads at rock-bottom fares, giving people without their own carriages a new freedom to live further from their work and to travel for leisure to the theatres and parks. Electric traction brought a reliable form of mechanisation and Southport, thanks to its bosky nature, felt able to adopt the normal, side-running, overhead trolley system and merge the poles and wires against the ample cover of trees without resorting to cable, conduit or surface contact traction to conserve the amenities. As the tram was patronised mainly by those who could not afford their own carriages, it was generally stigmatised as the working man's carriage. There were exceptions, such as the well-furnished trams to Birkdale Park and Hesketh Park and Liverpool's exclusive 1st class trams.

Southport has a niche in tramway history. The pier tramway was one of the pioneers of passenger cable haulage in 1864 and new research reveals that it was the first known cable railway on which cars were equipped with grippers and handbrakes for driver operation – nine years before San Francisco. The pier is now the second longest in Britain and one of the few remaining piers with a tramway. Southport Tramways Company was only the second system in Britain to have tramcars fitted with windscreens, in 1901; London trams didn't get windscreens till 1930. The Company pioneered the economies of one-man operation and regenerative braking in 1903. Southport also had 17½ route miles of street tramways for a population of 76,000 at its peak in the late 1920s. Local guide books used to boast that the resort 'has probably a greater length of tramway in proportion to its population than any town in the kingdom'. The density of the network here was exceeded only in large city centres. Nobody in the town lived more than a 5-minute walk from the nearest tram stop and this intensive network prevailed right up to the end of the Corporation bus system in 1974.

The tramway era in Southport, from 1873 to 1934, coincided with the main period of the development of the borough. This span of years was Southport's golden age. Southport had two tramway systems for most of the period and three systems running together during the transition from horse to electric power.

The Southport Tramways Company had the pioneer and premier lines, from Birkdale station via York Road, Lord Street and thence via two routes, Roe Lane and Cambridge Road, to the Botanic Gardens at Churchtown, opened in 1873-78 in the horse era and electrified in 1901-02.

The Birkdale & Southport Tramway

Company was the second horsecar company, running inland from London Square to Kew Gardens in 1883, Brighton Road, Birkdale, in 1884, and on to the Crown Hotel in 1894.

Still there was no public transport for residents living between Roe Lane and Scarisbrick New Road apart from the railway stations at St Luke's and Meols Cop. In 1900 Southport Corporation opened three electric tramways from High Park, Blowick and St Luke's to Hoghton Street and developed a one-way tram circuit around the town centre block.

Now there were three tramway operators in Southport, but not for long. The Corporation replaced the Birkdale & Southport horse tramways with electric lines to Kew Gardens and the Cemetery between 1900 and 1902 and the Southport Tramways Company electrified the line to the Crown Hotel in 1902 and extended the York Road line to the Smedley (Trafalgar Road) in 1903. That year a one-man car was built to work between London Square and Birkdale station.

The Corporation took over the Southport Tramways Company in 1918 to create a unified tramway system and between 1919 and 1929 the tramways were modernised, upgraded and extended to Bedford Park. But they were not extended far enough and the modernisation programme did not continue into the 1930s so, just as the system reached its peak of glory, it began its demise.

The tramways served only the old built-up area. Corporation motor buses were introduced from 1924 to run out to the less densely populated, inter-war suburbs of Marshside, Crossens and Ainsdale. From 1931 the buses gradually took over the tram services and the last car ran at the end of 1934.

In its golden age, Southport was exceptionally well served by public transport. The five railways that converged here gave Southport more route miles of railway and more stations than any other town of its size. There has been a total of 22 railway stations and one halt in the borough at various times over the period since 1848. From 1906 to 1938 Southport had 15 stations and one halt open simultaneously, nine of them served by frequent electric trains. But that's another story.

*

James Dean was born in 1920 and therefore only 14 when the tramways closed, but they etched an indelible mark on an impressionable mind and he shares with us his remarkable observations for one so young. He said:

'My interest in trams started when I was about four or five years old, in 1924 or '25, when I first saw Southport's red cars travelling in the streets. I've been fascinated by tramcars ever since. I've seen trams in Liverpool, Manchester, London, Birmingham, Leicester, Newcastle, Gateshead, Glasgow, Edinburgh, Dundee, Aberdeen – and in 1927 I just got a glimpse of the Glossop Tramways in their last year. Those little green trams of the Urban Electric Supply Company were wiped out by North Western buses in 1927, much to my anger at the time – and I was only seven then.'

James studied the history of the Southport tramways back to 1873 through municipal and newspaper archives in the reference library and twice lectured on the subject to the Liverpool joint meetings of the Light Railway Transport League and the Tramway & Light Railway Society. He was a member of the League to promote modern tramways and of the Merseyside Tramway Preservation Society, which now restores trams at Birkenhead. James was known in these circles as the Dean of Southport Tramways.

I have known James since he was 48. He was a walking encyclopædia on tramways and the only living person in the 21st century with a photographic memory of Southport's track layout and overhead wiring and the details of construction of the individual tramcars of a system that disappeared in 1934. James could recall the fleet number of each car and describe its saloons, stairs, fenestration and other details as if they were members of his own family.

In his retirement James started writing this book about his pet subject and between the ages of 67 and 76 he produced coloured drawings of Southport tramcars and tramway scenes, some of which are reproduced in this book. Wayfarers Arts sold framed prints of 24 of his drawings and the Botanic Gardens Museum held a three-month exhibition of his pictures in 1989.

His neatly handwritten manuscript covered the history and development of the system from 1873 to 1903 together with some of his memories of the period 1924-34 before he had a slight stroke in 2001 at the age of 81. This slowed down his brain and his movements, and he shuffled with a stick. He could not draw any more and had great difficulty in writing. It would have been a pity if his knowledge, manuscript and drawings had gone unharnessed so, with his blessing, I have completed the history of the system from 1903 to 1934 and compiled and edited the text of this book from his unfinished manuscript, a series of tape-recorded interviews of more of his memories of 1924-34 and almost daily telephone consultations with him as the work progressed. All the first-person comments and memories in the context of this narrative are James's as he was the only one of us to witness the heyday and demise of the Southport trams.

To complete the story of Southport tramways from 1903 to 1934 I have done further research in the Tramways Committee minutes and newspaper files in the Atkinson Reference Library at Southport and gathered useful and interesting contributions to both the general narrative and appendices from Graham Fairhurst, T. B. Maund and Ron Phillips, who have also done research on Southport's trams and buses, and from the library of the National Tramway Museum at Crich, Derbyshire. The result is a relatively definitive work on the subject and an important era of local history. My thanks are due to James for vetting the first draft and to Ron for vetting the second.

Unfortunately, James died shortly before I completed the typescript and he never saw the finished product that bears his name. It's a suitable memorial to him.

Cedric Greenwood

About the authors

JAMES DEAN was born on 23 March 1920, at Rossmore Nursing Home in Leicester Street, Southport, to Gertrude (née Hulme). His father, also James Dean, was director of a firm of Manchester cotton importers. The family lived at 63 Windsor Road, Southport,

and James jnr went to Metfield Preparatory School in Hartwood Road and University School in Cambridge Road, matriculating in art, English and maths. His mother died in 1933 and his father died in 1937, so James had lost both his parents by the age of 17. He went to live with relatives at 96 Preston New Road for the next two years.

He started work in 1937 as a clerk in the Union Bank at Manchester, commuting daily by train, and was transferred to the Southport branch on Lord Street. But James and banking were not compatible and after 18 months he was sacked. In 1938-39 he was a progress clerk with the Brockhouse Engineering Company (the former Vulcan Motor Works) at Crossens, then making parts for Bristol Blenheim bombers as the clouds of war were gathering. In 1939 he applied for a short service commission as a pilot in the RAF, training on biplanes at Perth and Kinloss. He became a Pilot Officer in 1940, a Flying Officer in 1941 and a Flight Lieutenant in 1942. He flew Fairey Battles from RAF Manby, Defiant night fighters from RAF Barrow, Lysander bombers from RAF Jurby and Spitfires from RAF Kinloss. He was seconded to the Fleet Air Arm flying Barracuda torpedo bombers on North Sea patrols based at RNAS Arbroath, firing torpedoes and bombing U-boats. At the end of the war he was transferred back to the RAF and flew Proctors from RAF Hereford.

James married Joan Marshall of Birkdale in 1942 and she moved around the country with him as he was posted to different air stations, both billeted in civilian lodgings nearby. Their son Geoffrey was born in 1944 and Joan returned to live with her parents at Birkdale. James was demobbed in 1946 and inherited his parents' home at 63 Windsor Road, Southport, where the three lived for the next 30 years. James's early drawings of Southport street scenes with trams, buses and cars got him a job as a cartographer and surveyor of sites in the Wigan area for the Directorate of Open-cast Coal Production. But the pay was poor so he left to be a salesman for the Liverpool paper merchants C. M. Madden & Sons, of Edge Hill, trying to re-start the paper bag business after the wartime paper shortage. 'I never made very much but I bore with it

Heinz as the most interesting period of his life.

His son Geoffrey was a 'chip off the old block', sharing his father's vigour, strong opinions, sense of humour and animated enthusiasm about anything, especially tramways. The painstaking patience shown in his father's detailed drawings was inherited in Geoffrey's craftsmanship in modelling tramcars in 2.25mm and 4mm scale down to the tiniest details. As a young man Geoffrey worked nights as a freelance jazz and beat band drummer and used to pick the strands of his drum brushes to make handrails for his model tramcars! Each in his own way, both father and son were reproducing the past glories of the tramcar era. Geoffrey married and lived in Waterloo, working by day as a BSM driving instructor. By night he was a drummer with the Merseyside Big Band for 18 years.

James survived his wife and son, having lost Joan in 1995 and Geoffrey in 2002. He had a slight stroke in 2001, aged 81. Despite his misfortunes and advancing age, James was ever cheerful, always the complete gentleman and retained his boyish enthusiasm for trams. He still lived in the upstairs flat that had been the last family home in Part Street and got around town every day by cab and on foot, shuffling with his walking stick, and found a new vocation as an entertainer at the Royal Clifton Hotel, the Volunteer Arms and the Cheshire Lines, singing solo songs made famous in the 1950s and '60s by Tony Bennett, Perry Como, Bing Crosby, Bobby Darin and Frank Sinatra. He was best known for his rendering of Bobby Darin's 'Mac The Knife'. He died from a heart attack at home on or about 1 March 2007, shortly before his 87th birthday.

CEDRIC GREENWOOD was born at Carshalton in 1938 and went to school at Hove and Oxford, later boarding at Magdalen School while living at Wallasey and Herne Bay. He trained as a journalist with the *Kent Messenger* at Canterbury (1955-60). After deferred National Service with the RAF in Norfolk (1960-62), he married Ruth Amos at Margate and they had two sons, Karl and Ross, when Cedric was district reporter at Kendal covering part of Lakeland and the

James Dean at the age of 83 in 2003. *Cedric Greenwood*

from 1947 to 1953, when I got a job at Arthur Holland's toffee factory in Virginia Street, Southport, as a general dogsbody and eventually became a personnel officer.' This started him on a career in personnel. He became night personnel officer at H. J. Heinz's factory at Standish in 1957 then at Dunlop's new factory at Skelmersdale in 1965, eventually becoming assistant to the Group Personnel Manager.

In 1971 he was made redundant at the age of 51 along with the second in command of every department at that time. So, after a chequered career, frequently moving location, James found a job on home ground for the last 14 years of his working life as a night telephonist at Southport Promenade Hospital. His wife, Joan, was on the day shift at the hospital switchboard. The couple lived in Rufford Drive, Banks, from 1979 and after his retirement in 1985 they moved to a flat in Part Street, Southport. He looked back on his time as a surveyor and as a personnel officer at

Yorkshire dales for the *Lancashire Evening Post* (1963-68).

For the next 21 years he was a news reporter and feature writer with the *Southport Visiter*, rising to chief reporter and deputy news editor. He specialised in writing on the environment and transport and made a name for himself in a prolific period of in-depth feature writing: news-features, biographies and local history. A series of articles on local architecture was the basis of his first book, *Thatch, Towers & Colonnades* (1971, revised 1990), which put the spotlight on Southport's architectural heritage and was officially credited with prompting the Town Council to designate conservation areas in Lord Street and Birkdale. He also made himself unpopular with the Town Council with a series of reports and features consequent on a local scientist's discovery of raw sewage and heavy metals in the inshore waters. This became a national scandal and led, ultimately, to the clean-up of the Mersey and the eastern Irish Sea with sewage treatment and control of industrial waste dumping. Cedric and Ruth were divorced at Southport in 1981.

His newspaper career culminated as editor of the *Campbeltown Courier* (1989-91). This was the most interesting and stimulating time of his career, covering mainly sea stories around Kintyre, taking his own news and feature pictures, redesigning the paper and overseeing production. But the long working week, the days spent in court and council meetings and the persistent telephone interruptions made him decide, after 35 years in the job, to change horses at the age of 53.

While living at Southport he had bought a 1951 Wallasey Corporation Leyland bus out of service in 1973 and restored it at Burscough aerodrome. He owned it for 30 years, driving it regularly and running excursions over the extinct routes it used to run in Wallasey and Birkenhead. By virtue of having a PSV driving licence for his own bus, the only other job he was qualified to do was to be a bus driver.

He joined Chester City Transport to be near his own bus, then in the Birkenhead transport museum, and because Chester owned a 1953 Guy, which he regularly drove to take part in the annual Birmingham running day and the Welshpool steam gala. He drove Chester city and country bus services (1991-99) but decided to escape from Chester's jungle of signals and traffic jams to north Norfolk to finish up driving stage services with Sanders' Coaches of Holt (1999-2004). He says: 'The view from my windscreen was better than the view from the news desk or the press bench and this was a pleasant and therapeutic way to end my working life.'

He sold his Wallasey bus to the Birkenhead transport museum in 2003 and retired in 2004, but he keeps busy with part-time bus driving for Sanders, writing books, cycling, photography, line dancing and model trams and ships. His interest in bygone transport produced a series of narrated audiotape programmes, recently released on compact discs, about steam railways, pre-war electric trains, paddle steamers and tramcars he recorded over the period from 1967 to 1981. Since 1982 he has worked on a series of cine and video travelogues about canals, buildings and buses, tramways and light railways at home and overseas.

THE HORSE TRAMWAYS

Southport Tramways Company
Birkdale & Southport Tramways Company
1873-1902

The growing seaside health resort of Southport was incorporated as a Municipal Borough in 1867 and by the 1871 census the combined populations of Southport and the neighbouring village and villa park of Birkdale had reached 21,461. With the passing by Parliament of the Tramways Act in 1870 (then still the age of the horse) many cities and towns planned and constructed tramways under the new legislation and Southport's was among the first to open, in 1873.

The only public transport in Southport preceding the tramways were the horse-coaches operated by innkeepers and hoteliers to and from the canal wharf at Scarisbrick and the nearest railheads at Liverpool, Euxton and Preston, then the railways into town from Liverpool, Manchester and Preston. There was no competition for the horse trams in their own era; according to one guide book there

Left A rare view of a Birkdale & Southport horse tram, loading in London Square for Kew Gardens. This is car No 12, one of a batch of 'garden seat' cars built for the Company by G. F. Milnes & Company at Birkenhead in 1886-87. The route board above the windows reads: 'London Square – Chapel St. Station – Eastbank St. – New Infirmary'. A slip board in the middle windows reads 'Kew Gardens' while 'Scarisbrick New Road' was painted on the cream band below the windows. Passengers on the top deck are holding black umbrellas to shade themselves from the sunlight. The car is standing on the terminal loop around the cabmen's shelter in the middle of the square, stemming from the single track in London Street. The noble pile of yellow sandstone that forms the backdrop was Parr's Bank (now the National Westminster Bank), built in 1892-95 on the corner of St George's Place and London Street. Horse-drawn cabs await passengers on the rank outside the cabmen's shelter. The 10-sided gas lantern with a crown finial on a stout column in the foreground was one of about 50 sewer gas lamps around Southport that ventilated the sewer system and burned potentially explosive sewer gas, mainly methane, from the decomposition of sewage. *Courtesy of Martin Jenkins, E. J. McWatt and A. D. Packer, Online Transport Archive*

was just an assortment of horse-drawn 'hackney coaches, victorias, landaus, wagonettes, brakes and chars-a-banc' taking people to outlying villages like Marshside, Parbold and Sefton. The smooth rails of the tramway gave it an advantage over all other road vehicles in terms of comfort, speed and capacity. With the lower rolling resistance of steel on steel, the horses could pull twice as many passengers on rails.

The Oystermouth Tramroad was the first horse-drawn passenger railway, opened in 1807 around the shores of Swansea Bay, but the first street tramway in Britain was constructed at Birkenhead in 1860 by George Francis Train, the American shipping agent and entrepreneur. Train's pioneer tramways were not entirely successful because the stepped rails protruded three-quarters of an inch above the road surface and that was not popular with other road users. The 1870 Act provided that all rails must be flush with the road surface, which eliminated objections on that account, and allowed the local authority to buy the tramway company after 21 years.

Southport Tramways Company

Within a year of the Tramways Act the Southport Tramways Company was formed on 23 May 1871, and laid plans for a horse-drawn street tramway from St Cuthbert's Place, Churchtown, along Roe Lane (then Row Lane), Lord Street and Aughton Road to Birkdale station.

Immediately there was opposition from a number of residents headed by the Rector of North Meols. Charles Hesketh (1804-76) had been appointed Rector in 1835 and also became Lord of the Manor in 1842. The opposition deplored the construction of a tramway along Lord Street, considering it to be 'an intolerable nuisance'. They also feared that 'the rails would cause hindrance to the good people who owned horses and carriages and furthermore that the rumbling and jolting of the tram cars would cause fright to the horses and the awful possibility that they might bolt, resulting in untold injury and damage to property.'

In spite of the Rector's foreboding, the Southport Tramways Company obtained Parliamentary powers to build the line under the Southport Tramways Order in 1872. The Order provided for the 'business of tramways, railways and omnibus lines daily except Sundays in the townships of North Meols and Birkdale'. Sufficient funds were raised and construction commenced.

A prominent figure in the promotion of the tramway company was Walter Smith, a civil engineering contractor and entrepreneur involved in the construction of the railway from Waterloo to Southport in 1848, its extensions in 1851 and the line from Manchester to Southport in 1854. On completion of the Manchester line he organised a Temperance tea party for his navvies in Southport Town Hall, where he made his first public speech in the town and decided to settle there.

Smith became chairman of the Birkdale Park Land Company, was elected to the Southport Board of Improvement Commissioners in 1856 and, after the incorporation of the Borough in 1867, he was four times Mayor of Southport. He played a leading role in the town's affairs and was the founder and first chairman of the Southport Tramways Company (1871), the Winter Gardens Company (1874), the Botanic Gardens Company (1875) and the Southport & Cheshire Lines Extension Railway (1884), the railway from Aintree Central to Southport Lord Street. This terminus was alongside the Winter Gardens and the horsecars of the Tramways Company connected all Smith's enterprises, advertising the fact on their side panels as stages along the route. His losses on this last railway venture led to his bankruptcy, his resignation from the Town Council in 1884

and the ill health that hastened his death in 1887, aged 70.

Construction of the tramway under the supervision of Charles Beloe, a civil engineer, of 22 Lord Street, was completed by 24 May 1873. The original line was 3¾ miles long from St Cuthbert's Place, Churchtown, to Birkdale station, laid to the standard gauge of 4ft 8½in, with double track along Lord Street from Hill Street to the Winter Gardens and single track beyond in each direction with only four passing loops. The Company wanted to add a siding in London Square but this was refused by the Town Council. The rails were normal grooved horsecar-pattern tram rail, of lighter weight than the type of rail used for the later electric tramways. The exception was in Churchtown depot, where the six storage tracks were laid in ordinary, lightweight railway track with check rails, set in paving, similar to dockland railways.

The 1870 Tramways Act made tramway undertakings pave and maintain the carriageway between the rails and 18 inches on each side. They also had to pay rates on that roadway! The local councils in Southport and Birkdale also specified that the tracks should be paved in granite setts. Existing streets were paved in millstone grit setts or water-bound, dust-covered, graded limestone. The rails had to be laid flush with the road surface but the tramways were laid more level than the existing roads and when the work was complete the councils complained that in some places the new tramway paving was anything up to 5 or 6 inches above or below the roadway that flanked it. Many hundreds of yards of flanking roadway had to be relaid, notably in Roe Lane, Aughton Road, York Road and Weld Road, and the cost of this extra work was shared between the Tramways Company and the local councils.

The tramway commenced outside the Bold Arms in Churchtown and the tracks were laid through Botanic Road (then named Church Town), the village street with its thatched cottages and shops on each side. The line continued beyond the terminus around the acute corner into Cambridge Road and the main depot and stables that were being built there at the same time. Another depot line branched off the village street from the

Above A general view of Lord Street in late-Victorian times, looking south-west to the Scarisbrick Hotel (centre) and the distant clock tower of Lord Street railway station. A two-horse car of the Southport Tramways Company is bound for Churchtown bearing the common period advertisement for Zebra grate polish. *Courtesy of Martin Jenkins, E. J. McWatt and A. D. Packer, Online Transport Archive*

Right Horse trams on the Cambridge Road route to the Botanic Gardens terminated by the Winter Gardens at the south-west end of Lord Street, while Roe Lane cars operated to and from Birkdale station. This is car No 12, one of the batch of 16 Starbuck trams built for the opening of the Cambridge Road route in 1878. The back-to-back 'knifeboard' seating upstairs is quite clearly seen and the waist panels are painted dark brown as a Cambridge Road car. This photograph is an enlargement from a Victorian picture postcard captioned 'Cheshire Lines Station, Southport'. The colonnaded frontage of the CLC's Lord Street terminus, opened in 1884, is on the extreme left of the picture. The building behind the tramcar is the Opera House, part of the 9-acre Winter Gardens complex, which also included a conservatory, aquarium, concert pavilion and circus and occupied the whole block between the railway station and Coronation Walk, Lord Street, and the Promenade (Kingsway was not there then). The arcaded single-storey elevation beyond the tram was the main entrance to the whole complex. Walter Smith was chairman of the Tramways Company, the Railway Company, the Winter Gardens and the Botanic Gardens. The Opera House was destroyed by fire in 1929 and was replaced by the Garrick Theatre in 1932, now the Mecca Bingo Club on the corner of Kingsway. *Cedric Greenwood collection* direction of Mill Lane into Manor Road and the back yard of the depot, but that line was added later.

The line of route continued along Mill Lane, Roe Lane, Leyland Road, Queen's Road, Manchester Road and Lord Street to London Square. The indirect route via Leyland Road and Queen's Road was probably intended to avoid the gradient of Mount Pleasant on Manchester Road. The gradient from Holy Trinity Church up to Mount Pleasant – what was known as 'the great sandhill' – was steeper than it is today. It would have involved stationing trace horses opposite the church to assist outbound cars up the gradient because it is unlikely that the normal motive power of two horses per car could have hauled a loaded double-deck tramcar up the incline without assistance.

The tramway was a single line with short, double-track sections, or loops, where oncoming cars were timed to pass each other. The single line extended even into Lord Street from Manchester Road to Hill Street, but from there to the Winter Gardens the line along Lord Street was double track.

The company decided to order six tramcars to start operating a service between Churchtown and London Square before commissioning the rest of the line into Birkdale. As the depot in Cambridge Road was not then complete, the company built a small running shed and stables at the town end of Roe Lane opposite Leyland Road Methodist Church. This was later the site of Whiteside's Garage then Hatton's Garage and now Duerden's motor showrooms. It was a double-track shed with room for three cars on each track and stables at the rear, all belonging to Southport Tramways Company from 1873. Its use as a depot did not continue into the electric era.

The six cars were ordered from the Starbuck Car & Wagon Company, of Birkenhead. George Starbuck was another American, associated with George Train, and in 1862 he had established the first tramcar-building business in Great Britain in the town that had seen the birth of the street tramway in this country, supplying knifeboard-seat double-deckers to Liverpool, Brussels, Copenhagen, Berlin and Pernambuco, among others. To

Southport's first tramcar, horsecar No 1 of the Southport Tramways Company is seen across London Square as it stops in Lord Street by the corner of Nevill Street (left) on its way from Birkdale to Roe Lane and Churchtown. This was one of the first batch of six cars built for the Company by the Starbuck Car & Wagon Company at Birkenhead in 1873 with eight windows on each side of the saloon. The tramcar appears to belong to the Cheshire Lines Railway as this name is painted along the white rocker panel above the wheels, which became the traditional position for the name of a tramway company, but in those early days this company painted the names of the main stages on the route on the car body. This car shows 'Botanic Gardens' on the waist panel and 'Roe Lane' on the staircase, which dedicated the car to the Roe Lane route. These Roe Lane cars were distinguished by yellow waist panels below the windows. The name of the Cheshire Lines Railway dates the picture after 1884, when Lord Street station opened as the terminus of the Southport & Cheshire Lines Extension Railway from Aintree. The upper deck decency panels advertise Hatton Brothers' furniture shop at 28-30 Eastbank Street and 'Millinery, J. Broadbent & Co., Bon Marché, Chapel Street'. *Cedric Greenwood collection*

compete in an expanding market, the Starbuck Car & Wagon Company Ltd was formed in 1872 and the works expanded.

Southport's first six tramcars, 1 to 6, were duly delivered. They were Starbuck's latest 1873 design of four-wheel, double-deck vehicles with eight segmental-arch windows on each side of the saloon. The open-top deck was reached by a quarter-turn, direct staircase at each end. Passengers sat on continuous, longitudinal, wooden seats facing each other across the saloon. Upstairs they sat back-to-back on a longitudinal 'knifeboard' seat along the middle of the upper deck.

The horse trams were double-ended, like the later electric cars, so they did not have to be turned round at the terminus, although the horses did. The trace-bar was detached from the tramcar drawbar and taken together with the two horses and all their trappings to the other end of the car and re-attached for the return journey.

These early horse trams had four entrances/exits, one on each side of the platform at each end of the car. Passengers could board and alight on the offside as well as the nearside in those days as there were no regulations governing which side or end of the car one had to board or alight. The staircases, on the nearside of the driver's platform and the offside of the conductor's platform, arched over the nearside access at the front and the offside access at the back.

The cars came from the builders resplendent in the Company livery of mid-to-dark green and off-white. The dash panels, staircase stringers and waist panels below the windows were green, lined out in gold leaf, and the window frames and tapering rocker panels (below the waist panels) were white, lined out in black.

The tramway was completed on 24 May 1873, and passed muster by the Board of Trade inspector, Colonel Yolland, on 27 May. He described the line as being 'in fair order' but recommended the insertion of more passing loops between Leyland Road and Lord Street.

The opening date of Southport's first tramway is recorded in Bland's *Annals of Southport* as 31 May. The Company began working cars between Churchtown (St

Cuthbert's Place) and Southport (London Square) only, reversing in Lord Street on a crossover in the double track immediately north of the square. The line apparently opened without ceremony as it was not notified or reported in the *Southport Visiter*. The newspaper had previously reported on construction progress but only made a passing reference to the existence of the town's first tram service in its report of the Whit Monday bank holiday, 2 June, in the paper on the following day:

'The tramways did good business and the novelty of transit in Southport was no small attraction. Parties wended their way to Churchtown by the nearest route on foot or rode in the cars to the vicinity of the Strawberry Gardens.'

Tracklaying continued from Lord Street into Lord Street West, over the Birkdale Urban District boundary into Aughton Road, York Road and Weld Road, ending just short of Birkdale station in a loop-and-stub terminus outside the Park Hotel. The line was finished before the end of the year and the Company ordered another batch of cars from Starbuck, which could now be housed in the completed main depot and stables in Churchtown. These trams were similar to the original batch of six except that they were slightly shorter and had seven instead of eight arched windows on each side of the saloon.

About 100 yards beyond the terminus at the Bold Arms were the Strawberry Gardens, part of the grounds of Meols Hall estate, which the squire and rector, the Rev Charles Hesketh, opened to the public. The Strawberry Gardens proved to be extremely popular and in 1875 a much larger pleasure garden was opened on land donated by the squire on the opposite side of the road, behind the Hesketh Arms. It became known as the Botanic Gardens and incorporated beautiful flower gardens, rockeries and grottoes. A boating lake was formed on The Pool, a stream that runs through the gardens on its way from Martin Mere to Crossens. Eventually a fernery, a conservatory, fountains, a museum and refreshment rooms were added.

The Botanic Gardens gave the new name of

the village street, Botanic Road, and provided an ideal terminus for the tramway. The line was extended about 200 yards from the Bold Arms to the gates of the Botanic Gardens, where it ended in a passing loop and a stub-end just before the sharp left-hand bend into Bankfield Lane. There was now, in 1875, a complete tramline of almost 4 miles from the Botanic Gardens in Churchtown via Roe Lane to Southport town centre and beyond through the élite residential area named Birkdale Park to a terminus at Birkdale station. The horse trams did not have fixed stopping places; they stopped by request, but moved slowly enough for the more agile passengers to board and alight the cars while in motion.

The company's finances settled down to an acceptable level and further progress was being considered. The Rev Charles Hesketh had given the land for the development of Hesketh Park in 1865 on condition that the Commissioners laid a road around the park with sewers connected to the town system at the end of Lord Street. This paved the way for him to develop large villas around the park

and in due course a superior residential district was developed north-east of the town centre as smart and fashionable as Birkdale Park on the other side of town. It stretched along Cambridge Road towards Churchtown with detached houses, many of them three storeys high. Many businessmen and wealthy Lancashire mill-owners came to live there and commuted daily to Liverpool and Manchester. This was the territory of the privately owned horse and carriage but the Tramways Company considered that there was a promise of lucrative business and laid a second route between Southport and Churchtown in 1878.

From the Botanic Gardens the new route continued past the depot along the full length of Cambridge Road to Hesketh Park, around Park Crescent and along Albert Road to Lord Street. It was laid as single track with passing loops to the junction with the Roe Lane line at the corner of Manchester Road, where it entered Lord Street.

The Company ordered a further batch of double-deck trams from Starbuck, bringing the total fleet to 22 cars; as far as I can ascertain, there were 14 cars with seven-bay

Car No 5, one of the first batch of horse trams, clops and grinds along Lord Street near the Scarisbrick Hotel on its way to the Botanic Gardens. The conductor leaning out of the offside of the back platform illustrates the offside access for passengers boarding and alighting, a practice later banned by the Board of Trade. Behatted women and children are enjoying the view and the fresh air from the knifeboard seat on the top deck. Yellow waist panels under the windows distinguished this as a Roe Lane car for those who could not read. On the right is the rear view of a horse-drawn wagonette. *Graham Fairhurst collection*

saloons (ie with seven windows on each side) and eight cars with eight-bay saloons.

The Company wanted to open the Cambridge Road route on 8 June 1878, the Saturday before Whit Monday, and asked the Board of Trade for an inspection on 1 June. Owing to the short notice, the Board of Trade authorised opening on that date before inspection with retrospective authority to follow! The Cambridge Road horse trams ran between the Botanic Gardens and the Winter Gardens at the south-west end of Lord Street. The Winter Gardens terminus was adjacent to the Lord Street terminus of the Southport & Cheshire Lines Extension Railway when that opened in 1884. There was now a frequent service along Lord Street with both Roe Lane and Cambridge Road cars running the full length of the street.

As there were now two tram routes, the cars dedicated to each route had three distinguishing features. Roe Lane cars carried the name ROE LANE in gold-leaf capitals on the staircase stringers for those who could read and, for those who couldn't, the waist panels below the windows were painted yellow, lined-out with black. Cambridge Road cars bore the name CAMBRIDGE ROAD in gold capitals on the staircase stringers and the waist panels were painted dark brown, lined out in gold-leaf. The dash panels and staircase stringers remained green. By night the Roe Lane cars showed a red light and the Cambridge Road cars a green light at each end. Each horsecar carried two oil lamps, which served as saloon lights, marker lights and route lights. Each lamp was strategically located above the nearside bulkhead window at each end of the saloon, showing a white light in the saloon, and was fitted with a red or green route colour lens on the outer side. These were the only lights the horse trams carried, inside or out. In winter, 'heating' was provided by straw on the saloon floor.

The basic service on Roe Lane was at 15-minute intervals and Cambridge Road cars ran every 7½ minutes in summer and every 20 minutes in winter. The 1889 timetable shows the first car leaving Churchtown at 6.30am and the last car arriving at 10.14pm. In the horse tram era, platform staff were on duty throughout the working day – no shifts, no meal breaks – and were paid only a few shillings a day. The horses were treated better, working shifts of only 3 to 4 hours a day, and were well fed. Passengers paid differential fares 'inside' the saloon and 'outside' on top. The Ward, Lock guide of 1883-84 said: 'The fare from London Square to Birkdale or Churchtown is threepence inside and twopence outside.' These fares were relatively expensive for the time because of the large stud of horses required. Each horse consumed about 2cwt a week of maize, oats, bran, lentils and chaff and required the attention of ostlers, shoesmiths and vets. Fares dropped after electrification and horsecar fares were not equalled again till the 1920s and '30s.

The Birkdale & Southport Tramways Company

By 1881 the population of Southport alone was approaching 33,000. High Park and Blowick had been absorbed into the borough in 1865, and Churchtown and Crossens were annexed in 1875. High Park was a relatively new district but all the others (including Birkdale and Ainsdale, added in 1912) were old villages with Norse names. To cover this growing area there was only one tramway along the north-east/south-west axis of Lord Street with one line to Birkdale station and two lines to Churchtown, but nothing into the hinterland.

The seal of the Birkdale & Southport Tramways Company. *Geoff Price*

The Birkdale & Southport Tramways Company (the word 'Tramways' in the title was variously spelled in the singular or the plural) was formed in 1879 to serve the inland area of the town. Thomas Weld-Blundell, of Ince Blundell Hall, was its first chairman. His family estates included Birkdale and Ainsdale since the early 1630s and he was responsible for creating Birkdale Park as a high-class residential estate, although this was already served by the Southport Tramways Company. The Weld-Blundell family died out in 1957 and their manorial lands were sold, but they left their name in Weld Road and Blundell Drive in Birkdale.

The new Company advertised a start on construction under the title of the Birkdale & Southport Steam Tramway. Steam trams were replacing horse trams in industrial towns and on rural tramways. The Ward, Lock Guide of c1883-84, after describing the tram ride from Birkdale to Churchtown, reported: 'The cars of the other company are propelled by steam...' but this is the only known record of steam traction on the Birkdale & Southport and might have been taken from the prospectus. Residential Southport had conventional horsecars when the new Company opened its first line from London Square to Kew Gardens on 12 May 1883. The lines were laid to the standard gauge of 4ft 8½in with centre-groove, lightweight tram rail, all single track with passing loops.

There was no physical connection with the Lord Street line of the Southport Tramways Company. A turning loop was laid around the cabmen's shelter in the middle of London Square on the end of a single line in London Street. This obviated the need to turn the horses round to the other end of the car in the town centre. The line up London Street turned right into Chapel Street then left into Eastbank Street and out of town along Scarisbrick New Road.

This was a developing residential district around the axis of the new main road to Scarisbrick, Ormskirk, Wigan and Manchester. Scarisbrick New Road was laid out by the Scarisbrick estates to replace the former Norwood Road and Manchester Road approach to Southport, now obstructed by a railway level crossing at Blowick, and the older stagecoach route via Foul Lane, Wennington Road and Manchester Road. The area was being developed with large, detached villas like those in Birkdale Park and the Hesketh Park district.

The line extended beyond the end of the houses in Scarisbrick New Road into flat, open country. This was an area that, when built up, would become the suburb of Higher Blowick along the axes of Haig Avenue, Everard Road and the outer end of Southbank Road. After bridging Fine Jane's Brook the line crossed part of Blowick Moss to terminate in a final passing loop and stub outside the Richmond Hotel and the entrance to Kew Gardens. Here, a good 1¼ miles from Lord Street, was another leisure park with a boating lake, a zoo and a German 'Bier Garten'. The gardens took their name from their London counterpart and transferred the name to the suburb now known as Kew.

As implied by its title, the Birkdale & Southport Tramways Company intended to serve Birkdale as well as Southport. Its depot and stables were situated in Boundary Street by the Southport/Birkdale boundary. There was a junction on Scarisbrick New Road with a line along Sefton Street to the depot. The line ran four blocks along Sefton Street and straight across the T-junction with Boundary Street into an entry between two houses and the tramshed behind the back garden walls.

Karwowski Motors occupy the former car shed and stables of the Birkdale & Southport Tramways Company in Boundary Street, still known as the Tramshed Works in the address on the letterhead.

(The former tramshed became Butterfield's engineering works and is now the Tramshed Works of Karwowski Motors.) There was also a set of right-hand points at the end of Sefton Street into Boundary Street allowing for the proposed extension into Birkdale.

The company appears to have been run on a shoestring and most of its tramcars were second-hand from other tramways. Records of the fleet are scanty but we know that cars 1, 2 and 3 came from St Helens & District Tramways. These were short, four-wheel, single-deck vehicles with five-bay saloons (five windows each side) and a 'turtle-back' (humped) clerestory roof, the type of car usually pulled by one horse. They had short, open platforms with entrances/exits on both sides.

Cars 4 to 10, or possibly 12, ex-Birkenhead Street Railway, were bought from the successor Birkenhead Tramways Company. These were four-wheel, double-deck horsecars, built by Starbuck in 1876 with seven-bay saloons. The body of one of these cars, No 7, latterly used as a hut in a coalyard in Banastre Road close to the old depot, was rescued for restoration in 1970. This is the second oldest surviving street tramcar in Britain and has been restored as a Birkenhead Street Railway car; at the time of writing it is on display in Woodside Ferry tollhouse.

The roofs, windows and rocker panels of the Birkdale & Southport trams were off-white and the waist panels were scumbled in imitation of grained wood, lined out in gold-leaf with a gold-leaf fleet number in the centre of the panels. On the earlier cars the fleet number was encircled by an oval red garter inscribed 'Birkdale & Southport Ty. Co.'. On later cars the off-white rocker panel carried the legend 'Birkdale & Southport' in bold gilt capitals, shaded black.

The routes were painted in black capitals on roof-mounted roof boards above the eaves of single-deckers or on the off-white fascia-boards or letterboards above the side windows of double-deckers: 'London Sq., Scarisbrick Rd. & Richmond Hotel'.

With sufficient trams having arrived to run a service and the line completed from London Square to Kew Gardens with a depot access along Sefton Street to Boundary Street, the Company commenced operation on the line from London Square to Kew on 12 May 1883.

The Birkdale extension

There was a saying about this time: 'If you want to go to Southport get a Birkdale car; if you want to go to Birkdale get a Southport car.' At this stage the Birkdale & Southport Company trams ran entirely in Southport. Only the Southport Company trams ran into Birkdale.

Track construction continued from the right-hand turnout from Sefton Street into Boundary Street for three more car lengths, then turned left into Mosley Street. The extension continued into Everton Road and St Peter's Road, turned left into Liverpool Road and, after a further quarter of a mile, terminated at the corner of Brighton Road. This extension was laid, like the rest, as single track with passing loops, and the distance from the depot in Boundary Street was perhaps three-quarters of a mile.

On 5 November 1884 the service from London Square to Birkdale via Sefton Street commenced. The route painted on the letterboard above the windows was 'London Sq., Liverpool Rd. & Brighton Rd'. When the line was extended in 1894, cars carried supplementary destination boards on brackets on the side window pillars: 'To Crown Hotel'.

The Company received more trams during 1886 or 1887 and these were built with the new transverse 'garden seats' on the top decks instead of the longitudinal back-to-back 'knifeboard' seat. Each seated two passengers and they were arranged transversely each side of a central gangway. They had swing-over backrests that could simply be reversed at the terminus. There was no change to the seating in the saloon with longitudinal seats each side of the standing area.

By now the practice of boarding and alighting had been regulated by the Board of Trade: one could only board or alight from the nearside of the rear platform. (There were, however, special regulations at a later date for front-exit electric cars and 'toastracks'.) There was therefore now only one entrance/exit on each platform. The outside, quarter-turn staircase was still in the usual position but the

The crew and horses pose for a classic portrait of car No 22, built by Milnes in 1878, the highest-numbered car in the Southport Tramways Company fleet, at the terminus outside the gates of the Botanic Gardens in Churchtown. The car has brown waist panels to show that it runs via Cambridge Road. The oil lamp with a green route colour

lens is above the nearside bulkhead window between the driver and conductor. These doubled as saloon lights; the glow from the oil lamp at each end of the saloon provided the only lighting inside the car. *Graham Fairhurst collection*

side of the car below stairs was filled in to prevent passengers boarding and alighting on the offside.

George F. Milnes, former secretary to George Starbuck, took over the tramcar factory in Birkenhead in 1886, shortly after these changes in horsecar design, and he supplied the next batch of trams to the Birkdale & Southport Company incorporating these new design features. They were four-wheel, double-deck, open-top horsecars, shorter than the Starbucks with six segmental-arch windows each side of the saloon and reversible 'garden seats' upstairs. I am not certain how many of these new Milnes cars came to the Birkdale & Southport Company but there were at least seven, which took the fleet numbers 4, 5, 11, 12, 13, 14 and 18, replacing some of the ex-Birkenhead cars and interspersed among the remaining second-hand cars.

The last development of Southport's horse tramways came in 1894, when the line along

Liverpool Road was extended from Brighton Road for about half a mile to the ultimate terminus at the Crown Hotel, the end of the built-up area, and this remained the furthest outpost of the Southport tramways to the end of the electric era.

It appears that by 1896 the Company had pensioned off all the second-hand cars with which it began operations in 1883. Duncan's *Manual of Tramway Companies* for 1896 records that the Birkdale & Southport Company was reduced to six cars and 24 horses to operate the two routes totalling 4 miles, which must have provided a sparse service.

Change of ownership

Finally, the tracks of the two tramway companies were bought by the two local authorities, Southport Corporation and Birkdale Urban District Council, on both sides of the boundary, while the British Electric

Traction Company (BET), the largest British financial group of tramway companies, bought the majority of shares of both operating companies, which still owned the cars. Both moves were a prelude to electrification.

Southport Corporation made the first move in 1888, when it opened negotiations to buy the tracks of the Southport Tramways Company and lease them back to the Company to continue to operate tram services, but the company rejected the offer of £40,000.

The 1880s and '90s were the dawn of the electric traction era. Although still in its infancy, the technology of electric traction was advancing. Among the pioneers, the Volk's Electric Railway at Brighton (1883-84), the Blackpool promenade line (1885), the Blackpool-Fleetwood line (1898) and the Manx Electric Railway and its cars (1893-99) still operate today.

This was also the period of municipalisation, when borough councils began to acquire and operate public utilities, such as water, gas and electricity. An Act of Parliament in 1896 allowed local authorities, which could already own tram tracks, to run their own tramcars on their own public highways.

In the same year Southport Corporation re-opened negotiations with the Southport Tramways Company to buy the tracks for the Company to operate on lease. After rejecting the previous offer of £40,000 the Company accepted the second Corporation bid of only £17,000. Thus Southport Corporation became the owner of the tramways from Churchtown to Lord Street West and the Company agreed to continue working the lines on a 21-year lease, expiring in 1917, on payment of £2,700 a year.

The Town Council set up a Tramways Committee in 1897 and began talks with the Board of Trade with a view to planning a comprehensive electric tramway system to serve the whole borough. The committee also began to watch tramway developments in other Lancashire towns from 1899. Electric traction was still in the formative development stage and few towns had made the switch to it.

The fortunes of the two Southport companies picked up when BET took control in 1899. In that year Duncan's *Manual of*

Tramway Companies recorded that the Birkdale & Southport Company had 12 cars and 41 horses and that Emile Garcke, the founder and managing director of BET, and Vincent Kitchener, BET's district superintendent, were among the four company directors. Oddly enough, Garcke included the Birkdale & Southport Company in his annual *Manual of Electrical Undertakings* and in 1901, the last year of operation, the Company was shown as operating 14 cars with 54 horses.

Initially BET was to electrify and develop the entire system along the lines planned by the Corporation and operate all the tramways in the town, leasing the tracks from the Southport and Birkdale Councils. BET's engineer, Stephen Sellor, submitted plans in December 1898 for the 1899 session of the Board of Trade, for the electrification of all the existing company horsecar lines in Southport and Birkdale, including Sefton Street, plus three new lines that were, in the event, operated by the Corporation: to St Luke's via Manchester Road, to Blowick via Sussex Road, and to High Park via Bispham Road. They also planned three electric lines that were never built: an alternative route to Blowick via Kensington Road, an extension from Bispham Road to the far end of Russell Road, and a link between the existing lines in Weld Road and Liverpool Road through the main street of Birkdale.

As municipalisation and traction technology advanced towards the turn of the century, Southport, like many other boroughs, felt that it should run its own trams on its own public highways. The Council decided that the Corporation would relay, electrify and operate the tramways within the borough, taking over the Birkdale & Southport Company from BET but leasing tracks to the Southport Company from Churchtown to Lord Street West, as that operation extended into Birkdale Urban District. BET would relay and electrify the lines in Birkdale and operate them on lease from the District Council, as originally envisaged.

Southport Corporation agreed to supply current at 500 volts dc from the municipal power station at Crowlands to the Company lines in the borough and to revise the lease of the tracks. It took 18 months for the Board of Trade, then busy with new electric tramway schemes all over Britain, to approve the terms of the new lease, which commenced on 15 July 1901, and ran for 21 years, expiring in 1922, on payment of 4½d a mile for use of the track and current.

BET also negotiated with Birkdale Urban District Council over the remaining three-quarters of a mile of horsecar line from Aughton Road to Birkdale station and bought the tracks on behalf of the Council in 1901 for £2,000. The Council leased the tracks back to BET on condition that the Company would extend and electrify the lines. The Council delegated its powers under an Electric Lighting Order to BET to generate current for the tramways and for general lighting purposes in the district from a power station to be built on Birkdale Common, off Shaftesbury Road.

Meanwhile, Southport Corporation acquired the Birkdale & Southport Company lines within the Borough on 1 January 1900 for £12,500, giving the Company running powers until the end of 1901. These were the lines from London Square to Scarisbrick New Road and Mosley Street. The Corporation could not acquire the track beyond Mosley Street as that was in Birkdale Urban District, but the Company agreed to sell the Birkdale section to the District Council for £5,000 and continued to ply through to the Crown Hotel until 14 December 1901. The Corporation bought eight horses and two horsecars at the stock sale on 17 December, to continue operating the Southport section of the line for a further 12 months pending electrification of new lines to that part of town.

The end of the horse tramway era overlapped the beginning of the electric traction era in Southport by nearly 2½ years, during which both horsecars and electric cars could be seen plying the streets of Southport and Birkdale. The story of the horse tramways is concluded in the context of the next two chapters but, to round off the story of the horse tramways in this chapter, the last remnant connected with electric cars in Scarisbrick New Road and operated between Sefton Street and the boundary in Mosley Street only. The last horsecars ran on this section on 12 December 1902.

THE COMING OF THE ELECTRIC TRAM

Southport Corporation Tramways
1900-1902

Holroyd Smith's pioneer electric street tramway on Blackpool Promenade in 1885 was the first in Britain. Four-wheel, double-deck, horsecar-type trams picked up power from a central conduit between the rails. Unfortunately, blown sand drifted down the slot and rendered the system inoperative and the trams had to revert to horse traction. In 1899 Blackpool erected overhead electric wires.

Credit for the successful operation of a trolley pole with a copper-bronze, grooved wheel running along an overhead copper conductor wire must go to the United States of America. This device was pioneered by Charles van Depoele at South Bend, Indiana, in 1885 and improved and perfected by Frank Sprague at Richmond, Virginia, in 1887-88. Sprague went on to pioneer multiple-unit electric traction at Chicago in 1897. His early trolley poles had heavy lead weights at the base to keep the wheel on the overhead wire. Later, metal springs, some in tension, others in compression, were used to ensure that the trolley pole maintained the correct angle and kept the wheel in contact with the wire.

The International Thomson-Houston Company and American engineer William Graff-Baker introduced the first overhead trolley line to Britain in 1891, when six imported American, four-wheel, single-deck trolleycars ran experimentally at Leeds on a 2-mile double-track extension of the city steam tramway system from Sheepscar to Roundhay Park, with a half-mile single-line branch from Harehills to the depot.

The swivelling trolley head was invented in Britain by Alfred Dickinson and pioneered in 1893 by South Staffordshire Tramways. Use of the swivelling trolley meant that the overhead wires did not need to be suspended directly over the centre of the track and the side-running trolley was used extensively in Britain

and France. In 1895 American-built, four-wheel, double-deckers started running in Bristol with overhead trolley current collection, and George Milnes of Birkenhead supplied a large number of Bristol trams in the late 1890s; however, these early electric cars still looked like horsecars with trolley poles although they were larger and more robust.

Other builders were coming into the field, among them the Brush Electrical Engineering Company of Loughborough, Hurst, Nelson & Company of Motherwell, and Dick, Kerr & Company of Preston. In June 1900 the 'new Liverpool car', designed jointly by Dick, Kerr's Electric Railway & Tramway Carriage Works and Liverpool Corporation Tramways' Manager, C. R. Bellamy, eclipsed the earlier design with a full-length upper deck with 'garden seats' for 34 passengers, semi-circular canopies over the platforms and reversed stairs for safety. The saloons had three large rectangular windows each side with inward-opening, hopper-style, top-light ventilators above the transoms. These cars were mounted on Brill 21E four-wheel trucks with a 6-foot wheelbase, built under licence to a design by the J. G. Brill Company of Philadelphia. This design became standard throughout Great Britain for many years.

Although steam trams of the 1880s had top covers and wind/smoke screens, the new electric cars were built with open tops because no satisfactory method had been evolved to allow the movement of the trolley pole, based on its iron mast in the middle of the open top deck. There was also the problem of clearance under bridges. The height from rail level to the top of the trolley mast was about 14ft 9in. The addition of a top cover or roof brought the height of the car to about 16 feet; the trolley mounting would have to be fitted above this. It was not until the dwarf trolley base with horizontal springs was invented in 1903 that the problem was solved. It was then that Bellamy designed his famous covers for Liverpool trams, known as Bellamy roofs.

Electric traction for Southport

In 1899 the Southport Tramways Committee went on a fact-finding tour of the few electric tramways operating in south Lancashire at the time. In 1898 Liverpool had opened its first overhead-wire tramline from the Victoria Monument in South Castle Street to Dingle with German-built single-deck motor cars and trailer cars. The Blackpool & Fleetwood Tramroad had also started running from Gynn Square to Fleetwood in 1898; this was an overhead-trolley light railway using single-deck bogie cars. Blackpool Corporation had just changed over from conduit to overhead wire on the Promenade in 1899 and was running four-wheel and bogie cars. Bolton Corporation had opened its overhead trolley line to Tonge Moor in 1899, using the then new Dick, Kerr four-wheel, short-canopied, open-top trams, similar to those supplied to Liverpool in 1899 and to the Liverpool Overhead Railway's tramway between Seaforth and Waterloo.

Southport Corporation decided to electrify its tramways on the overhead wire principle, using Liverpool as its model. The Corporation's application for a £55,000 loan to build a tramway system was the subject of a Local Government Board inquiry in June 1899, and Board of Trade consent to its tramway scheme was confirmed by Parliament in October of that year. This gave the Corporation powers to electrify four lines, to High Park, Blowick, St Luke's circular and Kew Gardens, plus any others it wanted to build within the borough. The original estimate for the rolling stock was prepared at this time and it suggested the purchase of 15 single-deck motor cars and four trailer cars, indicating that the committee had been impressed with Liverpool's German motor and trailer car operation.

However, Liverpool did not continue with the foreign single-deckers and by 1899 a number of Brush and Milnes four-wheel, open-top, double-deckers of the Bristol type with short canopies were appearing as new lines opened and, finally, Dick, Kerr's new 1900 model of four-wheel, open-topper with a full-length upper deck as described above. So in 1900 Southport's original estimate of 1899 was altered and an order was placed for nine double-deck, open-top trams of the 'new Liverpool type', six single-deck, combination (open and enclosed) cars, and one normal single-decker, a total of 16 cars.

The bodies were built by the Electric Railway & Tramway Carriage Works Ltd in Strand Road, Preston, and mounted on Brill 21E four-wheel trucks with a 6-foot wheelbase, and motors and control equipment made by Dick, Kerr & Company Ltd on the other side of the road. The coachworks was a subsidiary of the Dick, Kerr engineering works, which also supplied the grooved rail for Southport. The two establishments combined to form the largest tramcar factory in Britain, known from 1918 as English Electric.

Construction

The Corporation set to work on 15 January 1900 laying rails and underground cables, repaving the roads and erecting traction poles with bracket arms and overhead electric conductor wires along new lines from Hoghton Street up Sussex Road to Blowick, Crowlands depot and High Park, and up Manchester Road to St Luke's Road and Ash Street. The permanent way and overhead electrification were constructed by direct labour under the supervision of the Borough Surveyor, Mr R. P. Hirst, the Borough Electrical Engineer, Mr R. S Downe, and the Corporation Tramways Manager, Mr R. J. Wilton.

Roads were excavated to a depth of 13½ inches and the rails were laid on a bed of broken stone and 6 inches of concrete, packed with stone chippings, sand and cement. The Dick, Kerr grooved girder rail was supplied in 40-foot lengths, weighing 87lb per yard, and laid to the standard 4ft 8½in gauge with tie-bars to maintain the gauge. Special trackwork, such as points and crossovers, was supplied by

Edgar, Allen Ltd of Sheffield. The movable points all had drains. The Corporation considered concreting the tram roads from kerb to kerb but decided to repave the roads with granite setts because of their durability and to give horses a better grip as most traffic was still horse-drawn. Lord Street and London Square were repaved with wood blocks to dampen the drumming of the trams on the rails. The routes were laid with single track and passing loops except for Manchester Road, which was double-tracked from Holy Trinity Church to Hartwood Road.

The tubular steel traction poles that supported the overhead wires stood 25 feet tall with 5 feet buried in the ground. Bracket arms, supported by ornamental iron scrollwork, were fixed about 22 feet above the roadway with vertical lugs towards their extremities to suspend the overhead wire about 21 feet above the rails. The stout bases of the traction poles, varying between 4ft 6in and 5 feet high, were embossed with the borough coat of arms. The poles were crowned with ball-and-spike finials, which were not merely ornamental but prevented rainwater from rusting the poles from the inside.

Side-bracket poles were employed almost universally on the system. The running wires were erected using rigid suspension with the insulators and copper wires fixed directly to the bracket arms, except on Lord Street and Sussex Road, where flexible suspension was tried with the insulators fixed to a transverse wire suspended between two lugs bolted to the underside of the bracket arm. This experiment proved to be successful, for in March 1901 a severe snowstorm brought down all the rigid overhead wiring, leaving Lord Street and Sussex Road intact. Having learned this lesson, the Tramways Department re-hung the wires with flexible suspension, although it took till 1906 to complete the conversion throughout the system.

Track-laying and electrification of the High Park, Blowick and St Luke's lines was complete by 25 June ready for the Board of Trade inspection and the inauguration of public service. Six miles of new tramway had been constructed in five months by muscle, pick, shovel and horses.

The electricity supply for the tramways came from the municipal electricity generating station built next to the gas works at Crowlands in 1894. Initially this provided a dc power supply to the town centre only. The power station was enlarged in 1898 and, in pursuance of the Corporation's fast tramway building policy, by the beginning of July 1900 two of the three traction generators had been commissioned and were supplying 500 volts dc to the tramway system. The tram depot was built on the same campus as the power station and the gas works: it was a 10-road, brick car shed built to house 40 cars. It was known as Crowlands depot till Canning Road was built in the 1920s.

It was stipulated that the nine double-deck tramcars should be delivered in time for the scheduled opening of the system on 18 July 1900, and they duly arrived by railway at Blowick sidings. The complete lower decks, including platforms and stairs, came on railway low-loaders (short, four-wheel flatcars). The trucks, complete with motors and wheels, and also the upper-deck fittings such as decency panels, railings, seats, trolley masts and trolley poles, were loaded separately, to be put together as kits. The whole lot had to be transferred by crane to road low-loaders hauled by steam traction engines along Butts Lane to Crowlands depot. Unfortunately one of the complete lower decks was dropped and damaged during transfer from rail to road and had to be returned to Preston for repair.

The Corporation now had only eight trams for the three routes when three cars had been allocated for each service. The double-deck cars in the Corporation fleet were given even numbers only and the first batch was numbered 2 to 18, but I do not know which one was the damaged car.

Opening day

The sun smiled down auspiciously on 18 July 1900, the opening day of Southport Corporation Tramways. The inauguration of electric traction was a historic occasion in those horse-drawn days and a great crowd gathered to see the opening ceremony. Four open-top tramcars were festooned in evergreens, bouquets of flowers and small

This was the opening day of Southport Corporation Tramways on 18 July 1900. A crowd sees off the civic party on two of the six inaugural cars from Hoghton Street terminus on a tour of the lines to Ash Street (via Hartwood Road), Blowick (via Sussex Road), High Park (via Bispham Road) and Crowlands depot. These were among the first batch of nine open-top double-deckers from Dick, Kerr & Co Ltd, of Preston. Chapel Street in the background still had horse trams. *Cedric Greenwood collection*

Union flags and the temporary tram terminus at the town end of Hoghton Street was overhung with bunting.

The civic party, totalling 100 guests, included the Mayor and Mayoress, the chairman of the Tramways Committee and the Chief Constable of Southport. Reporters from the town's two main newspapers, the *Southport Visiter* and *Southport Guardian*, were present to cover the event. The Tramways Committee chairman, Cllr G. F. Travis, was reported as saying that the council had been in 'a little bit of a rush' to open the tramways. It was only six months since the first rail was laid, the Corporation had taken delivery of only half of the cars it had on order, the initial service would consequently be only half what was intended and the staff uniforms were unfinished. The tramways were not altogether ready that day but the Corporation preferred to start in a rather modest way so that the tramwaymen might become fully accustomed to their duties before increased traffic was put on, he said.

As the horse trams in Southport had been mainly patronised by ladies, Cllr Travis invited the Mayoress, Mrs T. P. Griffiths, to start the first car, Mrs Travis the second car and Mrs Jones, wife of the chairman of the Electricity Committee, the third, presumably under supervision (it was a not uncommon courtesy in those days to allow a lady to start the inaugural electric tramcar). The crowd

watched the convoy of cars move off along Hoghton Street and turn right into Mornington Road. The civic tram procession toured all the electric lines, to Ash Street, Blowick and High Park, reversing at the terminals, and finally arrived at the nearly completed tram depot at Crowlands. The party inspected the running shed, the workshops, the paintshop and the power station.

The line leading to the depot from a triangular junction with Bispham Road was used solely for depot access and for test runs; it was not in public service generally, although from June 1908 passengers on the last cars at night were allowed to ride along the private track till just before the left turn into the tramshed.

The four tramcars that took part in the opening ceremony were joined by two more from the depot and the six cars returned to town to start running public services from 2.30pm. With only two cars on each route this service was rather sparse for the first day of operation. Souvenir tickets were issued for the occasion; they read: 'Southport Corporation Tramways opening day, July 18th, 1900; fare 2d. for one journey on any section. For ordinary fares see back.' On the reverse side of the ticket the ordinary fares were given as 2d to Blowick or High Park (with 1d and 1½d intermediate stages) and 1d on the Inner Circle to Ash Street. The next day, 19 July, saw seven cars in service with one spare car in the depot.

Three cars were on the High Park route, two on the Blowick line and two on the Ash Street line via Manchester Road.

The electric car fleet

About six weeks later, towards the end of August, the damaged double-deck car, now repaired, arrived from Preston together with seven single-deck cars, which took the odd numbers 1 to 13 in the fleet. The first six single-deckers (1 to 11) were combination (enclosed/open) cars with open-sided seating areas for smokers fore and aft of a central saloon. These were called 'California' cars as the design had originated there in 1893 and was very popular in those balmier climes. This design was quite popular in Britain in those days even for non-smokers, who enjoyed the fresh air and summer breezes – even Wigan and Manchester had California cars! The British climate, however, proved the California cars to be unsuitable for general, year-round use; the design was short-lived and never repeated. The seventh single-decker, No 13, was a conventional saloon car, which was often set aside from public service for official inspection trips and became known as the 'Committee Car'.

Two more California cars, Nos 15 and 17, were delivered in December in time to augment the roster of cars on the Inner Circle

service on the completion of the circle from Ash Street back to town with the opening of the Scarisbrick New Road line to the Infirmary. This brought the Corporation fleet to a total of 18 electric cars.

The technical details of the tramcar fleet at this stage were as follows. All were built and equipped by Dick, Kerr & Company, Preston. The delivery of the nine double-deckers was sandwiched between a massive order of 300 destined for Liverpool. Southport was probably the first authority outside Liverpool to be operating the 'new Liverpool' type of tramcar with the full-length upper deck. The Corporation fleet comprised:

Nine double-deck, open-top cars
('new Liverpool' type); even numbers 2 to 18
Overall length
  27ft with open platforms and reversed stairs
Saloon
  16ft long, 6ft 7in high, 6ft 6in wide with three rectangular windows each side
Seating
  22 inside on two continuous longitudinal benches, 11 each side; 34 outside on transverse seats with reversible backs; total capacity 56
Equipment
  Brill 21E, 6ft wheelbase, four-wheel truck with 30in diameter wheels

This side view of a 'California'-type car, loading in London Square in the winter of 1900, shows the unusual arrangement of this combination car for all seasons: a short, central saloon with curtains and back-to-back, cross-bench seating on open-sided platforms. Striped canvas blinds could be used as windbreaks on the offside of the open seating areas, which were also the vestibules to the saloon. Eight of these cars were built by Dick, Kerr for Southport in 1900 and they were used on the more lightly loaded Inner Circle and Blowick routes. The photograph shows a rudimentary lifeguard tray at each end of the truck before being fitted with the standard gate-and-tray lifeguard in 1902. The steeple of Christ Church is in the background; the spire was removed in 1952. *James Dean collection*

Two 25hp Dick, Kerr 25A motors
Two Dick, Kerr 1A controllers
Ratchet handbrakes and electric emergency
brakes
R. W. Blackwell trolley mast and pole,
centrally placed with outside springs in
tension and swivel trolley-head

**Eight single-deck combination ('California')
cars with clerestory roofs; odd numbers 1 to
11, 15 and 17**
Overall length
27ft with open-fronted platforms
Saloon
6ft 6in wide with two segmental-arched
windows each side and clerestory roof
Seating
16 in saloon, eight each side on
longitudinal benches; eight on two back-to-
back cross-bench seats on each platform
with three-pane glass screen between
forward- and rear-facing seats; total
capacity 32
Equipment
As for double-deckers except that
controllers were type 1B and trolley mast
was based on decking mounted on
clerestory. Total height of trolley mast and
pole was equal to that on open-top double
deckers

**One standard single-deck saloon car
('Committee Car'); No 13**
Overall length
26ft with short, open-fronted platform at
each end
Saloon
6ft 6in wide, four windows each side with
curved top corners
Seating
26 in saloon, 13 each side on longitudinal
benches
Equipment
As for California cars

All Southport's double-deckers, both of the
Corporation and Company, were built with
full-length top decks, full-canopied platforms
and reversed stairs. The passenger mounted
the platform and, after passing the conductor,
immediately on the left was the foot of the
staircase. It went up to the back of the car,

curving in a 90-degree right-turn over the
conductor's head, and ended up on the semi-
circular end of the top deck. Direct stairs, on
the other hand, began to the right of the
conductor and curved 90 degrees to the left,
facing forward.

Reversed stairs were considered safer than
direct stairs. If you slipped when coming
downstairs as the car was stopping, the
bulkhead would break your fall on the platform,
whereas if you fell down direct stairs you could
shoot off the open platform into the street.
Reversed stairs went out of fashion in later years
because, as the cars were double-ended, they
limited the driver's headroom and his visibility
of traffic overtaking on the nearside. This did
not matter in 1900; being electrically driven, the
trams were the fastest vehicles on the road. In
Southport they got round the visibility problem
by putting a thick glass panel riser in the
staircase at the driver's eye level.

On opening day the cars had no destination
indicators but very shortly afterwards they
were all fitted with reversible destination
boards (eg TOWN/BLOWICK) that slotted
into brackets on the front ends of the cars.
Routes were identified only by their
destinations initially, later supplemented by
route letters and coloured lights (see
'Consolidation' chapter).

Southport copied not only the Liverpool
design of tramcar but also the Liverpool livery
of the time: crimson lake dash and waist
panels and ivory rocker panels and decency
boards, lined out in gold-leaf, black and
brown, with 'Preston standard' gold fleet
names and numbers shaded blue. Trucks and
other ancillary equipment, including railings
and trolley masts, were painted ruddy brown
(officially 'red oxide'). Collision fenders were
black. The surfaces of floors, platforms and
stair treads were finished in grey.

Crowlands depot was completed in August
1900 and was said to be one of the finest
examples of tram depot architecture in Great
Britain. The Accrington pressed brick
building, still extant with minor alterations,
on the corner of Cobden Road, has a
decorative façade topped by a striking trinity
of curved Dutch gables with stone copings and
finials. The three-bay façade framed three
portals for the tramcars with full-height

Inside the Corporation tramway workshops at Crowlands depot in 1901 we see Dick, Kerr car No 6, a 56-seat, open-top double-decker of 1900, showing a 'High Park' destination board. We also see two triangular-frame jacks for lifting the body off the truck and the block and tackle for hoisting motors from the truck. Each car was powered by two 25hp motors. *James Dean collection*

double doors. These portals had semi-elliptical arches each with five spaced keystones. The broad central bay featured a more elaborate gable with a stone-framed clock under a hood moulding. The private single line to the depot had three single left-hand turnouts through the three portals. Inside the shed the centre track separated into four roads and each side track into three, giving a total of ten roads, each four cars long; the capacity was thus 40 cars, which was considered to be sufficient for the foreseeable future. The shed, initially 150 feet by 122 feet, included offices at the front, and the ten roads led behind sliding partitions to the workshops at the back. This building is still in use today as the bus garage, slightly and tastefully modified at the front and much extended at the back for buses, with access from Cobden Road.

The electric lines

The original three electric tram routes started from the town end of Hoghton Street. They were:

Town to High Park via Hoghton Street, Mornington Road, Derby Road, Sussex Road, Tithebarn Road, Bispham Road and Old Park Lane, terminating in High Park Place.

Town to Blowick via Hoghton Street, Mornington Road, Derby Road, Sussex Road and Norwood Road to a terminus at the corner of Hart Street.

Town to Ash Street via Hoghton Street, Manchester Road, Hartwood Road, St Luke's Road, Rose Hill (St Luke's station bridge) and Ash Street to its junction with Scarisbrick New Road.

Although the routes can be followed on the map on page 6, bear in mind that the trackwork in 1900 was not as well developed as shown on the map, which depicts the system at its maximum extent in 1928.

In July 1900 all routes commenced from a single-line terminus in Hoghton Street with a passing loop and a stub headshunt outside the Hoghton Arms. At Mornington Road the High Park and Blowick cars turned right into a passing loop and continued on single track along Mornington Road, then round a left-hand corner into Derby Road for about 150 yards to the inner end of Sussex Road at what came to be known as the 'Jam Chapel' corner. St Mark's Methodist Church was built in 1905 on the corner of Derby Road and Church Street at a cost of £25,000. A major benefactor was William Hartley, of 2 Wellington Terrace, Lord Street, owner of Hartley's jam factories at Aintree and elsewhere.

The trams turned right into Sussex Road and continued for a further 200 yards before arriving at the next passing loop at Zetland Street. This length of single track from Mornington Road to Sussex Road, with two blind corners where drivers could not see oncoming trams, caused no end of problems. Inward and outward trams often met in Derby

Road and the inbound tram had to reverse to Zetland Street loop. As a result of this chaos, passing loops were added at Mornington Road/Derby Road corner and at Derby Road/Sussex Road corner. Another loop was also installed on the crown of Sussex Road bridge over the Preston line after the first few weeks of operation.

On the town side of the bridge the Sussex Road line crossed the St Luke's Road line of the Ash Street semi-circle at right angles and a single-line curve around the southern corner of the crossroads formed a junction between the two single lines. This would be used in future as a depot access line only by trams running light to or from Scarisbrick New Road, the Cemetery and the Crown Hotel.

The High Park cars continued over the crown of the bridge on Sussex Road. The car had just cleared the trailing point when, still on the downward slope, the lines diverged, the Blowick line going straight ahead and the High Park cars taking a left-hand single turnout into Tithebarn Road. While still descending the curve the car ran into a passing loop with a slight right-hand bend in the middle of the loop as the road levelled and straightened out. This was almost like riding a rollercoaster, especially if one was seated at the front of the upper deck.

The Blowick cars, on the other hand, proceeded straight on down the Sussex Road ramp into the loop at Maple Street at the foot of the slope and continued to the end of Sussex Road and the right-hand bend into Norwood Road. This bend was double-tracked with a long loop in later years. The trams ran along Norwood Road only for about 300 yards before arriving at Blowick terminus, just short of the two railway level crossings by Blowick station: the ungated gas works siding and the gated main line to Manchester. At that time this was the end of the built-up area of Southport, apart from an odd building or two. The tramline finished in a passing loop and a stub end in the middle of a wide space formed by the junction with Hart Street. Between this junction and the railway crossings the Blowick Hotel stood on the left-hand side and on the right were the railway sidings, where the new tramcars had arrived and been unloaded.

Meanwhile the High Park tram, having cleared the loop in Tithebarn Road, was now heading for the long ramped bridge over the railway at Meols Cop station. The bridge carries the crossroads junction of Tithebarn Road-Bispham Road and Norwood Road-Norwood Avenue. The car swung through a slight S-kink between the alignment of Tithebarn Road and the bridge ahead then mounted the ramp and entered a length of double track that took it over the bridge and the crossroads. The double track extended over the upper half of each ramp, then the car reverted to single track as it descended into Bispham Road.

The route so far had been residential but over the bridge the tram continued through an area of small shops around Wennington Road crossing, where there was a loop. This loop became the terminus of a route from the Crown Hotel at a much later date, in 1925.

Our tram journey is now nearing its end. After Wennington Road loop the trams reached the right-angled triangular, single-track junction with the Canning Road line to the depot. About 150 yards further on the line took a left-hand bend into Old Park Lane, following a rather winding course with odd cottages interspersed among the semi-detached houses. At the end of Old Park Lane the tramcar terminated in High Park Place. Here were more shops and the tramline terminated alongside a cabmen's shelter on its left in the middle of the square. There was a gap of about 4 yards or so beyond the end of the Corporation tramline to the Southport Tramways Company horsecar line as it turned the corner from Mill Lane into Roe Lane but there was no physical connection between the two lines at that time.

The Inner Circle

The third electric tramway was a semi-circular route to Ash Street, which was called the Inner Circle from the outset although there was no outer circle and the circle would not be complete until December 1900, involving the use of Scarisbrick New Road and Eastbank Street, which were still being served by horsecars of the Birkdale & Southport Company. The Ash Street cars, like the High Park and Blowick cars, started from Hoghton

Street terminus but instead of turning into Mornington Road they continued along Hoghton Street to Holy Trinity Church.

At this crossroads the Corporation electric tramway met the Company horse tramway but the two lines converged and diverged here without touching. The Corporation electric line turned right from Hoghton Street into Manchester Road while the Company horsecar line turned left from the lower end of Manchester Road into Queen's Road. By September 1901 there would be a tramway crossing here with double tracks right down Manchester Road and a single line from Hoghton Street to Queen's Road with single-line connecting curves around the north and south corners.

Initially Manchester Road was laid with double track from Holy Trinity Church up the rise of Mount Pleasant to the point where it met Roe Lane at Leyland Road Church and turned right into Hartwood Road and back on to single track. From Holy Trinity corner the road started to climb and was, in effect, a long crescent with a series of slight bends to the left, finally straightening out at the top of Mount Pleasant to the Leyland Road junction. As this double-track section connected single lines in Hoghton Street and Hartwood Road, outward-bound cars had to run on the wrong side of Manchester Road for about one car length to enter and leave this double-track section, as can be seen on the map. It should be remembered that motor traffic was scarce in those days and that, even when the internal combustion engine became more prolific, such manœuvres by tramcars were accepted as the norm.

The Manchester Road tracks were strung with overhead wires suspended independently from traction poles with short bracket arms on each side of the road instead of the more general practice of supporting both wires from poles with longer bracket arms on one side of the road. The short bracket poles were not opposite each other; each bracket arm supported only one wire and the up and down wires were further apart. The wires were not directly above the tracks, but this was acceptable with swivel-head trolleys. At the wide road junctions at both ends of this section, at Holy Trinity Church and Leyland Road Methodist Church, the overhead wires had to be suspended from long span wires supported by traction poles.

At Leyland Road junction the Corporation electric and Company horsecar lines converged and diverged again, the horsecars turning left from Leyland Road into Roe Lane and the electric cars swinging right into Hartwood Road. Very shortly the electric single-line made another right turn into St Luke's Road and a passing loop. St Luke's Church was passed on the left-hand corner of Hawkshead Street. At the next corner the line crossed the Sussex Road single track and a single-line curve (the depot access line described earlier) came in from the left as the trams headed for the bridge over the railway at St Luke's station.

The scene changed as the line approached the station. St Luke's was a suburban junction station, where the Manchester and Preston lines of the Lancashire & Yorkshire Railway bifurcated. The bridge spanned two island platforms and six railway tracks. It was therefore a long bridge with a fairly flat summit and a long tramway loop past the station booking office and the T-junction with Hart Street. This was the last passing place before the tram terminus in Ash Street just short of Scarisbrick Road crossing.

The station booking office atop the town side of the bridge was a typically substantial and elaborate railway building in pale yellow-ochre glazed bricks relieved with brown glazed brick string courses and corbelling under a hipped roof with a mock-Tudor gable over the archway. A covered footbridge and staircases led down to the two island platforms with full-width glazed canopies, one on the straight line to Blowick and Manchester and the other on the curve leading to Meols Cop and Preston. Situated about 3 minutes' journey time from Chapel Street terminus, St Luke's was a stop for all businessmen's expresses to and from Manchester as well as the local trains to Crossens and Preston.

When the bridge was built, several years before the tramway was laid, the ramps rose above the ground level of the houses in St Luke's Road and steps had to be provided to give access to them from the raised street level; their front garden gates and railings are now alongside the footpaths on the bridge ramps.

This area around St Luke's station had been Little London, a hamlet that had been overwhelmed by the urban development of Southport some 30 years previously. There were still several old houses that had been shrimpers' and fishermen's homes, and other remnants of Little London were the rebuilt Blue Anchor public house in Tithebarn Road and the London Hotel on the corner of Windsor Road and Kensington Road. In the railway sidings at the St Luke's end of Windsor Road were the cattle and sheep pens on the site of the original terminus of the West Lancashire Railway to Hesketh Bank before the line was completed to Preston and extended to Southport Central station on Derby Road.

As it turned out, the Inner Circle tram route was never a financial success and was subject to two-way working, one-way working, extensions, suspensions and early abandonment. From 1914 the tracks of the Inner Circle were used by circular sightseeing tours, which were very popular and lucrative but they operated only on fine summer days and it was always the regular stage services for residents that consistently brought in the revenue.

The Tramways Committee thought at first that the situation in Southport would be similar to that in Blackpool, where holidaymakers rode the trams along the Promenade to the Tower, Palace Ballroom, Golden Mile, Louis Tussaud's Waxworks and the Pleasure Beach and north to Gynn Square to connect with the Blackpool & Fleetwood Tramroad. Although Southport had no wish to emulate Blackpool's brash and vulgar entertainments, it did have the Winter Gardens indoor entertainment complex, the second longest pier in Britain and a fairground being developed at the south end of the Marine Lake. As far as the tramways were concerned, Southport was completely different from Blackpool in that its trams did not run along the Promenade and nowhere in Southport would a tram passenger have caught sight of the sea.

Town Centre and Kew Gardens

After opening day, 18 July 1900, no time was lost in removing the Birkdale & Southport Company's horse tram track in London Square, London Street, Chapel Street and Eastbank Street as far as Talbot Street loop. The horsecar services to Kew and Birkdale via Scarisbrick New Road and Sefton Street were cut back to that point and passengers had to walk the few hundred yards between Talbot Street and the town centre while the town centre trackwork was relaid.

There was a central gas lamp with a circular seat around it in the middle of the crossroads at London Street, Chapel Street and Hoghton Street in the leisurely days of horse trams and this had to be removed to extend the Hoghton Street line into Chapel Street. The line along Chapel Street was the first leg of the one-way tramway circuit of the town centre, which Americans would call 'the downtown loop'. The heavier-section electric tram rails were laid as single track along Chapel Street with a right turn into Eastbank Street. In Eastbank Street Square the line passed left of the central cabstand before turning into Lord Street.

With the double-track horsecar line of the Southport Tramways Company still in situ along the middle of Lord Street, the new single-track electric line was taken around the corner from Eastbank Street Square into Lord Street for one block to London Square. There were now three tracks along this section of Lord Street, with the electric line being laid between the horsecar tracks and the footpath along the gardens side of the street. Thus the electric cars on this section were all travelling north-east on the wrong side of the road, passing to the right of the horse trams going south-west! With horsecars heading north-east on the seaward side of the road there were two lines of trams going north-east and one going south-west in the middle!

At London Square the new electric line swung in a wide sweep to the right, keeping well to the left of the cabmen's shelter in the middle of the square, to a loading point alongside the footpath on the north-east side of the square. When the circuit was complete, this was to be the main loading point for the electric cars to High Park, Blowick and the Ash Street semi-circle, and the temporary horse trams to Kew Gardens and the Crown Hotel. The single line went through a reverse curve out of London Square into London Street to an equal-turnout facing point, left into Hoghton Street and right into Chapel Street. The former terminal loop in Hoghton Street was now a short stretch of double-track from the triangular single-track junction with London Street.

With the trackwork complete around the town centre circuit the next stage was the erection of the traction poles and overhead wires. This was done, again in typical Southport fashion, by means of side bracket arms, some of them, particularly in Eastbank Street and Lord Street, stretching 10 feet or more over the streets. As stated previously, flexible suspension was used on Lord Street. Here also the poles were erected among the trees, which stood about 7 or 8 feet back from the kerb and marked the front boundary of the long gardens of the early-Victorian houses of the past.

It was a mystery to me why the overhead wires around the town centre circuit were double right from the very start, as if for a two-way service, although the trams ran only one way in a clockwise direction. Cars used the left-hand wire but not the right-hand one, which was strung around the inside of the circuit. If you looked up from the top deck of a tram, the left-hand wire was polished by the action of the trolley-wheels whereas the right-hand wire was green with the weathering of the copper. I was puzzled by this for some time in my early years. I can only conjecture that it was a supply wire. The Corporation was committed to the supply of electric current to the Southport Tramways Company within the Borough of Southport. The Company, having been absorbed by the British Electric Traction Company Ltd in 1899, was preparing to electrify its horse tramways from Churchtown to Birkdale via Lord Street.

The town centre one-way circuit of tracks and wires was commissioned on 10 October 1900, and used by all electric cars from Hoghton Street, travelling clockwise. Sufficient progress had been made on electrifying the line along Scarisbrick New

This is London Square in the summer of 1902 with Corporation car No 14 loading a good queue for Scarisbrick New Road and Kew Gardens. The outside springs on the trolley base are clearly silhouetted. On the extreme right is the back end of a Company car loading at the London Square stop on Lord Street for Churchtown. This splendid view is taken from Parr's Bank, now the National Westminster Bank. London Square and Lord Street were paved with wood blocks and horse-drawn landaus waited for passengers outside the cabmen's wooden shelter, which had been extended since horse tram days to include a waiting shed for tram passengers and the adjoining brick lavatories. Bath chairs are for hire (bottom right). *Online Transport Archive*

Above This rare photograph was taken during the brief period at the turn of the century when Southport tramways were in transition from horse power to electric power. It shows a horsecar of the Birkdale & Southport Tramways Company turning right from Lord Street into London Square under the new electric wires erected for the Corporation's single-line circuit around the town centre. It is running on the right hand side of the road on the newly laid third track that was used by trams from Eastbank Street Square to London Square between the commissioning of this circuit in October 1900 and the realignment of tracks on the inland side of the road for normal double-track

working at the end of November, when the left-hand line was lifted. The picture shows traction poles continuing along Lord Street for the STC electrification but without bracket arms or wires. The horse bus on the extreme left of the picture, loading at the corner of Nevill Street, might have operated between Birkdale and Churchtown during the relaying and electrification of the STC lines, although the horse trams are reported to have used temporary rails linking the old and new tracks. The horse tram in the picture is BST car No 5, built by G. F. Milnes at Birkenhead and displaying a 'Birkdale' destination board. This route via Sefton Street to the Crown Hotel was cut back to Mosley Street in December 1901, and was the last horse tramway in Southport when it closed on 12 December 1902. The incomplete state of the traction poles and the absence of electric cars suggests that the photograph could have been taken shortly before the town centre circuit was electrified on 10 October. *James Dean collection*

Left This is the same junction viewed in the opposite direction after the completion of the trackwork and electrification on Lord Street, viewed from London Square. Corporation cars are now running on the left-hand line from Eastbank Street Square to London Square, sharing tracks – but not overhead wires – with Company cars from Birkdale to Churchtown. The third track, the original horsecar line to Churchtown, on the shops side of the street, has gone and the electrified double tracks are offset on the gardens side of the street. Dick, Kerr car No 24 of 1902 is about to take the right-hand turnout into London Square to load for Kew Gardens. This picture shows the London Square end of the three-wire section from Eastbank Street Square and, as can be seen, the Corporation cars tapped the centre trolley wire on their one-way circuit of the town centre; the two outside wires were used by Company cars running the full length of Lord Street. The Corporation, which owned all the tramway infrastructure within the borough, provided separate wires for the Company cars so that their consumption could be metered. *Courtesy of Martin Jenkins, E. J. McWatt and A. D. Packer, Online Transport Archive*

Road to complete the Inner Circle and for clockwise and anti-clockwise cars to start running both ways between the town centre circuit and Ash Street from 3 December. On the same day the horse trams to Kew Gardens and the Crown Hotel were reinstated through the town centre, running round the new circuit, interspersed between the electric cars and considerably slowing them down. From 17 December 1900 electric cars replaced the horse trams to the Infirmary but the horse trams continued in service between the Infirmary and Kew Gardens until 5 January, when alternate electric cars to the Infirmary continued to Kew Gardens. Horse trams continued to mix with electric cars between the town centre circuit and Scarisbrick New Road to work the Sefton Street line to the Crown Hotel for a further 12 months until December 1901.

For the first few years of electric traction the tracks on Eastbank Street were single from Chapel Street inward to Lord Street and double from Chapel Street outward to the bridge. Some time between 1903 and 1909 the track was doubled between Chapel Street and Eastbank Street Square, where they converged to single before the cabstand, enabling trams to reverse there. The purpose of the outbound line from the square to a trailing junction with Chapel Street was another mystery. I believe that service cars reversed in the square and returned up Eastbank Street on temporary diversion for track relaying but only once did I ever see a tramcar on that stretch of track.

It was a straight line from Eastbank Street to Kew Gardens but for a slight left-hand bend into Scarisbrick New Road. The double track along Eastbank Street converged to single track up the north-west ramp of the bridge and divided to double again from the crest of the bridge along Scarisbrick New Road to St Philip's Church. The line reverted to single track before Ash Street and remained single the rest of the way to the terminus with passing loops at the Infirmary, Ash Lane (Haig Avenue) and Kew Gardens.

Two lines to the Cemetery

The Corporation planned to add two more routes to the system, to the Southport/Birkdale boundary near Southport Cemetery, one via Shakespeare Street and the other via Ash Street. The Birkdale & Southport horsecar line along Sefton Street would then be abandoned.

Meanwhile the Corporation relaid the horse tramways from Lord Street to Botanic Gardens for the first stage of electrification of the Southport Tramways Company within the borough between March and June 1901. The route opened on 1 August (see the next chapter) and later that month the Corporation started two rather obscure tram services sharing tracks with Company cars on Lord Street, Queen's Road and Albert Road:

Opera House to Blowick and High Park, two late-evening cars from the crossover outside the Opera House on the corner of Lord Street and Coronation Walk, going via London Square then following the normal routes to Blowick and High Park.

Park Circle to Hesketh Park and Kew Gardens, from Eastbank Street Square via Lord Street, Albert Road, Park Road, Queen's Road, Hoghton Street, Chapel Street, Eastbank Street and Scarisbrick New Road.

Both these services were short-lived. The regular Park Service was withdrawn at the end of October 1901, and operated only as a bank holiday service until it was eclipsed by the start of the Grand Tour in 1914. Scarisbrick New Road trams ran every 15 minutes to the Infirmary and hourly to Kew Gardens. The Opera House service to Blowick and High Park, after the show, apparently assumed that these were communities of seasoned opera-goers but it was little used by residents. The service was reduced in the winter to a one-car shuttle service between the Opera House and London Square and that was withdrawn shortly afterwards. The Opera House cars were the only ones known to use the south curve from Eastbank Street Square into Lord Street, but there was no junction in the overhead wires and the conductor had to jump the trolley from one wire to the other using the trolley rope (this was before the introduction of bamboo poles). The normal Blowick service was not well patronised either and was halved from 15 to 30 minutes in December 1901.

Meanwhile, in the midst of all these works, the Tramways Manager, R. J. Wilson, who had come from Sheffield tramways to supervise the inauguration of the Southport system, resigned his post in November 1901 to become construction manager of George Hill & Company, electrical equipment manufacturers, of Manchester, and was succeeded as General Manager by his former Depot Superintendent at Crowlands, Thomas Kendrew, at the same rate of pay, £3 a week. He was manager of Southport's trams and buses for 36 years.

The Birkdale & Southport Company's running powers on the Crown Hotel line expired on 14 December 1901. At the height of its mission to promote electric traction, the Corporation, which already owned the horse tramway and depot, now found itself the reluctant owner of eight horses and two trams from the Company stock sale necessary to continue operating the short Sefton Street-Mosley Street line for a further year pending the opening of the Shakespeare Street and Duke Street electric line to the Cemetery.

The horse tramway from London Square to the Crown Hotel was suddenly lopped at both ends and reduced to a short section in the middle of the route. The Corporation decided it was time to stop horsecars sharing tracks with electric cars and cut them back from London Square to the junction of Scarisbrick New Road and Sefton Street, where passengers changed cars. At the same time the Birkdale section, from Mosley Street to the Crown Hotel, was abandoned as the Corporation could not inherit the Company's powers to run in the neighbouring Urban District, and the Company was wound up shortly after selling the track to Birkdale UDC. This section would be electrified and re-opened 11 months later by the Southport Tramways Company running via Upper Aughton Road (see the next chapter).

On 29 September 1902 Southport Corporation started the construction of the two new routes to the Cemetery and the Birkdale boundary. The Shakespeare Street and Duke Street line was to be the main route. This came off the Kew Gardens line in a double-track junction at the foot of Eastbank Street bridge and swung right into St James Street. This was known as Tabernacle junction

after the Baptist Tabernacle in the fork of Scarisbrick New Road and Southbank Road. While the Kew line made a slight left-hand bend into Scarisbrick New Road the new line continued straight ahead for about two car lengths alongside the kerb of a triangular island with a cabmen's shelter and public lavatory in the middle of the road junction before turning right into St James Street and reducing to a single track on the curve. After crossing Portland Street the single track continued along Shakespeare Street with its small shops. At the next corner the line turned left into Duke Street on a passing loop that went right around the corner so that drivers of inward and outward cars could wait if they saw an oncoming car on the single-line section in either street.

The track along Duke Street crossed the single line of the Sefton Street horse tramway at right-angles and, as the horse trams would continue to run for only a few more months, a manufactured tramway crossing was not installed; the horsecar lines were cut, flush against the electric car track at the same level, and two grooves for the horsecar flanges were chiselled into their upper surfaces. Immediately beyond the crossing the electric line went into another passing loop then continued along Duke Street to Cemetery Road with the Cemetery on the opposite, left-hand corner.

The tramway made an equal facing turnout left and right into Cemetery Road, making a single-track triangular junction with the other new line being laid along Cemetery Road. The line continued as single track along Cemetery Road and the terminus known as 'Cemetery' was 330 yards beyond the Cemetery, at the Birkdale boundary, where Cemetery Road became Eastbourne Road. The Corporation had no powers to run its trams into Birkdale Urban District but the anchor pole for the overhead wires was just over the boundary in Birkdale.

The second route to the Cemetery was the line via Scarisbrick New Road and Ash Street. It will be recalled that the double track along Scarisbrick New Road became single at St Philip's Church, followed, after a length of some 50 feet, by a left-hand turnout into Ash Street (north) for the Inner Circle. Now a right-hand turnout was added for the Cemetery cars and this was laid within those 50 feet of single track immediately before the left-hand point to ease the radius of the right-hand curve as this turn was more acute owing to a slight bend in Ash Street where it crossed Scarisbrick New Road. At the same time a single-line crossing was laid to join up the two sections of Ash Street. It was thought at the time that the Tramways Department had ideas of operating an extended Circle route, which it did, but many years later. There were two passing loops on the extension, in Ash Street and at the Cemetery gates.

These extensions were electrified with overhead wire suspended, as usual, from side-bracket poles. Their ornamental cast-iron bases displayed the borough coat of arms, as usual, but their finials, as I observed in later years, were similar to the British Electric Traction Company's 'flower-pot' type, as used for the Southport Tramway Company in Birkdale, whose lines were being electrified at the same time, instead of the Corporation's usual ball-and-spike design.

The construction of these two new routes was carried out to improved standards, compared with the earlier electrification. Heavier track was laid, the points were rubber-cushioned to reduce noise and fitted with curved tongues to give a smoother turnout than the older straight tongues. The improved overhead was of a design that the Corporation had begun re-erecting over the rest of the system earlier in 1902 and was one of the chief factors to influence the Tramway Department's later decision to replace the trolley rope with the bamboo pole.

This 1½ miles of new electric tramway to the Cemetery and the Birkdale boundary, via Duke Street and via Ash Street, was constructed in two months and ready for commissioning on 13 December 1902.

More double-deckers

To serve the extensions, eight more open-top, four-wheel double-deckers of the 'Liverpool type' were delivered from Dick, Kerr during the early part of 1902. This time they arrived by train at Meols Cop station goods yard to be transferred to the adjacent tramway on Bispham Road for conveyance to Crowlands depot. These cars received the even fleet numbers 20 to 34, the Corporation continuing its policy of numbering its double-deckers in an even sequence with no complementary odd numbers.

In appearance these cars were almost identical to the original batch of 1900. Their dimensions, seating capacity, trucks, motors and other equipment were standard, but the last four cars, 28 to 34, delivered on 18 May, incorporated improved ventilation, top-deck lighting, handrails, fenders, trolley masts and destination displays. They featured internally lit, single-aspect destination boxes, mounted on brackets above the handrails at each end of the top deck. The conductor could now change the destination at the terminus by turning the blind with a brass handle to any one of the 12 destinations listed instead of having to keep a stack of loose destination boards and exchange them in the end brackets. This new feature was fitted retrospectively to the older trams.

The new arrivals brought the Corporation fleet to a total of 26 trams, all four-wheelers, comprising 17 open-top double-deckers, eight single-deck California cars and one standard single-deck saloon car (the 'Committee Car'), which was rarely used. This would be the Corporation tram fleet for the next 12 years.

When the two new routes to the Cemetery were opened on 13 December, the Duke Street route was joined to the High Park route, making a cross-town service. On the previous day, 12 December, the last horse trams in Southport ran on the Sefton Street line to Mosley Street. The remaining two horse trams and seven of the horses were sold, but the Corporation kept one horse to pull the overhead line tower wagon as there was no works car in the tram fleet. The connecting curve between Scarisbrick New Road and Sefton Street was removed, but the Sefton Street horsecar line survived in situ, disused, for the next 30 years.

Service adjustments and experiments

The Ash Street trams to the Cemetery did not continue to the Birkdale boundary but turned right from Cemetery Road into Duke Street and worked a one-way circular route back to town via Shakespeare Street. Cars ran every 20 minutes but after one week passenger receipts were so poor that the service was suspended. Whether the first week was long enough to be able to judge is open to doubt but this route had a chequered and short career.

In the run-up to Christmas 1902 a new circular service was introduced from London Square via Hoghton Street, Queen's Road, Leyland Road, Hartwood Road and round the Inner Circle back to town. The route along Queen's Road and Leyland Road was on new track electrified on lease to Southport Tramways Company. This so-called Park Service (not to be confused with the Park Circle) dropped passengers for Hesketh Park at the corner of Queen's Road and Leyland Road, about 100 yards from the park gates! Cars operated clockwise only around this circle. The Inner Circle was retained to maintain the service in Manchester Road but was curtailed at Ash Street as before.

The Park Service lasted no more than two or three weeks. The Tramways Department decided it was not a good move at all and reinstated the full Inner Circle in January 1903. I would not have thought that the Christmas period was the best time to make alterations to the tram services; the festive season was not typical of the normal situation and I doubt very much if the results were indicative. Furthermore, I feel that the trial periods were too short.

Other service alterations included the withdrawal of cars to Kew Gardens for the winter, but those to the Infirmary were increased from a 15-minute to a 12-minute headway. To justify the use of the Ash Street line to the Cemetery, one car per hour on the High Park-Cemetery service (outward via Duke Street) returned to town via Ash Street and Scarisbrick New Road. The confusion it caused made it not worthwhile and after a

short period the service on the Cemetery route returned to normal. This meant that the new line along Ash Street and Cemetery Road was not used between Scarisbrick New Road and Duke Street, except by the first morning trams running light from the depot to the Cemetery and possibly the last cars at night – although the very last trams to the depot at night usually went through town to load at London Square and serve Sussex Road and Tithebarn Road.

In contrast with the Ash Street line the Duke Street service to the Cemetery proved to be very popular and an excellent revenue-earner. The cross-town operation between High Park and the Cemetery was only an operational expedient and any cross-town passengers had to re-book on the car in town: 2d to High Park and 1d to the Cemetery. The High Park and Infirmary services and the summer service to Kew Gardens were also mainstays of revenue. The Blowick route covered its costs but was a lighter-loaded service operated mainly by the single-deck California cars. The poor performer was the Inner Circle. One would have thought that it would have provided a useful link service but it seemed that nobody wanted to ride all the way round the town, except for joy-riding. Incidentally, the Park Circle (Hesketh Park-London Square-Kew Gardens) brought in the highest receipts per car mile but that now ran on bank holidays only!

Corporation cars shared tracks with Company cars on the town centre circuit along the centre block of Lord Street, on the bank holiday Park Circle along Lord Street and Albert Road, on the short-lived service along Lord Street to the Opera House and on the even briefer Park Service along Queen's Road and Leyland Road. As the Corporation owned all the lines in the borough, it could introduce a service on any line if it so wished and that could include sharing tracks with Company cars, but these were the only known instances where this occurred.

Electrification in Churchtown and Birkdale

Southport Tramways Company
1901-1903

After the opening of its electric lines to High Park, Blowick and Kew, Southport Corporation began work on 18 March 1901 to relay and electrify the Company tramlines within the borough on the two routes between Lord Street West and the Botanic Gardens, via Cambridge Road and via Roe Lane.

All the new tramway infrastructure for the Company within the borough was carried out by Corporation workmen to the same standards as the municipal tramways (see the previous chapter), under the supervision of the Borough Surveyor, the Borough Electrical Engineer and the Corporation Tramways Manager, as before but with flexible suspension of the overhead wires with the benefit of experience. The Company's electric lines in Birkdale were installed to similar standards by the British Electric Traction Company on behalf of the Urban District Council.

The horse trams continued running throughout this upheaval by means of the constant provision of portable, temporary tracks linking the old lines and the newly laid rails. Again the track was supplied by the Dick, Kerr Company of Preston and laid on a 6-inch concrete bed on broken stones and paved with wood blocks along Lord Street and granite setts beyond. The wires, supported by side-bracket traction poles, were suspended 20 feet above the road but dipped to 16ft 6in under Churchtown railway bridge in Cambridge Road, where they were suspended from the bridge.

While some environmentally conscious authorities, such as London and Hastings, opted for the less satisfactory cable, conduit or surface-contact systems in preference to overhead wires, Southport's policy for side-running trolley wires was dictated by the desire to merge the traction poles and overhead wires against and amongst the foliage of the trees along Lord Street and the Company's bosky suburban roads and they tried to camouflage the poles by painting them green. Hence the tracks along Lord Street and around Hesketh Park were offset to the gardens side of the road, which provided the greater tree cover. Side-running trolley wires were negotiated by swivel-head trolleys overhanging one side of the car and this also kept the live wire a safe distance from the passengers on the open top decks of the cars, especially when passing under Churchtown railway bridge.

It will be recalled that the Corporation's existing town centre tramway circuit was laid alongside the kerb on the inland side of Lord Street with trams running on the wrong side of the street from Eastbank Street Square to London Square. This line was now extended the full length of Lord Street from Manchester Road to Duke Street and the kerb was set back by 7 or 8 feet to the line of trees fronting the civic buildings and private front gardens on that side of the street and the traction poles were planted between the trees. Thus the laying of the electric tramways created the wide carriageway we know today. The exception was the area of Christ Church graveyard, where the footpath jutted out and remained about 2 feet from the tramline, but this was realigned later.

At the same time the adjacent horse tramline along Lord Street towards Birkdale was relaid in heavier rail for electric traction, providing a double track offset to one side of the road, on which the wrong-road running of the trams would be reversed to normal left-hand running. The other horse tramline towards Churchtown was then abandoned and later removed. Churchtown trams would run along the crown of the road. The double tracks occupied a 13-foot strip allowing 8ft 6in clearance for motor traffic on the gardens side of the street and 24 feet on the shops side in a carriageway with a total width of 45ft 6in from kerb to kerb. This left enough room for two lanes of motor traffic and parking space on the shops side of the street.

This transformation of Lord Street was quite a major and extensive undertaking. The curves from Eastbank Street Square into Lord Street and from Lord Street into London Square were both relaid to cross the new Birkdale line so that trams on the town centre circuit would use the new Churchtown line between the two squares and points had to be installed at these two locations. Points were also installed with a new south curve from Eastbank Street into Lord Street (towards the Winter Gardens), although, in the event, this curve was hardly ever used.

The up and down overhead wires along the central section of Lord Street between the two squares were relocated over the centre of the Birkdale line and the original bracket arms were replaced by longer ones with a reach of up to 18 feet, supported by ornate wrought-iron brackets. There were now three wires along Lord Street from Eastbank Street Square to London Square: the Corporation cars used the centre wire on their one-way circuit and the Company cars used the two outside wires on the up and down lines.

The rest of Lord Street was electrified with overhead poles, brackets and wires on this new alignment. To limit the reach of the bracket arms, the wires for both lines were suspended fairly close together over the Birkdale line, which meant that the trolley poles of the cars on the Churchtown line projected at a wide angle to the offside, as can be seen in the photographs.

The Company's first electric line was the Cambridge Road line to Botanic Gardens; the former single track with passing loops was replaced with double track all the way from Lord Street to the terminus except a short section that was interlaced, effectively a single track, through the narrow part of Albert Road

from Saunders Street to Leyland Road. Interlaced track saved pointwork in the track and overhead on the two passing loops and at each end of the section.

The double track around Hesketh Park was offset to run alongside the park. The inside rail was only 2 feet from the kerb and the traction poles were planted inside the park just behind the railings. This was a golden opportunity to make the line into a reserved-track tramway with a kerb between the outer track and the rest of the roadway, which is very wide, but this was not done because there was so little road traffic at the time and the concept of tramway reservations lay in the future. Nonetheless it caused some confusion among motorists driving into Southport when faced with an outbound tramcar for Churchtown on the left-hand side of the road. The road beside the tramway was wide enough for three lanes of motor traffic but there were no road signs or lane markings directing motorists along the path they should follow relative to the tramway.

At the south-west end of Lord Street the double track converged to single between the railway station and Duke Street and remained single through Lord Street West as far as the borough boundary at the corner of Westcliffe Road.

Overhead wire fittings such as hangers and ears were of English make and the Corporation was already replacing the American wire fittings on its own new overhead wires with better-quality English fittings, even though they were slightly more expensive. The overhead line on the sections of route leased by the Southport Tramways Company was separated from the Corporation wires by section insulators. Thus the current used was registered on separate meters at Crowlands power station, which supplied 500 volts dc to the Company lines within the borough to the boundary in Lord Street West.

The Corporation had taken up the horse tramway, laid the 3 miles of double track and installed the overhead electrification for the Cambridge Road line from Lord Street West to Botanic Gardens in 19 weeks ready for the Board of Trade inspection on 1 July, the day before the Company cars arrived. Two

Corporation cars were used to test the gauge and clearances.

The electric service begins

Southport Tramways Company took delivery of a fleet of 20 open-top, double-deck electric cars with bodies and trucks built by the Brush Electrical Engineering Company at Loughborough. The first cars, for the Cambridge Road line, arrived by railway at Meols Cop station on 2 July 1901. Delivery was completed by rail on the Corporation tramway along Bispham Road and Old Park Lane to join the Company's unfinished Roe Lane line to the depot in Cambridge Road.

Following staff training, the Cambridge Road line opened on 1 August 1901 in bright sunshine tempered by a sea breeze. On this occasion three cars, gaily festooned with bunting, evergreens, flowers and ferns, carried 80 guests on a round trip along the line from the Winter Gardens to the Botanic Gardens and back, stopping on the curve between Park Crescent and Cambridge Road for photographs and adjourning for lunch at the Prince of Wales Hotel.

The Company chairman, Mr John S. Raworth, said he was amazed at the rapidity with which the Corporation Tramways Department was making progress on Company lines while still laying its own new lines elsewhere in the town. Great lengths of roadway were up, not mere sections of 100 yards, and the work had been done two or three times quicker than the Company could have done it.

Work had been going on apace along the Roe Lane route to Churchtown and this was completed by the end of August. Both lines had been relaid and electrified in less than six months. The total length of route was 5 miles 280 yards. Of this, 3 miles 1,344 yards was double track and 1 mile 706 yards single track. It is interesting that the *Tramway & Railway World* trade magazine recorded these events in the same issue as it reported that London County Council was only then advertising for tenders for reconstruction and electrification of its horse tramways. The Roe Lane route commenced operation in September 1901. Both services terminated at

Lord Street West, where passengers changed to the Company's horse trams in Lulworth Road pending the electrification of the Birkdale section.

As in horse days, Roe Lane cars would turn right from Lord Street into Manchester Road, left into Queen's Road, right into Leyland Road and left into Roe Lane. However, the Leyland Road line was not ready at the inauguration and for the first few weeks the Company cars used Manchester Road to reach Roe Lane, sharing tracks with Corporation cars on the Inner Circle. The Manchester Road double tracks were linked up through crossroad junctions with the Company lines at Holy Trinity Church and Leyland Road Church.

Roe Lane cars were diverted via Leyland Road after the first few weeks of electric service and it would be many years before Manchester Road would be used again as a through route to Roe Lane. The Roe Lane route was single track with passing loops for most of the way from Queen's Road to Botanic Road but there was double track along the wider part of Roe Lane from High Park Place to a point halfway between Wennington Road and Norwood Avenue.

The electric cars

The dark mid-green and off-white livery of the new electric cars mingled with the crimson and cream of the Corporation trams on Lord Street. Unfortunately the tinted picture postcards of the period rarely showed the correct livery of the trams. Generally speaking all trams were shown as dark red and white, which was the most common tramcar livery of the period and reasonably acceptable as far as Southport Corporation cars were concerned. Only now and again have I come across views depicting the Company cars in their true green colour, although the trees would always be tinted green.

In 1899 the Southport Tramways Company had become a subsidiary of the British Electric Traction Company, which bought the majority of shares in various private tramways throughout Great Britain and operated them under their respective local titles and different liveries, but they all

A handsome portrait of Southport Tramways Company car No 7, built by Brush in 1901 and posed for the photographer on the curve from Cambridge Road to Park Crescent. The 56-seat body is painted dark mid-green and off-white with lined-out panels and the company's garter insignia under the centre windows. The Brush 6-foot-wheelbase, double-sprung truck is clearly shown. These cars were in advance of their time being complete with windscreens on the platforms and internally lit destination boxes. This car displays the destination 'London Square' in black letters on white and the route is fully described in sign-painted lettering on the rocker panels. The top deck was lit at night by the two 'oyster' lamps on stanchions, one at each end. The picture was posed before the car entered service with curtains in the saloon windows and lifeguards under the platforms. The company favoured this wide road junction to photograph its cars. Here the overhead wires were supported by a span wire from an anchor pole planted just inside Hesketh Park (right). All the traction poles around the park were inside the railings as part of the policy to camouflage the poles and wires against the trees. Observe also the ornate gas lamp post with its circular seat in the middle of the road junction. *James Dean collection*

displayed the BET magnet and wheel emblem on their side panels. The BET Company worked hand-in-glove with the Brush Electrical Engineering Company Ltd, at the Falcon Works in Loughborough, which built and equipped many of the tramcars for BET subsidiaries. The design of the Southport Company cars was by John Raworth, who was a director of the Brush Company as well as chairman of the Southport Company.

Early in 1901 20 of Raworth's design of four-wheel, open-top, double-deck trams were ordered from the Brush Company. They came complete with windscreens and automatic lifeguards, which were non-standard at the time, and were heralded as the most luxurious four-wheel, open-top cars in the country! They were designed for patrons from Cambridge Road, Roe Lane and Birkdale Park. They looked resplendent in their green and white livery, lined out in gilt, with gilt numerals, shaded black. In the centre of the waist panel below the lower saloon windows was the STC circular garter sign with the BET magnet and wheel in the centre. The main places along the route were painted on the white rocker panels: 'CHURCHTOWN', 'SOUTHPORT' and 'BIRKDALE' above 'BOTANIC GARDENS', 'HESKETH PARK' and 'WINTER GARDENS'.

The saloons were better furnished and ventilated than on the Corporation trams, with cushioned seats, sash windows, ornate lampshades and millboard ceilings painted white and picked out in gold, embossed patterns. The platforms were vestibuled with windscreens for the driver and conductor and reversed stairs led to the upper decks. (Reversed stairs, it will be recalled, were considered safer than direct stairs because passengers could not fall into the street.) Before the end of the year the order had been completed and all 20 trams had been delivered to Churchtown depot.

The details of the Brush cars were as follows:

20 double-deck, open-top trams (Raworth's design); Nos 1 to 20
Overall length
　26ft with vestibuled platforms and reversed stairs
Saloon
　15ft 6in long, 6ft 6in wide and 6ft 6in high with cushioned, longitudinal seats and five half-drop windows each side
Unladen weight
　7 tons
Seating
　24 inside on two longitudinal benches (12

each side); 32 outside on transverse seats with reversible backrests; total capacity 56
Equipment
    Brush type A four-wheel truck with 30in wheels and 6ft wheelbase
    Two 25hp Brush motors, two Brush controllers
    Brush patent trigger lifeguards
    Ratchet handbrakes and electric emergency brakes
    R. W. Blackwell trolley mast and trolley, centrally placed with interior spring under compression; swivel trolley-head

The cars were notable for being only the second fleet of open-top, double-deck trams in Great Britain with windscreens on the platforms – 26 days after those of the Isle of Thanet Electric Tramways & Lighting Company. The Thanet trams were built by the St Louis Car Company, of the USA, and ran across exposed, open country and clifftops between Margate, Broadstairs and Ramsgate. The Southport cars had only a three-pane windscreen while the Thanet trams were glazed right around the offside of the platforms and the stairs. Single-deckers on the Kidderminster & Stourport Electric Tramway were fitted with windscreens as early as 1898; they, too, were Brush cars for a BET subsidiary.

The windscreens were not necessarily welcomed by the drivers and appeared to be the subject of controversy. The *Southport Guardian*, reporting on the delivery of the new cars, said:

'It is a double-decked car of a type that does not meet with universal approval, having glazed ends with moveable sashes for the protection of the driver but which in rain or snow will have to be opened in order that the driver may see where he is going and, having to stand by a narrow opening, is likely to feel bad effects from draught.'

Windscreen wipers were a long time in the future and Southport tramcars were never fitted with them.

We can be sure that the passengers approved of the saloons. The Company philosophy on their furnishing was reflected in the contemporary trade press report in the *Tramway & Railway World* of 12 September 1901, which said, with reference to the interior photograph illustrating this chapter:

'As will be seen from the photograph of the interior of the car they are most luxuriously fitted up. The neighbourhood through which the cars pass is a residential one, inhabited chiefly by retired manufacturers, merchants and

The interior of the saloon of car No 7 at the depot in 1901, with cushioned longitudinal seats for 12 passengers on each side. Other features are the ornate lamps, transom lights and ceiling, the half-drop windows, the leather straps for standing passengers and the perforated plywood backrests on the seats. The 125 volt dc, 16 candlepower incandescent lights were in cut-glass globes on scroll brackets. The transom lights were patterned on ruby stained glass and the patterns on the millboard ceiling were embossed. There was a sliding door in the middle of the bulkhead at each end of the saloon, giving access from the platforms, and bevelled mirrors above the bulkhead windows. Through the bulkhead glazing we can see the reversed staircase with a written warning that passengers who alight while the car is in motion do so at their own risk.

Curtains were fitted to the windows before the car entered service. *Cedric Greenwood collection* tradesmen from Manchester, Liverpool and other Lancashire towns. A large number of well-to-do businessmen from south Lancashire also have their homes in Southport and travel by train to and from their business daily. The Tramways Company took this into account in selecting their cars and fitted them up in a more expensive manner than would have been advisable in a less wealthy district.'

The electric cars on both routes from Botanic Gardens were terminating in Lord Street West, the southern extent of Southport Corporation's electrification within the borough, and passengers had to change to horse trams on a shuttle service from Lulworth Road to Birkdale station. As the company depot was in Cambridge Road, Churchtown, two horse trams still trundled through Southport early every morning to take up service in Birkdale and returned to Churchtown depot at night. The company had to retain at least four of its horsecars for this purpose, which meant that at least 16 horses still had to be stabled, fed and watered. The redundant horses and horse trams were sold by this stage.

Birkdale electrification

It was imperative that the electric tramway be completed as soon as possible, and in November 1901 contractors for British Electric Traction began lifting the horsecar lines and replacing them with the heavier electric tramway rails from the temporary electric car terminus in Lord Street West along Aughton Road and York Road to Birkdale station.

The single track in Lord Street West became double as it crossed the boundary into Lulworth Road, Birkdale, and the double track, which was little more than an extended passing loop, continued around the left-hand bend into Aughton Road and reverted to single line. The Company lines through Birkdale were all laid as single track with passing loops. At the corner of Aughton Road and York Road a junction was laid in double track with a single-line spur continuing up Aughton Road and a single line along York

Road to Birkdale station, ending in a loop before the stub terminus outside the Park Hotel. The spur line in Aughton Road continued up to the town side of the railway level crossing with the intention of extending it along the projected route to the Crown Hotel, which would join the old Birkdale & Southport horsecar line in Everton Road.

Aughton Road and York Road were part of a district known as Birkdale Park. Both roads were narrower then than they are today; there was room for motor traffic to pass on each side of trams on the single line but not on the loops. York Road was a typical Birkdale suburban road, tree-lined on both sides with elegant houses standing in large grounds.

The Corporation and Company agreed to supersede the 1896 lease agreement with a new 21-year lease dating from 1901 by which the Company would pay the Corporation 4½d a mile for the use of the track and current. They also agreed to mutual running powers on each other's lines where and when necessary, as on Lord Street, Manchester Road and Queen's Road. The Corporation also offered to supply current to the Company lines over the boundary until Birkdale power station was commissioned.

Southport Tramways Company built its own generating station on Birkdale Common, near the Crown Hotel. Under the Birkdale lease agreement the Company was obliged to supply all the general power and lighting needs of the Urban District, paid for by the Council, and free street lighting along the tram routes as well as its own traction current. A new subsidiary was formed, the Birkdale District Electric Supply Company Ltd, with John Raworth as chairman. Construction began on 1 March 1902, and the single-storey, brick and stone-dressed building and square, wooden cooling tower were complete by 1 July. After the installation of machinery and equipment, the power station was commissioned on 1 August, supplying dc electricity to Birkdale and its tramways through 20 miles of feeder and distributor cables.

The electric supply undertaking was sold to Birkdale Urban District Council in 1906 and passed in turn to Southport Corporation on the amalgamation of the borough and the urban district in 1912, but the dc supply to

Birkdale continued long after amalgamation and long after the trams had finished. It was 1950 before the dc system in Southport and Birkdale was replaced by ac supply.

The tramway overhead in Birkdale followed the Southport pattern of side-bracket standards with short to medium-length arms. The wires were hung with flexible suspension but in Birkdale were hung more directly above the track than in Southport, although the Company cars, like Southport's, had swivel-head trolleys and were quite adaptable to side-running.

You could always tell whether you were in Birkdale or Southport by the difference between the tramway traction poles. The Birkdale poles were of the British Electric Traction Company's pattern with the magnet and wheel emblem embossed on the cast-iron base instead of the borough coat of arms. The collars on the joints between the sections of the pole differed in pattern and the capping finial was of the well-known 'flower-pot' type instead of the traditional ball-and-spike finial seen in Southport. This type of pole was to be found in profusion among BET company-owned tramways in the Black Country and many other parts of Britain.

On 27 March 1902 passengers on both the Cambridge Road and Roe Lane routes were able to travel through to Birkdale station by electric tram while horsecars still ran in Southport on the Sefton Street and Mosley Street line for nine months longer. Birkdale & Southport Company horse trams had ceased running between Mosley Street and the Crown Hotel the previous December.

One would have thought that the Southport Tramways Company must have had a certain amount of temerity to dare to introduce tramcars into this preserve of the private, horse-drawn landau or even the odd 'horseless carriage'. Fortunately there were many who appreciated the advantages of the new electric cars over their horse-drawn predecessors. There was the little, elderly lady who asked the tramway inspector, 'If I put my foot on the line will I be electrocuted?'

'No, madam,' he replied, 'not unless you put your hand on the overhead wire.'

Then there was the gentleman in the top hat who asked an inspector what would happen if there were a thunderstorm and lightning were to strike the car.

The inspector replied, 'No need to worry, sir – we have a conductor on board each car.'

The cars were, in fact, equipped with Garton lightning arresters.

The Crown Hotel line

The next step was to press on with the construction of the route to the Crown Hotel. No more than 500 yards of new tram route was required along Aughton Road and Upper Aughton Road to link up the Birkdale station line at the York Road junction with the former Birkdale & Southport Company horse tramway in Everton Road, but it included a level crossing with the Lancashire & Yorkshire Railway line to Liverpool, which presented something of a problem, whereas the former B&S tram route bridged the railway on Eastbank Street. Upper Aughton Road began on the inland side of the railway crossing and shops stretch along the left-hand side to the junction with Mosley Street, where the single-line horse tramway crossed Upper Aughton Road into Everton Road.

The horse tramway was cut off at the end of Mosley Street and the new electric line was laid around a half right-hand bend from Upper Aughton Road into Everton Road and on towards the Crown Hotel as the horsecar tracks were lifted. A relaid loop in Liverpool Road marked the original horse tram terminus at Brighton Road and there was a final loop just before the stub terminus at the corner of Halsall Road. Liverpool Road was lined with fine houses and long gardens (later cut back for road widening) giving way to shops on both sides on the wider stretch from St John's Road to the Crown Hotel. The terminus was virtually at the end of the built-up area of Birkdale at that time with only a few well-built houses and scattered farm buildings between there and Ainsdale.

The overhead wiring was supported by bracket poles with arms of medium length erected on the west side of Liverpool Road. On the wide bend at Shaw's Road the arms were quite long over the passing loop and the up and down wires were hung wide apart so that they were almost directly above their respective tracks.

The small power station on Birkdale Common could be seen from the trams on this stretch of Liverpool Road between Shaw's Road and the Crown Hotel. The common was a rural tract on the edge of the built-up area; it lay inland of Liverpool Road, bounded by Shaw's Road on the north, Shaftesbury Road on the west and Halsall Road on the south. In 1908 the Company erected a small depot alongside the power station with access by a long siding from Liverpool Road.

Railway signals for the trams

Having described the route to the Crown Hotel, we must go back to Aughton Road railway crossing, where there was a break in the route and progress was delayed. The railway to Liverpool was still worked by steam and would

be for another two years. The Lancashire & Yorkshire Railway Company was to electrify the line in 1903-04 but this should not be a problem as it was to be a dc third-rail pick-up. There would be a break in the conductor rail over the road crossing while the tramway overhead wires, 20 feet above the road, would in no way interfere with the railway circuitry. At the insistence of the Board of Trade, however, trams were not allowed to carry passengers over the level crossing until signals were installed on the roadside, interlocked with the crossing gates.

Electric trams began plying to the Crown Hotel on 4 November 1902, but the outer end of the route, from Upper Aughton Road, had to run as a connecting shuttle service with passengers changing cars at the level crossing and walking across the railway to the car on the other side!

Although this picture belongs to the period covered by the next chapter, it illustrates the railway-style semaphore signals erected on the roadside traction poles to protect Aughton Road railway crossing in Birkdale. This view of Aughton Road from the railway crossing shows the signal mounted on the other side of the nearest traction pole on the left for cars approaching the crossing from town. There was another signal to protect the crossing for trams approaching the crossing from Upper Aughton Road and both signals were operated by a lever in Aughton Road signal cabin. This was the tram route to the Crown Hotel via Everton Road. There are, in fact, three tramcars and no other vehicles in this bosky Birkdale scene. Car No 4,

nearest the camera, is standing at the tram stop flag on the same pole as the signal on its way to Roe Lane. It is waiting for two trams ahead to clear the junction at York Road and the conductor is leaning out from the back platform before giving the driver the bell to proceed. A car from Smedley, pulling out of York Road into Aughton Road, is waiting for an oncoming third car, which can just be seen, to clear the single track beyond and enter the double-track junction. The car from York Road to Cambridge Road usually ran just in front of the car from the Crown Hotel to Roe Lane, which followed on sight. *Cedric Greenwood collection*

This went on for 4½ months while the railway company took its time to supply and erect semaphore signals on tramway traction poles and install the mechanism to interlock them with the crossing gates and operate them from Aughton Road signal cabin. No 1 lever in the cabin not only operated the tramway signals but also de-energised the tramway overhead wire for 50 yards each side of the crossing. The equipment was installed during 14-16 March 1903 and immediately after it had all been inspected by Major Druitt for the Board of Trade on 21 March the through tram service via Roe Lane to the Crown Hotel was inaugurated by a car carrying Company officials. That evening the through service was highlighted by an illuminated car, bedecked with flags, which had been waiting in the depot at Churchtown for the past two months, just for this day.

The roadside signals for the trams were of the normal railway semaphore design, red with a white band on the facing side and white with a black band on the back, with red and green spectacles behind the pivot, illuminated at night by an oil lamp. One signal was erected each side of the crossing about halfway up a traction pole. As the poles were sited on the right-hand side of the road going out from town, the signal for outbound cars was on the right and the signal for inbound cars on the left. The signal arms were lower-quadrant, horizontal for stop and dropping 45 degrees from horizontal to give a clear road to the trams to proceed. While the signal in Aughton Road dropped to the right of the pole, ie away from the road, the signal in Upper Aughton Road also dropped to the right, projecting into the road, which was the opposite of railway practice. By night the oil lamps and coloured spectacles showed a green light when the gates were open for the trams and a red light when the gates were closed.

The complete system

The final phase in the initial development of the Southport tramways was the extension of the line along York Road and Trafalgar Road for about 600 yards to the Smedley Hydropathic Hotel, now the General Register Office, a division of the Office for National Statistics. The Company had planned to extend the Smedley line into Grosvenor Road and Crescent Road to join up with the Liverpool Road line, but that link was abandoned with the agreement of the District Council in March 1903. Work began on the Smedley extension in April and opened on bank holiday Monday, 3 August 1903. It was a single line with no passing loop, rendering the Weld Road line to Birkdale station as a short spur, although four out of every five cars still terminated at the station.

The Company operated trams on the following routes, which could be readily identified by coloured Maltese crosses on metal squares slotted in brackets on the ends of the upper-deck panels instead of route numbers or letters:

Green cross	Botanic Gardens-Cambridge Road-Lord Street-Birkdale station
Red cross	Botanic Gardens-Roe Lane Lord Street-Crown Hotel
Yellow cross	Botanic Gardens-Cambridge Road-Lord Street-Smedley
No cross	London Square-Birkdale station

The colours of the crosses were another tradition inherited from horsecar days, when Cambridge Road and Roe Lane cars carried green lamps and red lamps respectively. The electric cars also had internally lit destination boxes with roller blinds with black lettering on a white background. Birkdale cars showed Crown Hotel, Birkdale Station or Smedley. Churchtown cars showed either Roe Lane or Cambridge Road as a route indication instead of the destination, Botanic Gardens, but all the Company cars carried the words 'All the green cars run to Botanic Gardens' painted on the side decency panels upstairs.

Cars ran on the Cambridge Road route to Birkdale station every 10 minutes, on the Roe Lane route to the Crown Hotel every 15 minutes and on the Cambridge Road line to the Smedley every half hour. The London Square-Birkdale station short-working was also half-hourly. Between them they provided a 5-minute service along the full length of Lord

Above Two Company cars pass on the loop on the Birkdale station spur in Weld Road, viewed from the railway level crossing. An open-top double-decker is leaving the terminus on the green cross route to Cambridge Road as the sole single-deck 'demi-car' arrives on its dedicated short-working from London Square to Birkdale station. On the right, beyond the colonnaded shops, are the facade of Birkdale Police Station and the clock tower of Birkdale Town Hall. Birkdale was an independent Urban District until its amalgamation with Southport in 1912. This picture postcard was sent in 1906. Birkdale Town Hall was demolished together with the police station, library and ambulance station in 1970 and they were replaced by Weld Parade of shops. *Picture postcard, Cedric Greenwood collection*

Below Another picture postcard, this time showing Liverpool Road, Birkdale, with a Company car passing Clifford Road (right) and approaching the loop on the bend before the branch line along Shaftesbury Road to the sub-depot and power station. This was the last loop before the Crown Hotel terminus. Later the road was widened on the left-hand side and the loop was lengthened. *Geoff Price collection*

Street in each direction, cars every 4 minutes on the Birkdale side of London Square and every 7 or 8 minutes along Cambridge Road. The London Square-Birkdale station short-working was not introduced until December 1903, and was operated solely by the demi-car.

The 'demi-car'

The first few years were the worst, financially, for both the Corporation and the Company tramways as both systems initially ran at a loss. The Company was the third largest money-loser among British Electric Traction subsidiaries in the whole British Empire after Auckland and Mumbles. (The Mumbles Railway, acquired by BET in 1899, continued to be worked by steam until it was electrified in 1929.)

The Southport Company sought to economise on running costs by designing an experimental car, which was delivered from Brush in the summer of 1903 and underwent extensive trials before going into service in December. This car, No 21 in the fleet, was particularly interesting and unusual. It was the first one-man-operated tramcar and the first pay-as-you-enter vehicle in Britain and was the pioneer of regenerative braking and all sorts of experimental technology.

The car was designed for lightly loaded service in off-peak times and dedicated to the

service between London Square and Birkdale Station. It certainly looked rather odd as a very short, half-length single-decker and was known as the 'demi-car'. Several other towns had them from 1904 onward. Passengers dropped their penny fares in a box beside the driver, who issued the tickets with a ticket rack and Bell punch. The fare was 1d any distance between London Square and Birkdale station.

The philosophy behind this design was explained in the British Electric Traction Company's *Monthly Gazette* of October 1903:

'The car has been designed by Mr Raworth, chairman of the Southport Tramways Company, for use on lines which at certain periods cannot support the comparatively high working expenses of a full-sized car. This condition obtains in Southport. The population here (inclusive of Birkdale) is 61,000 and the tramways of the Company and the Corporation together cover 17 miles of route so that there are some 3,600 of population per mile.

Time is not valuable to the majority of residents at Southport and the result is that the cars may often be seen running comparatively empty. Of course, in the season when the "trippers" arrive they change all this but "trippers" only go to Southport in the summer and interest and the sinking fund are always present. Last

Southport's 'demi-car' was a pioneer of one-man operation and economy of electric consumption by regenerative braking. Built by Brush in 1903, it is believed to have been the first tramcar of its kind in both respects. It was designed by the chairman of Southport Tramways Company, John Raworth, who was also a director of the Brush Electrical Engineering Company, Loughborough, which built all the Company's tramcars. The demi-car was designed for low-frequency service in low-density areas during slack periods of the day, and worked between London Square and Birkdale station exclusively. It was a double-ended car with seven cushioned longitudinal seats each side in the saloon and a three-seat wooden bench for smokers on each platform next to the driver. Passengers on the platform seat were protected by glazing, on which can been seen the words 'smoking compartment', but there was no windscreen for the driver as his brake spindle was outside

the dash panel. The demi-car did not lead to any more cars of this design being ordered by the Company or the Corporation and it was withdrawn from service by 1911 and scrapped by the Corporation on the take-over of the Company in 1918. *Cedric Greenwood collection* year the Company made a loss of £2,000 and the Corporation a loss of £1,200 and, though these losses were due, perhaps, partly to accidental causes, it was recognised by both authorities that improvement in the economical working of their respective lines was imperative.

It will be seen that this car enables a much more frequent service to be run on lines which at present can barely support a 15 or 20 minutes' service and will bring the benefits of electric traction to districts which at present cannot support them. It is estimated that the use of these cars during the slack periods of the day and year will convert the losses of last year into possibly handsome profits for the Southport Company and Corporation.'

This was the year in which the Company also began running its double-deckers on one motor to save electricity.

The demi-car was a double-ended four-wheeler with a front entrance and exit on each side so that passengers paid the driver. The short saloon, with only two segmental-arched windows on each side, seated 14 passengers – seven each side – on cushioned, longitudinal seats. A third segmental-arch window, which appeared externally to be an extension of the saloon, was actually a windbreak for the smokers on the three-seat bench on the offside of the motorman's platform at each end, giving a total seating capacity of 20 passengers.

From each side the car appeared to have no back platform, so the words 'Passengers enter by the driver's platform' were painted on the rocker panels below the end window where passengers would normally be looking for the boarding steps. Passengers entered by the front platform and put their fares in a box by the driver. The rear step on the offside was folded up and locked by closing a folding, lattice iron gate.

As passengers dropped their fares into the box the driver admitted them into the car by raising a bar across the entrance to the seating area. Lifting the bar shut off the current to the motors and, if the driver became incapacitated while the car was in motion, a passenger only had to raise the bar to stop the car. The car could not be started again until the bar was slotted in place.

This car had no windscreen for the driver as his brake handle spindle was on the outside of the dash panel and the orbit of the handle overhung the front of the car, but there was a short, arched windscreen for the smokers on the front offside of each platform. The driver's brass controller looked like the engine-room telegraph on the bridge of a ship, the handle moving forwards and backwards in a vertical plane like the joystick controller of modern trams. The forward position gave a top speed of 17mph and to stop the car it was only necessary to pull back the handle.

At only 4½ tons the car consumed less power than the normal 7-ton car but it also carried fewer passengers. The regenerative braking reversed the motor field coils and, with the momentum of the car, the motors worked as dynamos, pulling up the car gradually and uniformly and passing current back to the supply lines, thus saving more electricity. This electric brake could be applied with force for an emergency stop without the wheels skidding.

The disadvantages of the system were a tendency for motors to overheat from constant use; power surges in the overhead could fuse the lights in tramcars in that vicinity and could even damage the generators at the power station. No more of these cars were ordered by the Company and the Corporation did not take up the idea. The demi-car was retired from service prematurely, at least by 1911, when the Board of Trade banned regeneration after a collision between two tramcars at Rawtenstall. It was stored at the back of the shed for some years before it was scrapped in 1918.

However, regenerative braking was developed by trolleybuses, which were not included in the ban, and by some of the larger tramway undertakings, such as London, Edinburgh and Glasgow, in the 1930s. Regenerative braking is now standard on modern trams and trains with electronic control systems. Southport's demi-car was ahead of its time.

Together with the Southport Corporation routes to High Park, Blowick, Kew and the Cemetery (described in the previous chapter), the Southport tramway scene was now set for the period up to the First World War and the amalgamation of the Corporation and Company systems in 1918.

CONSOLIDATION

Southport Corporation Tramways
Southport Tramways Company
1902-1918

From the electrification in 1900-02 to the amalgamation of the two systems in 1918 was a period of slow progress for Southport tramways. It saw the introduction of bamboo poles to replace trolley ropes, improvements in lifeguards and route identification, electric signalling from Mornington Road to Sussex Road and advertising, parcels services and post boxes on trams. A start was made on enclosing the top decks of cars and sightseeing tours with wide open 'toastrack' cars. The period from 1910 was marred first by industrial unrest and then by war, which put a great strain on the tramways.

The Edwardian years were the halcyon days when the streets were empty and quiet but for one or two electric cars swishing along the overhead wires under the trees. New electric traction motors hummed quietly and steel wheels drummed the rail joints with a gentle, steady rhythm.

Board of Trade Regulations governing tramways in 1903 set a national speed limit of 8mph, raised to 12mph on some stretches, and reduced to 4mph through curves and facing points. These were considered safe speed limits having regard to the service handbrakes in the era before air brakes. The tramcars were not, however, fitted with any speed meters; the measure of speed was left to the driver's judgement. Board of Trade circulars in 1909 and 1911 recommended that 'speed indicators' should be fitted to tramcars but Southport Tramways Committee ignored them and thought it 'unnecessary'. In view of the sedate speed at which tramcars were generally driven in Southport, they were probably right.

Every one of Southport's cars was fitted with two 25hp motors, one on each axle of the four-wheel truck, sufficient for the speed limits of the time and Southport's flat terrain. In January 1903 Southport Tramways Company began running its double-deckers on one motor to save money on electricity with the result that they ran at half the normal speed. The Corporation then tried the idea but found the operating speeds too slow and reverted to two-motor operation, although from September 1904 this economy was applied to single-deckers working the lightest loaded services, B Blowick and C Inner Circle.

As mentioned earlier, while the Corporation had flagged tram stops, the Company had no fixed stopping places at first, continuing the horse tramway practice of obligingly pausing anywhere that anyone wanted to board or alight. The Corporation complained that the slower Company cars, moving at half speed and stopping anywhere, held up the Corporation cars on the common section of track on Lord Street, and in 1903 the Corporation compelled the Company to limit car stops to fixed stopping places. This was done only on Lord Street at first, from 7 June, but fixed stops were later extended throughout the Company routes from Churchtown to Birkdale.

The Company also perpetuated a horse tramway practice of charging differential fares in the saloon and on top to encourage hardier passengers to relieve the demand for the comfort of the saloon. The open top decks were for smokers and usually the preserve of male passengers as females in the voluminous skirts of the time could not negotiate the steep, narrow staircase. Differential fares (eg 4d inside and 3d outside for the ride from Botanic Gardens to Lord Street West) were not uncommon in the early days of electric trams and lasted some years into the electric era. The practice was finally eclipsed by the need to enclose the top deck in deference to the British climate and fares were standardised.

The regulation speed limits were gradually increased over the years but they were not applied universally; each town had its own speed limits as it had to apply to the Board of

Above Corporation and Company standard cars on Lord Street at London Square in 1902. The Company car (left) is approaching the stop at Boots on its way to Churchtown and the Corporation car following behind (right) is about to turn right from Lord Street into London Square as it loops the town centre circuit on the Infirmary service. We can just see – over the roof of the shelter – the top deck of a third car unloading passengers in London Square. St George's Place is in the background. *Courtesy of Martin Jenkins, E. J. McWatt and A. D. Packer, Online Transport Archive*

Below A good general view of Lord Street showing a Company car stopping at the corner of Nevill Street (right) and the crossover used by Birkdale-London Square short-workings of the demi-car and Sunday trams. *Picture postcard, Southport local history collection, Sefton Library Service*

Above Company termini: the crew and passengers of a Company car, which has just arrived at the terminus at the Crown Hotel, Birkdale, pose for this postcard picture entitled 'Liverpool Road South, Birkdale'. Nelson Rimmer's general store on the corner of Halsall Road (right) housed Liverpool Road South Post Office. *Cedric Greenwood collection*

Below The Smedley tram terminus was in Trafalgar Road, Birkdale, and the track ended flush with the crossing of Grosvenor Road. The terminus took its name from the Smedley Hydropathic Hotel (right), one of several hydropathic establishments with specialist baths for water cures in this health resort. *Picture postcard, Geoff Price collection*

Trade to raise the speed limits for different stretches of its own system. As late as 1914 the Southport Tramways Company issued a notice to its drivers about maximum speeds of 10mph on open stretches such as Cambridge Road, Roe Lane and Liverpool Road, 8mph on Lord Street and most other streets and 4mph on Botanic Road, Aughton Road railway crossing and all curves.

Corporation cars did not run on Sundays, the day of rest. The Town Council had decided to observe the Sabbath this way, a policy that, while not common, was not unusual on Edwardian small-town systems. The Parliamentary Order for Southport tramways specifically banned tramcars from plying for hire on Sundays but the Order for Birkdale did not and four Company cars did run regular, scheduled Sunday services in Birkdale from 9 November 1902. They did not stop at the boundary in Lulworth Road but continued along Lord Street to London Square, reversing on the crossover outside Boots the chemists, although no fares were collected within the borough so as to conform with the order not to ply for hire within the borough on Sundays.

With their depot in Churchtown, the Company trams also had to traverse Southport at the beginning and end of Sunday duties in Birkdale and gave free rides on these cross-town depot workings. This dead mileage was relieved when the four-car shed opened at Birkdale power station in 1908. Heaven's advocates raised hell. Great was the indignation against tramcars desecrating the peace of the Sabbath day. The strongly Protestant citizenry protested in letters to the press and public speeches, citing Sunday as the day of rest, but the Sunday patronage proved a need and helped to offset the financial losses, which the Company could not sustain for ever. The controversy rumbled on, as did the Sunday trams, for 16 years until it was resolved in 1918, so the course of this dispute will be summarised later.

During the period covered by this chapter there were many reports in the Tramway Committee minutes of tram conductors being rewarded 10 shillings by the Department for stopping runaway horses in the streets.

Interurban schemes

The Edwardian period was a time of enthusiasm, foresight and a desire for progress and it seemed that the potential for interurban travel by tram was more fully realised in those early days than later on. 'Interurbans' were introduced in North America – and in the Isle of Man – in 1893. The technology evolved historically from extensions of electric streetcar lines to roadside and cross-country routes linking up strings of towns and carrying passengers, mail and freight. The first decade of the 20th century saw the rapid development of the technology and the network, which was a boon to the rural community and farmers' access to markets. By 1917 a total of 18,000 miles of interurban lines served 45 states of the Union and six Canadian provinces. Big, powerful, electric, 'mahogany and varnish' cars, some with railway post offices and dining saloons on board, sped passengers across the wide open spaces. 'Trolley freight' cars delivered goods, produce and livestock, exchanged with the steam roads. Even the *Southport Visiter* noted on 28 May 1903 that 'the first sleeping cars on any electric tramway' would start between Columbus and Cincinnati, Ohio, on 1 July that year. By contrast with Southport's trams, the standard North American interurban car of this period was 50-60 feet long with four 50-100hp motors and a top speed of 50-60mph. These figures increased in the 1920s and '30s.

Paved roads, private cars, buses and lorries and the inter-war recession saw the decline of the interurban empire, like that of the British tram, over the period from 1925 to 1963 and today only one 90-mile passenger line and a few small trolley freight operations survive – plus the 18-mile Manx Electric Railway.

The Manx Electric Railway was authorised under Manx law. Similar lines on the British mainland were authorised under the 1896 Light Railways Act, designed to encourage cheap extensions of steam railways into rural areas for farmers, such as the Kent & East Sussex and the Welshpool & Llanfair (both now preserved), but tramway promoters could also take advantage of the less expensive procedure and less onerous conditions of a

Corporation car No 14 has just arrived at Kew Gardens terminus out in the country, the point where the proposed light railway to Ormskirk would have joined up with the Southport system. The driver (left) and conductor (right) pose for the photographer at the Ormskirk end of the car before reversing. The driver has to take his controller handle and reversing key to the controller at the other end of the car and the conductor has to turn the trolley with the hooked bamboo pole seen under this side of the car, reverse the seats on the top deck and turn the destination blinds in the boxes on the top rail.

This was one of the original batch of nine double-deckers built by Dick, Kerr for the opening of the

Corporation system in 1900. On page 35 we saw this car in London Square in 1902 but since then these cars were fitted with lifeguards under the platforms, route letters on the top rails and route lights on the destination boxes (1902-03), adapted to carry advertising (1907) and vestibuled with windscreens on the platforms (1909-10). The only advertisements on this car are those for Hovis bread etched on opaque red or blue glass on the transom ventilators. Notice how neatly the upper deck decency panels have been picked out and lined out in crimson and cream. The staff uniform included French-style pill-box hats. The Kew Gardens route was a summer service only from 1902. This photograph was taken about 1912. Service cars stopped running to Kew Gardens in 1914 and reversed at the Infirmary or Haig Avenue, but the Grand Tour continued to run to the end of the track here until the tour was withdrawn in 1924. *W. A. Camwell, James Dean collection*

Light Railway Order to serve more than one local authority. Two such lines from Southport were promoted under the Act: the Ormskirk & Southport Light Railway and the Southport & Lytham Tramroad. Neither, however, materialised. Had they done so we might have seen London Square looking something like a smaller version of Manchester's Piccadilly, which was the hub of the greater Manchester joint tramways network.

The Ormskirk line was planned to run beyond Kew Gardens along the country road for 6 miles to Ormskirk town centre. It would have been operated by a private company and Southport Tramways Committee expressed its willingness to give the Company running powers over the Corporation metals from Kew Gardens along Scarisbrick New Road to and from the town centre circuit subject to agreement on a car mileage payment to the Corporation.

Had the Lytham scheme materialised it would have made a great difference to travel between Southport and the Fylde coast. The distance between Southport and Lytham was only 7 miles across the Ribble estuary compared with 30 miles by train, changing at Preston. The first scheme, of 1896, was for a swing bridge across the shipping channel approached by a causeway and pier on each side of the estuary with through running of trams into Lytham town centre and eventually on to Blackpool. The trams would have left Southport along existing tracks to Hesketh Park gates and new street track along Park Road West to the reserved track along an embankment across the marshes.

The second scheme, dated 1898, replaced the swing bridge with a transporter bridge (like the one at Widnes from 1905 to 1961) and replaced the last 2½ miles of causeway to the bridge with a moving platform like a mobile pier running on track laid on a concrete bed along the shore. The idea was taken from the 18-foot-gauge Brighton & Rottingdean Seashore Electric Tramroad of 1896-1901 except that this would not be the passenger vehicle but a platform to carry the trams across the salt marshes, mudflats and high water to the bridge. A ride on an open-top double-decker on the mobile pier and the transporter bridge would certainly have been one of the most exhilarating and exciting rides in Great Britain.

The sea-going tramway scheme was abandoned in the final Southport & Lytham Tramroad Order in 1900 for a pier at Hesketh Bank to a transporter bridge over the channel 2 miles further up-river from the first site. The project remained live until 1909, when the Southport & Lytham Tramroad Company was wound up. The promoters were unable to raise the necessary funds because of problems with the Widnes transporter bridge from new.

A more detailed description and history of these two interesting interurban tramway schemes has been kindly contributed by Graham Fairhurst in Appendix 1 (Ormskirk) and by T. B. Maund in Appendix 2 (Lytham).

The *Southport Visiter* mused on the prospects of the Ormskirk and Lytham light railway schemes in its editorial comment on 19 July 1900, regarding the previous day's inauguration of electric traction in Southport, and the editor hoped that the Liverpool Overhead Railway's tramway from Seaforth to Great Crosby would also extend to Southport. He wrote:

'It is the good fortune of Southport Corporation Tramways to have planned this tramway extension to coincide with the outcrop of private enterprise in tramways leading into the borough. If these enterprises succeed, the Corporation Tramways are bound to succeed handsomely. When Southport is linked by electric cars to Ormskirk on the one hand and to Lytham – and so to Blackpool – on the other, a through traffic of considerable proportions will be developed and, unless Southport is to be an exception to a well established rule, the borough will grow and thousands who never rode will get into the habit of riding.

A circular route should be as popular a way of spending half an hour as the Morningside [Marchmont?] Circle in Edinburgh. The Marine Drive is not to be brought into the scheme but it must in time. When the Tramways Committee has finished its other extensions, public opinion will press for the inclusion of a sea stretch to complete an outer circle, which would begin at Albert Road, touch

the Botanic Gardens and Kew Gardens, run down Scarisbrick New Road, cross to Birkdale and back along the Esplanade and the Marine Drive to the North Promenade. That round at a fixed fare of 4d would be an added asset of the first rank.

For the greater part of the development of tramways the town will look to the schemes that would connect Southport with Ormskirk, Liverpool and Lytham. The Southport & Lytham Tramroad Act has received the Royal Assent and unless the promoters think it prudent to delay going to the public for their capital until the wars are over, the line should be complete in under three years. The Ormskirk line, it is said, only awaits the grace of the overworked Board of Trade. The [tramway] extension of the Overhead Railway from Seaforth has begun and that too may reach us during the next decade. The public just now has faith in tramways and light railways.'

Faith, however, did not raise the cash required for any of these schemes. British tramways generally only linked up towns in the great conurbations around London, Birmingham, Manchester and Glasgow. Outside Manchester and Glasgow municipal systems were inclined to take a parochial view about through running between boroughs. Outside the conurbations, private companies succeeded in making interurban links such as Blackpool to Fleetwood, Llandudno to Colwyn Bay, Stourbridge to Kinver, Burton to Ashby, Redruth to Camborne, Grimsby to Immingham and Margate to Ramsgate. The lines from Southport to Ormskirk and Lytham would have resembled these in character. The light railways of Switzerland and Austria and the true interurbans of North America, carrying passengers, mail and freight on extensive rural networks, remained an unknown phenomenon in Britain. The Manx Electric, which carried mail till 1975 and still has vans available to carry freight, is the world's sole surviving example of pioneer North American interurban practice of the 1890s.

Company cars 16 and 11 pass in Lord Street at the junction with Eastbank Street Square about 1907-08, with the abandoned Maltese cross brackets still on the end panels. The wide angle of the trolley pole on the Churchtown-bound car illustrates the practice of side-running trolleys with the traction poles, bracket arms and both overhead wires on one side of the street; the wires for both lines were suspended fairly close together over the Birkdale line. The neo-Elizabethan timbered building on the right, looking like a bit of old Chester, is Lomas's (later Cannell's) high-class fashion store, opened in 1905. The only other vehicles in sight are a bicycle, two hand-carts and a distant horse-cart. *Geoff Price collection*

Improvements in equipment

Once the Southport Corporation and Company tramways had been laid and electrified in 1900-03, there followed a period of consolidation and stability with only a few minor changes. One of the first changes came in July 1902 when the Corporation abandoned trolley ropes and each car was equipped with a bamboo pole with a hook on the end to raise and lower the trolley. The reason for this change-over was that there was a lot of side-running in Southport with the wires offset to one side of the road and the trolley was always swinging wide over the side of the open-top cars. It was quite possible for the overhanging trolley rope of one car to get wrapped around the neck of a passenger sitting on the offside of the top deck of an oncoming car, or at least to remove his hat.

The Corporation led the way in the change-over to bamboo poles and the Company followed suit after an incident on 6 November 1902 (reported in the *Visiter* on 8 November) in which a woman passenger on the top deck of a car was hit on the neck by the trolley rope of a car passing in the opposite direction and was knocked off her seat. She had three severe cuts in the neck and suffered from shock.

Apparently the lower end of the rope, which was normally tied to a rail on the conductor's platform, had become detached and was blowing about.

The bamboo poles were about 16 feet long and carried on hooks on one side of the car under the rocker panel, just above the truck. There was a small loop of rope hanging from the trolley-head to hook it down.

All but the last four Corporation cars had been delivered without destination boxes, which were fitted retrospectively. They were single-aspect boxes showing only the destination in white letters on a black roller blind and were internally lit by night. In about 1902-03 the Corporation identified its different routes more clearly and for the benefit of those who couldn't read with large route letters and coloured lights (route numbers were not adopted till 1919). The route letters were painted in white on a black metal square placed in slots under the wooden destination box. The coloured lights were on a little ornamental black box supported by carved wooden scrolls on top of the destination box and they lasted till about 1921-22, when new combined indicators were installed with route number blind boxes on top. The routes from 1903 were identified thus:

Showing the K route letter for Kew Gardens, Corporation car No 12 passes along the single line through Chapel Street on the one-way town centre circuit in about 1910. This was still a two-way street for other traffic, although there are no other vehicles in sight. The octagonal turret and spirelet on the left was one of a pair on Broadbent's department store. The car is passing the corner of Tulketh Street. *Picture postcard, Cedric Greenwood collection*

H	High Park to Cemetery (both ways)	red light
B	Blowick	blue light
K	Infirmary or Kew Gardens	green light
C	Inner Circle	white light

As we saw in the previous chapter, the Company never used route numbers or letters but, from opening day in 1901, featured destination boxes on the top-deck rail and coloured Maltese crosses on the upper end panels below the destination boxes for easy identification of routes.

In February 1903 signals were installed to control High Park and Blowick cars working over the section of single track along Mornington Road and Derby Road with a blind corner at each end of the Derby Road track. A wooden box with a circular white carbon-filament light facing in each direction was fixed to a traction pole on the last passing loop in each direction before the single-line section: one in Mornington Road and one in Sussex Road (at Zetland Street). The conductor

of the first car to enter the loop inserted a key into the box and this lit up the light on the box at the next loop so that the driver of the next car travelling in the opposite direction could tell that an oncoming car was occupying the single track. He would then wait on the loop to await the other car's arrival.

The Mornington Road and Sussex Road signals were removed when the section of track along Derby Road was doubled many years later, in 1923. The double track extended around the corner at each end to give drivers visibility along both Mornington Road and Sussex Road before rejoining the single track.

Another factor that contributed to the safe operation of tramways generally throughout Great Britain was the edict by the Board of Trade in 1903 that required all tramcars to be fitted with lifeguards at both ends. At first the Corporation cars had rudimentary wire mesh scoops in front of the wheels but about 1902 they were replaced by the Tidswell standard type of wooden slatted gate and tray lifeguard on iron frames. A two-bar gate hung on a metal frame below the fender at each end of the car to about 4 or 5 inches above the road. The gate could pivot backwards if it came into contact with an obstruction, a dog or a body and was connected by a rod mechanism to a slatted tray held horizontally, also about the same height above the road and just in front of the wheels. A simple mechanism dropped the leading edge of the tray at a shallow angle on to the track. The gate and tray were about 5ft 6in wide, a little wider than the track gauge. The tray could slide along the rails and scoop up the body. The back of the tray had a vertical shield of slats to stop the body rolling back under the wheels.

All lifeguards in the country followed this pattern although some differed in minor detail. The Company cars were delivered in 1901-02 already fitted with a similar type of gate and tray lifeguard but made of wire mesh instead of wooden slats. It was simplicity itself to operate and saved an appreciable number of lives over the years, including dogs and cats. The lifeguard was not only actuated automatically but could also be operated by the driver from his platform by pressing one of the three foot pedals on the platform floor by the controller. The other two pedals were for the warning gong and for the sanders. There were sand hoppers under the longitudinal seats in the lower saloon and they dropped sand on the rails in front of the wheels in slippery conditions. All this equipment was, of course, duplicated at each end of the car.

In 1903 the Corporation Tramways Manager reported that 'the type of lifeguard originally fixed is inefficient' and he replaced the Tidswell lifeguards with a similar but cheaper, simpler and more efficient design by Hudson & Bowring following extensive trials with a dummy body on the depot line in Canning Road. The Manager told the Committee that the dummy was placed in every possible position, the car ran at it at speeds from 4 to 16mph and the tray picked it up every time. Later on, Southport trams were fitted with two-bar side gates below the offside of the platforms as well as a front gate.

Service changes

In the tramway mania of the early electric traction era, Southport had perhaps over-invested in tramways. The electric cars were seen as a status symbol in an otherwise horse-drawn, gas-lit environment. Patronage of the new electric trams in Southport was slow to grow and did not initially reach the expectations of the promoters. Perhaps Southport and Birkdale were over-endowed with tramways in proportion to the population at that time with 17 miles of route for 62,280 people (1901 census). In the fiscal year 1902-03 the Corporation trams lost £1,200 and the Company lost £2,368. In the same year Blackpool trams (which ran seven days a week) contributed £2,249 to the relief of the rates. In fact, Southport Corporation trams ran at a loss during nine years in the 13 years up to the First World War but finally made a profit overall from its post-war heyday.

As passenger traffic fluctuated and summer gave way to winter, the Tramways Department was constantly adjusting the frequency of cars and the provision of double- and single-deckers according to patronage. It was difficult to alter the frequency with long stretches of single track so some extra loops were installed.

The 12-minute headway on the Blowick and High Park services was reduced to 15 minutes in January 1902. The hourly extension from the Infirmary to Kew Gardens was suspended for the winter from 1902, except that, as a result of objections from Kew Gardens and Kew Bowling Club, a Saturday-only service was maintained over that stretch of line. The Inner Circle, which always logged the lowest car-mile revenue, had a chequered career: at least once during this period it was reduced to one-way operation – clockwise – then restored to two-way operation.

On bank holiday Whit Monday, 1 June 1903, three extra cars were put on the Kew Gardens service, two extra cars on the High Park-Cemetery service and one extra car shuttled between town and Maple Street on the Blowick line to relieve through cars to Blowick and High Park. Revenue per car mile in the summer of 1903 was: Cemetery section

Corporation car No 8, on the clockwise Inner Circle, passes the Market Hall on Eastbank Street opposite the junction with Chapel Street in about 1908. This domed, stone-faced building opened in 1881 and covered the block from Eastbank Street to Market Street. It closed in 1913 after it was gutted by fire. The new Market Hall opened on part of the site, fronting King Street, in 1931. *Picture postcard, Southport local history collection, Sefton Library Service*

10.1d, Kew section 10d, High Park section 9.6d, Blowick section 9.5d, and Inner Circle 7.9d. The bank holiday Park Circle service was netting 14.1d per car-mile.

The Lancashire & Yorkshire Railway began electrifying its line from Liverpool Exchange to Southport Chapel Street and Crossens in 1903 and the electric train service that began in March 1904 was serious competition for the tramways, offering fast and frequent trains between Chapel Street and St Luke's, Hesketh Park, Churchtown and Birkdale. The electric trains also served Ainsdale and Crossens, outlying districts never reached by the tramways and not served by bus until 1925.

Tramcar passengers had the strange experience of traversing Chapel Street twice in the same direction when the Corporation, in an attempt to route all cars via Lord Street, made High Park to Cemetery cars loop the loop of the town centre circuit. This practice lasted only for one month, June 1904.

The line between the Infirmary and Kew Gardens was something of a backwater of the system until the Royal Lancashire Agricultural Society held its annual show in the 12-acre park in July 1904. This illustrious patronage was good publicity for the gardens and the increased traffic in the years that followed was further boosted by the development of the existing menagerie as the main attraction in April 1906, when the name of the gardens and the destination on the trams changed to 'Zoo

This photograph of Chapel Street in 1902 clearly silhouettes the ornamental scrollwork on the bracket arms, the double overhead wire around the single-track, one-way circuit of the town centre and the guard wires above them. The guard wires were a Board of Trade regulation to prevent telephone lines falling across the tram wires and short-circuiting them or bringing them down. The regulation was lifted as superfluous about 1906 and they disappeared from the tramway scene, as did the overhead telephone wires. *Courtesy of Martin Jenkins, E. J. McWatt and A. D. Packer, Online Transport Archive*

Park'. In 1908 the Scarisbrick New Road line was reported to be the most profitable part of the system, the summer traffic to the gardens being augmented by winter traffic to the new football ground from 1905.

The winter service on Scarisbrick New Road was curtailed variously at the Infirmary or Ash Lane (now Everard Road and Haig Avenue). The Southport football ground opened in (what later became the Haig Avenue section of) Ash Lane in 1905 and this boosted receipts on the line on Saturday afternoons in the winter, when football special cars used the line beyond Ash Lane as a storage siding during matches. The County Show returned to Kew Gardens in August 1909.

Ash Lane linked Higher Blowick with Lower Blowick and is not to be confused with Ash Street, which also crossed Scarisbrick New Road half a mile along the line towards town, which is why Ash Lane was renamed. The Ash Street route to the Cemetery was evidently restored at some time after its false starts in 1902-03 but remained poorly patronised and was closed finally on 19 October 1909. From opening it was clearly surplus to the Shakespeare Street and Duke Street route to the Cemetery, which continued to be one of Southport's most profitable services. The half-mile of single line along Ash Street and Cemetery Road between the junctions at Scarisbrick New Road and Duke Street remained unused except by cars on depot workings and, from 1914, on summer sightseeing tours.

Developments in Birkdale meanwhile saw the Tramways Company sell its majority holding in the Birkdale District Electric Supply Company to the District Council in 1906 for £4,591 16s 9d, and in 1908 the Company built a small running shed for four cars alongside the power station on Birkdale Common. A long siding from Liverpool Road to the depot formed a junction south of Shaw's Road loop and ran along Shaftesbury Road for about 30 yards, turned left into an unmade road (later Grantham Road) then turned right through a gate into a field. The track was laid in granite setts up to this point but then ran for about 300-400 yards on ballasted sleeper track across the field, which was part of the Common, to the depot. Standard side-bracket traction poles supported the overhead wires across the Common. The depot was located on what is now the site of Lincoln Road Clinic and part of the original boundary wall still borders the south end of Grantham Close.

It was 1908 before the first advertisements

Company car No 2 passes Lord Street Station on its way to the Smedley terminus in Birkdale in 1904. The car is about to leave the Lord Street double track and enter the single track in Lord Street West. The location is Duke Street crossing and the stone plinth of the street lamp in the middle of the crossroads is a monument to William Sutton. Duke Street was named after this flamboyant Churchtown innkeeper, who was nicknamed 'Duke', and he is credited with founding the seaside resort by building a bathing house and shooting lodge here in 1792. It was called the Duke's Folly as it stood in a wilderness of sandhills, the South Hawes, but it was close to a fine stretch of bathing beach. In 1798 he rebuilt and expanded the lodge into the South Port Hotel, which he named after a nearby anchorage used mainly by smugglers. This became known as The Original Hotel. As the resort grew up around it, Sutton's primitive and run-down hotel became an eyesore and an obstruction in the middle of the street and it was demolished in 1854. The inscribed tablets of the monument are now set in the balustrade around the gardens on the right-hand side of the street. *Southport local history collection, Atkinson Reference Library, Sefton Library Service, courtesy of The Francis Frith Collection*

A medley of romantic and classical architecture of the period 1884 to 1905 (from left to right) forms the impressive backdrop, to the right of the trees, to Company car No 7 of 1901 as it passes the junction with London Square on its way along Lord Street towards Birkdale. The coloured Maltese cross has been moved up to a new slot on the top-deck rail above the destination box, leaving the extant brackets on the end panels, prior to replacement with advertising in 1908. The destination box is the rotating, four-sided kind with the destination, BIRKDALE, in black letters on opaque white glass. *Courtesy of Martin Jenkins, E. J. McWatt and A. D. Packer, Online Transport Archive*

appeared on Southport trams in a bid to improve tramway revenue, although it did nothing to improve the smart appearance of the cars. The advertisements took the form of enamelled steel panels screwed on to the outside of the top deck decency panels on both Corporation and Company cars. Corporation cars also carried advertising transfers in white lettering on ruby red on the transom ventilator glass in the lower saloons but the Company cars retained the dignity of their saloons with their ornate patterns on the ventilators. During the First World War the Corporation allowed coloured paper advertisements to be stuck on to the ventilators.

For the Company cars advertising on the side decency panels on the top decks replaced the sign 'All the green cars run to Botanic Gardens', which was a form of advertising for an associated private enterprise. To make way for advertisements on the end panels the Maltese crosses were moved up to brackets on the upper deck handrails above the destination boxes and additional Maltese crosses were carried on the upper deck side rails above the entrances in view of boarding passengers.

Also in 1908 the Corporation and Company sought extra revenue by starting a joint parcels and unaccompanied luggage service. Unaccompanied parcels, dogs, pushchairs, pigeon baskets and clothes baskets were carried on the driver's platform at 1d an item, bicycles 6d. Ticket-holders were allowed to take a basket of fish or a small (three- or four-hole) pigeon basket on the tram free of charge. It was reported that from 1 April 1908 to 27 February 1909 a total of 23,566 parcels and other items of unaccompanied luggage had

A classic portrait of Company car No 8 of 1901, pictured at the Botanic Gardens terminus in a full suit of advertisements after 1907. All the lettering on the coachwork was signpainted by hand and the enamelled steel advertisements were screwed on to the upper deck panels. The Company cars did not carry advertisements in the transom ventilator windows in the saloon, which retained the etched patterns in the ruby stained glass that we can see here. The lower wooden panel on the nearside of the three-aspect windscreen was intended to hide women's ankles on the stairs from the man in the street but the screen did not extend around the lower end of the staircase, which was exposed. The name John Lloyd, Manager, can be seen on the solebar below the rocker panel. The destination box is again the rotating, four-aspect type with black lettering on opaque white glass, showing the CROWN HOTEL. The Maltese cross above the destination box was repeated on the side rail

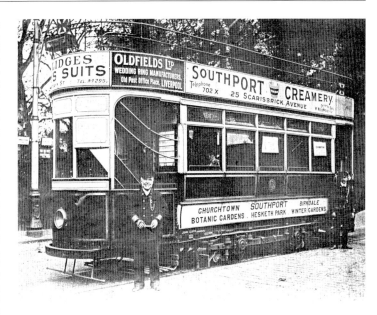

above the rear entrance; this car is on the red cross route. *Graham Fairhurst collection*

been carried on the Corporation trams alone, bringing in a revenue of £98 3s 10d, an appreciable sum in those days.

After a fire at the Zoo in 1908 with the loss of many of the animals, patronage of the Kew section began to decline and the Corporation tried to restore some of the lost traffic by issuing combined tram and Zoo Park tickets at a concession. The park was still a very attractive resort by day and night with its artistic flower beds, grottoes, maze, ferneries, conservatories, boating lake, rustic bridges, tea room, fairy lights and its dual-purpose dining hall and ballroom. Winter tram services were still cut back to the end of the built-up area, except on Saturdays.

The year 1909 saw the Lancashire & Yorkshire Railway electrify the Meols Cop triangle, enabling Crossens trains to call and reverse at Meols Cop station. The Corporation responded by increasing the speed and frequency of the High Park tram service to compete with the fast and frequent electric train service between Chapel Street and Meols Cop.

The ex-Birkdale & Southport tram horse, which the Corporation bought in 1902 to pull the tower wagon to work on the overhead line, died in April 1909. The Department

considered the cost of a motor wagon – and bought another horse. In January 1910 the new horse overturned the tower wagon, killing a tramways inspector. The Department then ordered a Leyland motor tower wagon for £475 and sold the horse when it arrived in June.

The accident occurred on 4 January at about 11pm after the last car had gone to the depot. Inspector Dominic Hoban was on the platform at the top of the tower helping two linesmen using a draw vice to tighten a slack wire in Tithebarn Road at the corner of Hawkshead Street. The vice slipped and hit one of the linesmen on the head, stunning him, and fell to the platform with a bang. This startled the horse, which 'immediately swerved round in a perilous fashion', said the *Visiter* report of the inquest. This caused the acetylene lamp to fall from the platform and crash to the ground, which caused the horse to swerve right round in a circle with such force that the tower toppled over and crashed across the road, hurling the three men to the ground. Inspector Hoban had severe injuries to the spine and face and a broken arm. He died in the Infirmary eight hours later. One linesman had back injuries and the other had bruises to one side of the body.

The *Visiter* described Inspector Hoban as 'one of the most familiar figures of the Tramway Department. His uniform and unfailing courtesy combined with a happy and attractive personality earned the cordial respect of large numbers of the public.'

In 1910 the Town Council decided to combine the Tramways and Electrical Departments and Committees as a matter of economy, appointing the former Borough Electrical Engineer, Mr A. S. Black, as Tramways & Electricity Manager with the former Tramways Manager, Thomas Kendrew, as his deputy. I think we can assume that these two officers continued to look after their own special interests. The Joint Committee decided to dispense with the post of deputy manager in 1912 but Mr Kendrew was retained on the staff.

In 1913 the Council changed its mind and decided to restore the two departments. The post of Tramways Manager was advertised at a salary of £200 and Mr Kendrew was only added to the shortlist of six candidates when one of them withdrew. The post was offered to another man but the Tramways Committee changed its mind and appointed Mr Kendrew

to his former post. In 1914 they raised his salary to £250. The whole episode sounds like bungling political interference. Apart from these three years, Mr Kendrew was Southport's transport manager from 1900 till 1940, when he retired.

During the period of industrial unrest from 1910, the coal strike in the spring of 1912 reduced coal stocks at Crowlands power station to five weeks' supply and the frequency of cars was reduced to 20 minutes on the Inner Circle and Infirmary routes and 15 minutes on the other routes to conserve power consumption.

On 1 April 1912 Birkdale Urban District, incorporating the townships of Birkdale and Ainsdale, became part of the County Borough of Southport. The Corporation thus acquired the tramways of Birkdale but the Southport Tramways Company still owned the cars and provided the services on the existing lease of the tracks. The Corporation made no move to extend its Cemetery Road line into Birkdale for some years to come.

Things looked bleak in the first half of 1913, a low point in the fortunes of the Corporation Tramways and a period of economies. The

Two Company cars, Nos 13 (left) and 8 (right), pass on the loop in Aughton Road, Birkdale, near the corner of Hollybrook Road. The photograph was taken by the Borough Engineer's Department to illustrate the need for the widening of Aughton Road as part of a road-widening

programme for the Southport Corporation Bill to go before Parliament in 1913, the year after the County Borough of Southport was extended to take in Birkdale, its tramway infrastructure and Ainsdale. *Graham Fairhurst collection*

year began with car-mile revenue down to 9.4d on the High Park section, 9d on the Cemetery section, 8.3d on the Zoo section, 7.7d on the Blowick section and 5.6d on the Inner Circle – compare these figures with those given earlier for 1903. Half-fare travel for schoolchildren was cut back from age 15 to age 12. The accumulated deficit on the tramways forced a halt to routine track maintenance and the Highways Department made no further track repairs except on the written orders of the Tramways Manager. Track maintenance continued to decline throughout the 1914-18 war.

Traffic picked up significantly in the summer of 1913 and restored confidence. The Inner Circle was restored to two-way operation, with cars working anti-clockwise again, and extra cars were put on the High Park-Cemetery service on Saturdays, short-working to an intermediate terminus at the Wennington Road loop on Bispham Road.

It is interesting to see that Southport was considering buses in 1912 and 1913 and that electric traction was the vogue in buses. The Electricity & Tramways Committee decided in November 1912 to apply to Parliament for a Bill to run trolleybuses from Park Road along the Promenade and Esplanade to Weld Road, and in October 1913 the Tramways Committee sent the chairman and Manager to see the pioneer 'trackless' trolleybus systems at Stockport and Leeds. Nothing came of this idea and when, eventually, the seafront service began in 1926 it was with a motor bus. The joint committee ordered two Tilling, Stevens single-deck, petrol-electric buses in January to substitute for trams at quiet times but the Tramways Committee cancelled the order in June and had to pay compensation.

By the end of this pre-war period, in the summer of 1914, traffic and revenue had risen again to healthier levels. Takings per car mile were Cemetery 12.8d, Zoo 11.5d, High Park 10.9d, Blowick 8.7d and Inner Circle 7.1d.

Upgrading the cars

Riding the open top deck of a tramcar was a great attraction on a fine summer's day but the open-top cars were losing potential revenue in the cold and the rain. Southport Corporation began enclosing the top decks of its tramcars with top covers in 1908 about the same time as many other tramway undertakings – although motor buses did not get top covers till about 1925. This was achieved by replacing the trolley mast with a sturdy plank to mount the trolley pole on the roof. The Corporation's first top covers came from the United Electric Car Company, the new name for Dick, Kerr's body works at Preston, formerly the Electric Railway & Tramway Carriage Works, following the acquisition in 1905 of two other tramcar builders, the British Electric Car Company and G. F. Milnes & Company. At a price of £110 each, two open-top cars gained a central, upper saloon, shorter than the lower saloon, with three segmental-arched windows each side and a roof that extended the full length of the car as canopies over the residual balcony at each end. The staircases still emerged on these balconies and there were sliding doors into the upper saloon.

These cars were so much appreciated by the passengers and crews that three more open-toppers were fitted with UEC top covers in 1909, still with short, three-bay saloons. All these cars appeared externally to have upper saloons with five-windows each side, but the end windows were outside the saloons and were windbreaks on the balconies. At the end of 1909 a further three open-top cars were covered; the fenestration was the same but these cars had longer upper saloons incorporating the outer windows with the saloon bulkheads directly above those of the lower saloon, giving better structural support and more enclosed seating.

Some of the first five top-covered cars with short saloons soon began to sag under the weight of the upper superstructure, carried on the bulkheads, with no direct support from the load-bearing bulkheads of the lower saloon, and between 1911 and 1913 the affected cars were rebuilt with the bulkheads in vertical alignment, giving longer upper saloons and shorter balconies to match the three cars of late 1909. I remember car No 20, one of the first pair of top-covered cars; it retained its short upper saloon to the end and was the first car to be scrapped in 1930.

The first windscreens on a Corporation tram were removable ones fitted

Above Trolleys under the trees: this well-wooded view of the town centre shows an open-top Company car passing along Lord Street (lower left) and a Corporation car with a top cover and balconies leaving Eastbank Street Square (centre). The top cover was the type fitted to five Corporation cars in 1908-09 with segmental-arch windows in the upper saloon. The narrower end windows were windbreaks for the inner seats on the balconies but cars rebuilt from 1909 incorporated them into an extended saloon. Southport's main public buildings are ranged behind the trees; from the right they are the West Lancashire Bank, the Atkinson Art Gallery, the Cambridge Hall (with the clock tower), the Town Hall and Christ Church. *Picture postcard, Ron Phillips collection*

Below In this view of Eastbank Street from the Scarisbrick Hotel we see a top-covered car with balconies on route H from the Cemetery to High Park followed by an open-top car on the clockwise Inner Circle route C. The double track along Eastbank Street converged to single track in Eastbank Street Square in the foreground but the left-hand line from the square to Chapel Street corner was seldom used as it ran counter to the one-way circuit of the town centre used by all regular service cars. The tramcar in the square is No 20, one of the first Southport cars to be top-covered in 1908, and it remained in this condition with its short upper saloon and long balconies until 1930, when it was scrapped. The photograph was taken before 1919, when route H became route 3 and route C became route 7. Again we see the West Lancashire Bank (left), which was taken over as an extension of the Atkinson Library & Art Gallery in 1923-24. *Geoff Price collection*

experimentally to one of the single-deck California cars in 1908 but the Tramways Committee thought it was 'not desirable or necessary' to fit them to any more Californias at that stage but from 1911 all the Corporation trams were fitted with home-made windscreens on the platforms – over 10 years after the Company cars, which were delivered with windscreens as new in 1901. This measure partially but effectively enclosed the open platforms as vestibules to the saloons, to the greater comfort of the drivers and conductors, although, like the Company cars, the offsides of the platforms, between the stairs and the saloons, remained unglazed until the rebuilding programme of the 1920s.

The Grand Tour

The most significant development of this halcyon period between the completion of the

tramways and the Great War was the departure into the tourist business and the arrival of the 'toastrack' car for the start of the Grand Tour of Southport at Easter 1914. If the public was not riding the tramcars for pleasure, as initially envisaged, then the Corporation would make them. And ride they did! In its first two years the Grand Tour, operating in the summer season only, was so popular among visitors – and so much more expensive than ordinary tram fares per mile – that it netted three times the revenue of any regular stage service in Southport.

Circular tours by open-top tram had proved popular at Scarborough, Torquay, Brighton and Hastings but in 1911 Blackpool set a new fashion in tramcar tours with entirely open, single-deck cars with 14 full-width bench seats placed transversely, which gave the cars the popular nickname 'toastracks'. These trams had no structure above the deck apart from the

This official photograph shows Southport's first 'toastrack' tramcar, a completely open cross-bench car designed for sightseeing tours of the town. The car entered service in 1914 on the Grand Tour, which operated every summer till 1924, and it is pictured at the start of the tour on the north-east side of London Square in June 1914. The classical concrete shelter in the background was removed to the south-west side of Eastbank Street Square for the construction of the Monument in 1923. Southport had four toastrack cars built in 1914-15 and three more in 1920,

when the Circular Tour began, and that tour continued until 1932. This car, No 21, could always be distinguished from the others by its ruddy-brown trolley mast and natural oak destination box on the mast; the mast and box were painted green on the later toastracks. Passengers could board at any point on either side of the car by mounting the running boards; safety bars were raised when the car was in motion. The two centre seats remained fixed back-to-back on each side of the trolley mast. *Southport Corporation picture postcard, Cedric Greenwood collection*

dash panel and controller at each end, the cross-bench seats ranged in between and the central trolley mast and pole. Each bench seated five passengers, there was no gangway, the car had no side panels and passengers could climb directly into their seats from either side of the car by mounting one of the full-length, side running boards, from which the conductor also collected the fares. The trolley pole was mounted on a tall iron mast amidships.

Southport began its venture into the tour business cautiously by selling 'circular tour' tickets on the Inner Circle in 1913 with cheaper fares for two people for the round trip. That autumn it placed an order for a £220 toastrack car body from the United Electric Car Company, Preston, which had built Blackpool's toastracks. The toastrack body arrived in March 1914 and was then mounted on a Brill 21E truck from a wrecked California car and numbered 21 in the odd-number series for single-deckers. (There was no car No 19 in the Corporation fleet until the take-over of the Company cars in 1918.) It was shorter than Blackpool's toastracks with 10 benches seating 50 passengers. The dash panels were painted in Corporation crimson and the trolley mast was ruddy brown, the same as the truck.

This car inaugurated the new Grand Tour of Southport (originally advertised as the Grand Circle) on 9 April, the day before Good Friday, 1914. The fare was 6d for adults and 3d for children for a 6½-mile ride, which lasted an hour – longer than Blackpool's. It was an expensive tram ride for the time, hence the high rate of revenue compared with other Corporation tram services, but the visitors loved it and the open car, parked on the corner of Lord Street and London Square, filled quickly. On Easter Monday the tour was so popular that the Corporation had to deploy four extra cars from the service fleet on the tour to meet the demand. The *Visiter* reported that '...among the owners of the horse charabancs there is a good deal of grumbling at the innovation of the Grand Tour as a very serious competitor to their drives round the town in the summer season'.

Between April and October 1914 the Grand Tour notched up record receipts: 27.8d a mile in the first four weeks and 32.8d a mile in the third week of August. It earned more than twice as much revenue than any of the stage services and three times the average.

The Tramways Committee, which had enjoyed a preview of the Grand Tour on 8 April, was so impressed by its initial patronage and revenue at Easter that on the following Wednesday, 15 April, they ordered three more £220 toastrack bodies from UEC for the 1915 season and placed them on trucks from three more California cars that had been withdrawn from service. This reduced the fleet of California cars to four, which continued in service till 1922-23. The three new toastracks were numbered 23, 25 and 27. Thus Southport became the second town in Britain with toastrack trams.

While Blackpool's Circular Tour used the Promenade, Lytham Road and the belt line around Marton, and Sunday was its busiest day, there was no tramway along Southport Promenade, no sea views from the Promenade anyway and no trams on Sundays. Southport, on the other hand, contrived to make the Grand Tour as long and devious as possible, as will be seen. The original Grand Tour replaced the bank holiday Park Circle service, which had last run in August 1913, and the tour cars were the only other trams ever to use Park Road.

To get to Kew Gardens and Hesketh Park on this convoluted mystery tour there were five points where the car had to reverse: two double reversals, at the crossing of Ash Street and Scarisbrick New Road, where passengers could remain seated as the car reversed around the corners, and three single reversals, at Kew Gardens, Hesketh Park and Hartwood Road, where passengers had to dismount from the car while the conductor flipped over the seat backs. But passengers were not allowed to leave the car at the parks or any other point of interest along the route and resume their ride on the next tour car as they could at Blackpool.

The route of the Grand Tour was as follows. Cars loaded in London Square, made their way through Chapel Street and Eastbank Street and headed out of town around Shakespeare Street, Duke Street and Cemetery Road. One wonders what first impression of

Southport this part of the itinerary gave the sightseers.

The object of the Grand Tour was to earn more revenue on the Zoo line and the Inner Circle. In this it certainly succeeded and the diversion via Duke Street just to make the tour longer was unnecessary. It would have been more straightforward if the cars had headed straight along Scarisbrick New Road from town, but to reach Zoo Park from Cemetery Road and Ash Street the cars had to reverse on the junction because there was no right-hand curve from Ash Street towards Kew.

The reversal ritual was repeated at Zoo Park terminus and again back at Ash Street junction, where the cars turned towards St Luke's and continued via Hartwood Road and Leyland Road, turned right into Queen's Road and left into Park Road. Instead of continuing around the left-hand curve into Albert Road and Lord Street, the tour cars reversed at Hesketh Park gates to return the same way to Hartwood Road and reversed again there to turn left into Manchester Road and so back to Lord Street.

That was the original Grand Tour but this itinerary was soon modified to cut out Hesketh Park and follow the Company's Roe Lane route into town along Leyland Road, Queen's Road, Manchester Road and Lord Street. When I rode the tour in 1924 it turned left out of Hartwood Road and went straight down Manchester Road. The tour toastracks terminated and loaded on a dedicated, newly laid curve from Lord Street into London Square, which kept them clear of the service tracks.

Wartime

The Great War of 1914-18 did not appear to put off holidaymakers from coming to Southport or riding the Grand Tour as the receipts in 1915 were slightly up on the first season. Passenger figures declined only slightly as the war dragged on, and the tour continued through the war and was well supported, but when war ended in 1918 inflation pushed up the fares by 50 and 100 per cent to 9d and 6d and ridership dropped.

The war years were difficult times for the tramways, which had to carry more passengers with fewer staff to crew and repair the cars and maintain the track and overhead lines. There was not only a shortage of staff but also a shortage of coal for the power stations and a shortage of materials and parts as the nation's industrial output switched to military needs. Many tramway drivers, conductors, track workers, linesmen and workshop craftsmen answered Lord Kitchener's call to arms. Women conductors, known as 'lady guards' or 'conductorettes' in Southport during the First World War, were drafted in from 1915 to replace the conductors who had gone to war and those who had moved up to the front platform to replace the absent drivers. At the same time up to 15,000 soldiers were camped and billeted in and around Southport and staying in the hospitals and convalescent homes, many of them converted from large hotels, and, with the shortage of horses and petrol too, more people were riding the trams.

In the restricted lighting conditions that prevailed during the war the electric cars droned eerily through the dark streets at night with dimmed lights in the saloons. Most cars still had open top decks where passengers were exposed to all weathers. The tramcars carried many more passengers, who crowded on, and standing passengers filled the rear platform and the top deck, even in the rain.

The result was that revenue reached new heights in the report for August 1915, with 35d a mile on the Grand Tour, 16.7d on the Cemetery section, 12.9d on the High Park section, 11.8d on the Blowick section, 11.6d on the Zoo section and 8.8d on the Inner Circle. There was no new tramcar production during the war and Southport made bids to buy or lease second-hand trams from other systems to help shift the crowds but the offers were declined; every town had the same problem. However, the Corporation did succeed in buying second-hand overhead arms and brackets from Northampton Corporation in 1917.

The Zoo Park service was discontinued altogether in August 1914 'for the duration of the war', never to re-open. The year-round tram service was curtailed at Haig Avenue or the Infirmary although the line to Kew Gardens was still used by tour cars from 1914

The presence of the conductress dates this photograph to the First World War, when the tramways were short of staff and rolling stock. This is one of the four Corporation 'California' cars that survived cannibalisation for 'toastracks' in 1914. The original appearance of these clerestory-roofed cars with cross-bench seats on long, open platforms was transformed in this reconstruction with windscreens, doors and roof-mounted advertising panels. Car No 7 was one of at least two fitted with doors in 1916. *Cedric Greenwood collection*

to 1924. The Blowick and Infirmary services were combined as a through service in December 1914. This was an operational expedient as the two terminals and the two lines, along Sussex Road and Scarisbrick New Road, were only half a mile apart, but it meant that all services were now cross-town, eliminating the congestion caused by tramcars terminating in London Square. It also restored double-deckers to Blowick, releasing Californias for the augmented Inner Circle service.

In 1915 cards were displayed in the tramcars and in the office window in Chapel Street advertising jobs for men not eligible for military service to take the places of staff who had joined the Army. Office and depot staff helped to crew the cars until the vacancies were filled but not enough men came forward and by November the Tramways Department had, for the first time, to find uniforms suitable for female conductors, who were employed at the same rate of pay as the men.

The Corporation trams suffered no war damage in the 1914-18 conflict but the fleet was reduced by one car. The sole standard saloon single-decker, the little-used 'Committee Car' No 13, was sold to the Electricity Department in March 1916 for £379 17s 5d. Its body was removed and its four-wheel motored truck, controls and trolley were used to equip a home-made, box-cab, electric locomotive to work coal trains over the private sidings from Blowick and Meols Cop railway goods yards along Butts Lane and Crowland Street to the Corporation gas works and electric power station. These lines, previously worked by horses, were electrified in June 1916 with overhead wire like a tramway and the Electricity Department provided the overhead, the traction, the driver and brakeman (see Appendix 4). The Electricity Committee re-sold the body of car 13 locally to H. Garside for £16, presumably for a chalet, shed or summerhouse.

By the end of the war in 1918 the Manager reported that the number of fitters in the workshops was reduced from 27 at the outbreak of war to 16 and only three of these men had more than three years' experience of fitting car trucks. The workshops were also having the utmost difficulty in obtaining the necessary parts and materials for repairs.

In his report for the fiscal year 1917-18, Mr Kendrew wrote:

'Owing to the shortage of suitable labour and materials, the maintenance of the cars has been difficult and arduous with the result that many of the cars have deteriorated considerably and will require extensive repairs during the coming year. As the tramways have now been in operation for nearly 18 years and only curved rails have been renewed, there are several lengths of straight track which require relaying. Some of the rails are very badly worn.'

By 31 March 1918 the total tramway staff of 83 included 32 women. Tram services were drastically reduced to 30-minute headways on the High Park, Cemetery and Infirmary routes, which led to overcrowding. The Manager reported poor timekeeping on the tram services because of novice drivers and conductors and the increased number of passengers, who crowded on to the back platforms, obstructing the conductors and the passengers boarding and alighting.

An interesting sideline that started during the war was a successful experiment with postboxes on late evening trams. These were provided at the request of the Postmaster for later posting of letters on the outskirts of town for next-morning delivery. They were fitted to the dash panels of the cars, initially on the Inner Circle from 1 November 1916, for a trial period. From February 1918 one postbox was placed on each route. Postbox cars ran on many tram systems in Britain and this service was developed during the 1920s.

Accidents

Although there was no war damage to the trams and nobody was killed by enemy action in Southport, there were four serious tramway accidents during the period 1914 to 1917, in which two pedestrians were fatally injured, one driver lost his leg and four cars were damaged. Three of the accidents and the two fatalities occurred in the restricted wartime street lighting conditions at night, when half the street lamps were switched off and the others were partly masked with black paint.

Two cars collided at the crossing of Sussex Road and St Luke's Road at about 2.15pm on 31 March 1914, when, according to the *Visiter* (2 April), a double-decker on its way to Blowick collided with the back end of a California car on the Inner Circle as it was clearing the crossing. The single-decker was derailed and spun round and the conductor's end of the car crashed through the brick wall and hedge into the front garden of Taylor Brothers' dental surgery on the corner of Pine Grove. As its wheels ploughed through the tiled footpath the sandy subsoil dragged the car to a stop short of the building.

The car, No 17, sustained damage to the dash panel and windscreen, and the conductor, Charles Johnson, was taken to the Infirmary with bruised legs and shock. Fortunately there were no passengers in the car. Tram services through the crossing were held up for more than an hour while the Manager, Mr Kendrew, supervised the recovery, using another tramcar to pull the damaged car back on to the rails and tow it back to the tramshed. It transpired that Mr Johnson was a part-time conductor deputising for the duty conductor, who had obtained leave to play football that afternoon. Car No 17 did not return to service, becoming the first of the eight California cars to be made redundant. Its truck was conveniently transferred under the new UEC body of the first toastrack car to inaugurate the Grand Tour the following month.

In the street lighting restrictions of the Great War an elderly man was fatally injured when the handcart he was pushing was in collision with a tramcar on the Scarisbrick New Road section of the Inner Circle on 17 November 1915. Charles Briggs, aged 72, of Matlock

Road, Birkdale, died in hospital on 3 December.

The inquest was told that Mr Briggs was an auctioneer's porter and was pushing a handcart loaded with furniture when the accident happened near the Tabernacle junction at 5.10pm. A man who was with him said that snow was piled along the side of the road so they moved over to the crown of the road as soon as an inbound Inner Circle car overtook them but immediately met an outbound car on the double-track section. The tram driver said the cart carried no marker light and he saw it too late in the intensified darkness after passing the lights of the oncoming car. His car caught the corner of the cart. The coroner exonerated the driver and recorded a verdict of accidental death.

In early morning fog on 15 October 1917 two tramcars collided head-on on the single line in Bispham Road. A car on service to High Park had just left the double-track over Meols Cop bridge when it met a car on its way from the depot to go into service on the Inner Circle. The inbound car overran the outbound car, whose driver, John Rimmer, received severe injuries to one leg, which had to be amputated above the knee. The other driver had cuts to the head and the only two passengers on the service car escaped injury.

A woman from Forest Road was knocked down by an Inner Circle car as she was walking across Ash Street at 7pm on 5 November 1917, but she was saved by the lifeguard and recovered in the Infirmary.

Another accident in the darkness of the restricted street lighting occurred in Duke Street near the corner of Cemetery Road at about 11.15pm on 12 December 1917, when a tramcar collided with a drunken jay-walker. Vincent Johnson, aged 62, was picked up on the lifeguard tray but had a fractured skull and was dead on arrival at the Infirmary.

His doctor told the inquest that Mr Johnson was addicted to drink, unemployed and of no fixed address. The tram driver said the man had been a passenger on his outward-bound journey to the Cemetery and alighted at Sefton Street. He was under the influence of drink and there was some difficulty in getting him off the car. On his return along Duke Street the driver first saw the pedestrian stepping into the road about 6 yards ahead. The car was going slowly, about 4-5mph, and making plenty of noise. He rang the gong and applied the brakes but the pedestrian stepped in front of the car and was knocked down.

The police witness said it was a very dark night, the nearest lit streetlamp was about 140 yards away and the scene of the accident was so dark that he could not see a woman who walked past him about 10 yards away; he only knew it was a woman by the sound of her footsteps. The jury returned a verdict of misadventure and exonerated the tram driver.

Amalgamation

The two Southport tramway systems merged into one in 1918 when Southport Corporation bought the Southport Tramways Company. Southport had become a County Borough in 1905 and the borough had been extended in 1912 by the formal annexation of Birkdale Urban District, including its tramway infrastructure. The amalgamation of the tramways followed six years later but four years before the lease of the Company tracks was due to expire in July 1922. Negotiations for the take-over began in 1917 and it was agreed that the Company should hand over to the Corporation on 1 January 1918, but, owing to a fault in the drafting of the agreement, the hand-over was deferred till 1 March, when the Company cars became Corporation cars.

This marked the end of 45 years of the Southport Tramways Company and the end of 45 years' service with the Company by John Lloyd, who had been General Manager for the last 21 years of horse traction and the first 17 years of electric traction. On 16 February all the Company staff met at Churchtown depot to honour Mr Lloyd on his retirement and the *Southport Visiter* reported the event on 19 February. Driver J. Tattersall presented him with a framed, illuminated address and an inscribed silver Waltham pocket watch on a double Albert chain, and Miss M. A. Hadley, the first 'lady guard' to be employed by the Tramways Company, handed Mrs Lloyd a silver dressing case. The framed address, adorned with the BET magnet and wheel emblem, the Southport coat of arms and a photograph of a tramcar, and signed by 65 staff, expressed their 'sincere gratitude for the genial, dignified and efficient manner in which you have at all times carried out your official duties, without intermission, for the long period of 45 years'.

On 1 March most of the Company staff were taken on by the Corporation, along with the cars, but some Company employees moved to the BET company system at Barrow-in-Furness – to be joined a few years later by four ex-Southport Corporation California cars that went into service in Southport livery (see the chapter on 'The heyday of the trams').

The 'new brooms' of the Corporation swept through the ex-Company fleet. The demi-car with its regenerative braking system, which had languished out of use for several years, was condemned and scrapped as unsafe and non-standard. The double-deckers were refitted with the standard Corporation destination boxes and Hudson & Bowring slatted lifeguards and the seat cushions were removed from the saloons because they said they were unhealthy and spread germs. So passengers sat on polished wooden seats – that

was clean and healthy! In due course these cars were rebuilt, repainted and renumbered.

The Company tram depot in Churchtown was sold in July 1918 for £6,000 and partly vacated for the new occupants, who allowed the green cars to continue using the running shed while Crowlands shed was extended to accommodate them. The new occupants of the former Company depot were BEV (British Electric Vehicles), manufacturers of narrow-gauge battery- and overhead-electric locomotives used in quarries and mines and steerable motor luggage trolleys used on railway stations.

Southport Corporation had to get a loan to pay the negotiated £35,000 purchase price of the Company. The largest element of the purchase price was £13,500 the Company claimed for the premature surrender of the leases in Southport and Birkdale. The Southport lease was not due to expire until July 1922, so the Company said it would wait until then for full payment. The Corporation paid 5 per cent interest to the Company in the meantime. After payment, the Company was wound up on 30 November 1922.

SUNDAY TRAMS

Southport Tramways Company
Southport Corporation Tramways
1902-1918

The acquisition of Birkdale's tram services in 1918 immediately re-opened the question of Sunday operations. No Corporation cars ran in Southport on Sundays but Company cars did run in Birkdale and over the boundary to the crossover by London Square throughout the period from 1902 to 1918, except for the eight months from November 1902 to July 1903, when cars terminated at the boundary. The Parliamentary tramways order for Southport and the lease of tracks to the Company did not allow trams to ply for hire within the borough on Sundays but the Birkdale order and lease provided for daily operation with Sunday provisions. The Company allowed free rides on the Southport section to comply with the order not to ply for hire in the borough.

This disparity posed a problem for Southport Town Council, which had to standardise practice on the amalgamation of the two systems. Either it had to stop Sunday trams running in Birkdale or start running them in Southport. In this issue the Council was torn between the strong Sabbatarian faction and the evident need for Sunday trams with their lucrative revenue, as proved by the Company operations. Now is the time for us to review the controversy, which had simmered on and off for 16 years.

The question of Sunday running was considered by Southport Tramways Committee early in 1900 before the July inauguration of electric traction. The Committee visited municipal tramways at Blackpool, Bradford, Halifax, Huddersfield, Leeds, Liverpool and Sheffield. They found that six of the seven towns had Sunday tram services. Some towns had 'church cars' to morning services but Southport decided it could do without Sunday trams initially in deference to the strong Protestant body of opinion in what was said to be the only town in the country with more churches than public houses.

Sunday tram services stemmed from the opening of the line to the Crown Hotel on Tuesday 4 November 1902. The following Sunday, the 9th, one car operated between the Crown Hotel and Aughton Road, connecting there with two cars operating between Birkdale station and Lord Street, reversing on the crossover at what the Company called St George's Square, referring to the gardens fronting St George's Place. Conductors collected fares in Birkdale only so as to comply with the terms of the Southport lease. The travelling public voted with their feet and the supply of 1,300 penny tickets sold out before the end of the day.

The *Southport Visiter* of 11 November reported:

'The electric trams of the Southport Tramways Company were running from Birkdale to Southport on Sunday for the first time on the Sabbath and during the afternoon and the later part of the day they were well patronised. These cars, it may be stated, have no connection with the Southport Corporation system of tramways. The Southport cars did not run.'

In its investigation of events, the newspaper revealed that:

'On Saturday evening Cllr Jones, chairman of the Electricity Committee, received a telegram from Mr Colebourne, London secretary of the Southport Tramways Company, stating that the Company would require current from 9 o'clock on Sunday morning till 9 o'clock at night. Under the Electric Lighting Act the Corporation is bound to supply current in any hour of the day or night for 365 days a year under a penalty. Whether the clause in the Tramways Order overrides this is a moot point.'

Apparently, Mr Colebourne was in Birkdale over the weekend to superintend the running of the cars.

Only one-third of the road staff were required for Sunday duty and they worked 4-hour shifts. The *Visiter* (13 November) reported:

'The clang of the bells was not heard on the day. The cars went at half speed all the time, except on passing places of worship, when they were slowed down to walking pace. Orders were given that no fares should be collected within the Borough of Southport.'

This was not good enough for Birkdale Cllr Rushworth, who told the *Visiter* that he was opposed to Sunday trams breaking the Fourth Commandment and the quietude of the Sabbath and he believed they would drive residents away and leave Birkdale with empty houses. That week Birkdale UDC voted 10-2 against Sunday trams. The District Council, however, had no power to stop Sunday trams because the clause in the original Order preventing Sunday operation of horse trams was not included in the revised Birkdale Order for electric cars. The indignation of Birkdale Council is hard to understand because the agreement for the renewed lease of the tracks included a clause compelling the Company to run a daily service and another clause for the cars to proceed at walking pace past places of worship on Sundays and not to sound their gongs. The Company had kept to its agreement.

Southport Town Council meeting on 13 November agreed that the Electricity Department could not have done anything else but supply current as requested but remitted the question of future supply to the Town Clerk and the Electricity Committee chairman.

It was reported that the Company chairman, Mr Raworth, had discussed the matter at length with the Town Clerk and the Committee. He said the exercise was an object lesson in what the Sunday running of tramcars ought to be. The drivers were instructed to drive the cars on series notches only so that the speed should never rise to the point at which it was necessary to use the gong. Some residents along the route were quite unaware that trams were running until they went out to chapel or church at 6 o'clock that evening.

He doubted that tram services could be made to pay in a town the size of Southport unless there was a Sunday service. Both undertakings were losing money and the Sunday service would help the Company to pay the lease to the Corporation and to set aside a depreciation fund to renew cars and infrastructure when due. The Sunday service would continue for a four-week trial period to assess the demand and remuneration, he said.

In advance of the second Sunday of operation the Company displayed a large notice in the *Southport Visiter* on Saturday 15 November, headed 'Sunday Trams'. It said that the first cars would leave London Square at 9.30am and Birkdale station and the Crown Hotel at 9.45 in time for the 10.30am church services in Southport and Birkdale.

'In consequence of the allegation that fares collected in Birkdale are, in fact, paid for travelling in Southport, passengers will be required to alight before crossing the boundary. A free car will be run in Southport between London Square and Birkdale. The Company is applying to the Southport Corporation for statutory permission to ply for hire in the borough on Sundays.'

Accordingly, Company cars were running in Birkdale and Lord Street again for the second consecutive Sunday. This time the Corporation had refused a request for traction current on the advice of the Town Clerk but the Company had inserted a jumper cable to by-pass the section breaker between the two overhead systems at the boundary to connect the Birkdale supply to its Southport section and this was sufficient to power the cars as far as London Square. Passengers changed cars at the boundary and were issued with gratuitous tickets for the Southport section.

The *Visiter* reported that 'Though there were not many passengers during the day, the cars were well patronised in the evening'. The report went on to say that the Company could be penalised if it did not provide a daily service in accordance with the terms of the Birkdale lease.

SUNDAY TRAMS.

THE FIRST CARS LEAVE:

BIRKDALE—CROWN HOTEL	—	—	—	9.45 A.M.
L. & Y. STATION	—	—	—	9.45 ,,
SOUTHPORT—LONDON · SQUARE	—	—	—	9.30 ,,

In time for the 10-30 a.m. Services in Southport and Birkdale.

In consequence of the allegation that fares collected in Birkdale are, in fact, paid for travelling in Southport, passengers will be required to alight before crossing the boundary.

A FREE CAR

Will be run in Southport between London-square and Birkdale.

The Company is applying to the Southport Corporation for Statutory permission to Ply for Hire in the Borough on Sundays.

The Southport Tramways Company placed this notice of Sunday trams in the *Southport Visiter* on Saturday 15 November 1902. *By courtesy of British Library Newspapers*

The Sunday tram service aroused vituperative opposition in public speeches and letters to the newspapers from Sabbatarians of Southport, led by the Wesleyan Church. The anti-Sunday tram faction was not entirely religious; working men opposed Sunday working on principle, except for cab proprietors, who opposed Sunday trams because they could cash in on the exclusive privilege of providing public transport in Southport on one day a week.

In deference to the opposition, the Company withdrew from the controversy and continued to operate entirely within Birkdale from the third Sunday, 23 November, but the number of passengers was halved from 1,400-1,500 to 600-700 each Sunday after the service was curtailed at the boundary. The Company chairman, John Raworth, published a pamphlet discussing the Fourth Commandment – 'Thou shalt do no manner of work on the Sabbath' – and entered into the controversy in the letters columns of the *Visiter*, writing from his home address in Christchurch Road, Streatham Hill, London.

The *Visiter* (25 November) said:

'Quite a number of the members of the Town Council are against Sunday running, not so much, perhaps, on strict Sabbatarian grounds as they fear it will convert Southport into a rowdy trippers' resort and tend to drive away the residential class.'

The editorial comment on 29 November went on to say that:

'It has become a settled policy that the example of Blackpool should not be followed. Many people here believe that the showy and sensational attractions offered by Blackpool would lead to disaster and that the introduction of Sunday trams would be quickly followed on an extensive scale by Sunday concerts, Sunday boating and driving and Sunday trading with the accompanying excitements indulged in by our neighbours.'

The Editor did not agree that trams should be run in Southport on Sunday just because they ran in Liverpool and Manchester and he doubted if they would increase the congregations of churches.

A meeting of Birkdale UDC on 2 December was advised by the Clerk that the Company had power to run on Sundays and the Council had no power to stop it. The Company applied to Southport Town Council for permission to ply for hire in the Borough on Sundays but the application was refused by the Council meeting on 9 December. The Company was reminded of a clause in the lease that the promoters should not ply for hire in the borough on Sundays except with the consent of the Council.

The controversy continued over the next six months with a public protest meeting in the lecture hall of Mornington Road Wesleyan Church on 8 December, petitions from the Southport & District Ratepayers' Association and local churches, debates in meetings of the Borough and District Councils and correspondence in the local newspapers. But it was not all one-way.

The Company House Proprietors' Association and 540 boarding house keepers petitioned the Town Council in support of Sunday trams. Cllr Stowe told the January 1903 meeting of Birkdale Council that he had attended St Peter's Church on many Sundays since the cars had been running and he never heard them passing by along St Peter's Road.

'A Resident' wrote to the *Visiter*:

'I consider it a wise policy on the part of the Tramway Company to run their cars on Sunday and trust they will not pay heed to these cranks that have raised such a chorus against Sunday cars. I have no doubt that these people will be the first to use the cars on a wet day and will say it is because of necessity. I note that one of your readers quotes passages from the Bible for his argument against Sunday trams but what does he say about the railway company running trains and shops that are open both in Southport and Birkdale? The cars will be a boon to many residents and visitors who are in favour of Sunday cars.'

The matter did not abate and eventually the Town Council decided to hold a poll of electors, to be conducted like a normal municipal election in the wards, on Saturday 4 July 1903. In the run-up to the poll, one of the main reasons advanced for running trams on Sundays was the need to recover more revenue to set against the expenditure on the system. The Council decided to submit the decision to the ratepayers in view of the deficit due to not running Corporation trams seven days a week.

The Tramways Company and the Wesleyan Church issued circulars for and against running trams on Sundays and the Area Church Council put up posters urging ratepayers to vote against it. Both sides displayed advertisements in the *Southport Visiter* on polling day urging electors to go to the polls and summarising their causes. The Rector of North Meols, the Rural Dean of North Meols and clergy representing eight churches in Southport subscribed their names to five reasons to vote against Sunday trams: they would (1) be unnecessary in Southport, (2) increase Sunday labour, depriving many of their due rest, (3) lead to Sunday desecration, (4) hinder the work of the Church, especially among the young, and (5) destroy the quiet

Sunday in Southport and the basis of its prosperity. Directly below it the Tramways Company listed five reasons to vote for Sunday trams: (1) the service in Birkdale had proved a great convenience to the residents, (2) no staff would work more than a six-day week or increased hours, (3) trams did not encourage Sunday desecration, (4) they did not hinder the work of the church and (5) operations would be quiet and orderly, as in Birkdale, where not a single complaint had been received from the public.

The *Visiter* reported that 'Cab proprietors were greatly in evidence in getting voters to the poll against the running of trams'. A crowd of about 2,000 people waited around the Town Hall between 8 and 9pm for the declaration of the poll. The result was a resounding vote against Sunday trams: 1,843 for and 3,639 against. All the wards with a strong working class population, including the villages of Marshside and Crossens, which did not have tramways, voted solidly against Sunday cars. Only Central Ward voted in favour: 233 for and 183 against. The Tramways Committee chairman, Cllr Travis, analysed the results dispassionately, saying that out of every six residents, one was in favour, two were against and three didn't care.

The Company responded contrarily by resuming the Sunday service to Lord Street the following day, 5 July. The *Southport Visiter* on the 7th said:

'At a late hour on Saturday night a representative of the Company waited on Cllr Thomas Jones, chairman of the Electricity Committee, and asked that current be supplied by the Corporation. This request was refused. The Company held that they are entitled to be supplied with current all the year round like any other customer and it is now a matter for the Corporation.

Again the Company attached jumpers to the connection at Westcliffe Road. No fares were being charged in Southport. Passengers paid to the boundary and were guests of the Company to London Square. A fair number of people availed themselves of the cars on Sunday, especially the voters for Sunday cars. On Sunday evening after

THE SOUTHPORT VISITER. SATURDAY, JULY 4, 1903.

DO NOTHING TO-DAY

YOU WILL REPENT OF HEREAFTER,

AND

VOTE AGAINST

THE RUNNING OF TRAMS

ON THE SABBATH!

SUNDAY TRAMS! AN APPEAL!!

CONCERTED ACTION BY THE CLERGY.

Ladies and Gentlemen,

In view of the Resolution of the Town Council to refer the proposal to run a service of Trams on Sundays to the Ratepayers for decision, we feel it our duty to offer a public expression of our opinion on a matter so closely affecting the interests of the town.

We venture to appeal most earnestly to the Residents of Southport to record their Votes against the running of Sunday Trams, and for the following reasons:—

1.—That whatever may be the case in other towns, Sunday Trams are not a necessity in Southport.

2.—That they would increase in several ways Sunday labour, and thereby deprive many of their Sunday rest.

3.—That they would inevitably lead to and encourage Sunday desecration.

4.—That they would hinder the work of the Church, and especially amongst the young.

5.—That they would destroy the Quiet Sunday in Southport, which has done so much to build up the prosperity of the town.

We are convinced for these five reasons that Sunday Trams would be prejudicial to the best interests of the whole community, and we earnestly implore the Ratepayers to realise their responsibility, and to do their duty on Saturday Next, July 4th.

We plead for the prosperity of the town, the welfare of the young, and the honour of God; and trust we shall not plead in vain.

J. DENTON THOMPSON, Rector of North Meols and Hon. Canon of Liverpool;
H. MONTAGUE DALE, G. Z. EDWARDS, and S. ERNEST SWANN, Assistant Clergy.

J. H. HONEYBURNE, Rural Dean of North Meols, Vicar of Christ Church, and Hon. Canon of Liverpool; E. P. COOK and P. GOUGH, Assistant Clergy.

C. S. HOPE, Vicar of Holy Trinity; H. E. MOCATTA, A. E. THORP, and G. RICHARDSON, Assistant Clergy.

F. SINKER, Vicar of St. Paul's; H. ICHET and W. BRADLEY, Assistant Clergy.

GRANTLEY C. MARTIN, Vicar of St. Andrews; F. G. GODDARD, Assistant Clergy.

C. T. PORTER, Vicar of All Saints' and All Souls'; J. WILLIAMS and F. W. SOAMES, Assistant Clergy.

C. A. CLEMENTS and A. URLING-SMITH, Assistant Clergy, St. Luke's.

C. H. HATFIELD, Vicar of St. Philip's.

THE SOUTHPORT TRAMWAYS COMPANY LIMITED.

REASONS FOR VOTING FOR SUNDAY TRAMS.

1.—THE SUNDAY TRAM SERVICE IN BIRKDALE HAS PROVED A GREAT CONVENIENCE TO THE RESIDENTS, AND WILL BE AS MUCH APPRECIATED IN SOUTHPORT.

2.—NO SERVANT WILL BE REQUIRED TO WORK MORE THAN SIX DAYS PER WEEK, AND THE TOTAL NUMBER OF HOURS WORKED WILL NOT BE INCREASED.

3.—THE RUNNING OF TRAMS DOES NOT ENCOURAGE SUNDAY DESECRATION.

4.—THEY DO NOT HINDER THE WORK OF THE CHURCH, BUT IN MANY WAYS WILL ASSIST IT.

5.—THE SERVICE WILL BE RUN IN A QUIET AND ORDERLY MANNER, AS IS DONE IN BIRKDALE. NOT A SINGLE COMPLAINT HAS BEEN RECEIVED AS TO THE CONDUCT OF THE SERVICE IN BIRKDALE ON SUNDAYS.

BY ORDER.

HOW TO VOTE TO-DAY, SATURDAY.

FORM OF BALLOT PAPER.—SUNDAY TRAMS.

FOR In Favour of the Running of a Service of Trams in Southport on Sundays.	X
AGAINST Opposed to the Running of a Service of Trams in Southport on Sundays.	

the rainstorm the cars were largely patronised by churchgoers. The Company secretary, Mr H. Colebourne, said that Sunday was a record day for passengers.'

On reviewing the legal situation, the Town Council reversed its decision and instructed its Electrical Engineer to supply traction current to the Company 'for purposes other than plying carriages for hire upon their tramways in the township of Southport on Sundays'. This formalised the existing Company practice of operating free of charge in the borough without the need for a jumper cable at the boundary.

Reporting operations on 28 July the *Southport Visiter* (30 July) said:

'On Sunday the Southport Tramways Company had four cars running, which were well patronised. They travelled from St George's Square to the Crown Hotel and Birkdale Station, passengers riding between the square and the boundary being allowed to do so free. The cars, having to come from the depot at Churchtown in the morning and to return in the evening, persons wishing to use them as they were passing to and from the depot were allowed to do so free of charge as the Company are not allowed to ply for hire in Southport. It is said that a goodly number availed themselves of the free ride.'

These Sunday operations continued and the controversy subsided but was not forgotten. There were, in fact, two municipal polls and one door-to-door referendum about Sunday trams in Southport during the 16 years under review and they reflected a progressive change of mind. Following a report by the Corporation Tramways Manager showing Sunday operations on 26 other small town tramway systems to be much more profitable in terms of pence per mile than weekday operations, the Corporation organised a second poll on 13 February 1913. Now that Birkdale was in the

Left Advertisements displayed by the Sabbatarians and the Tramway Company in the *Southport Visiter* on 4 July 1903, the day of the first poll on Sunday trams. *By courtesy of British Library Newspapers*

borough and Birkdale ratepayers were included in the poll, 2,242 people voted for Sunday trams and 2,763 against them.

After the acquisition of the Southport Tramways Company on 1 March 1918 the existing Sunday operations continued and the Town Council had to resolve the issue one way or the other. At the Council meeting on 21 March members voted 28-22 in favour of Sunday trams, despite a letter from the Southport Council of Churches. Next Sunday, 24 March 1918, saw tramcars running on all lines in Southport except the under-used Blowick section and the Inner Circle. The operations used 10 cars and 26 staff.

The *Southport Visiter* reported:

'Some of the cars in the earlier portion of the day carried only two or three passengers but in the middle of the day and in the afternoon they were better patronised. In the evening the extent to which the public took advantage of them was greater still, especially about the time the picture shows opened. The last cars left London Square at 9.45pm and when the various picture theatres discharged their patrons there were big rushes for the cars.'

The Southport Council of Churches organised its own referendum the following day, 25 March, employing 300-400 voluntary workers door-stepping from house to house. This time Birkdale swung the vote marginally in favour of Sunday trams. On analysis Southport still voted against their Sunday trams – 4,146 for and 4,524 against – but Birkdale residents did not want to lose their Sunday trams, which had served them for 16 years, and carried the day with a decisive 1,852 for and 906 against, producing a total tally for the borough of 5,998 for and 5,430 against.

The Town Council said it had made up its mind regardless of the outcome of the referendum, which, in the event, vindicated its decision. Opponents fought a rearguard action at the Town Council meeting on 9 April. Their motion not to run trams in Southport on Sundays, except from London Square to Birkdale, was lost by 20 votes to 31 (including the Mayor). So the Sunday trams continued on their way and the issue was never raised again.

THE HEYDAY OF THE TRAMS

Southport Corporation Tramways
1918-1931

By the end of the war in 1918 the tramcars and infrastructure were in a run-down state of neglect. War not only deferred the development of the tramways by five years but set it back further by the time it took to recover from the ravages of neglect. The same period saw the development of the internal-combustion-engined road vehicle as a war machine. Were it not for the intervention of war the future of road passenger transport in Britain might have been different.

As the Great War still raged on the continent, the Government rationed coal supplies from April 1918, and coal had to be saved at the power stations. The newly won Sunday services, which had begun on 24 March, were deferred to start at 2pm, too late for matins. On weekdays the Smedley service did not start till 10am and Cambridge Road cars reversed on a crossover in St Cuthbert's Place during the winter to save mileage and current on the last few hundred yards to the Botanic Gardens. The Inner Circle was cut back to St Luke's station and worked by one car till the service was suspended from 31 October 1919.

The shortage of coal was worsened by two national miners' strikes, 23 October to 8 November 1920, and 31 March to 4 July 1921. There were times when all trams were brought to a standstill by a shut-down at the power station, notably on Whit Monday bank holiday in May 1921, when fully laden cars were stranded for an hour. Sunday services were then suspended for a few weeks to save power and keep the weekday services going. The Tramway Manager's report for the fiscal year 1921-22 – also a time of severe recession – showed that total car mileage at 812,420 was a reduction of 26,072 miles compared with 1920-21. Coal stocks and services did not return to normal till 1923.

Railwaymen came out in support of the miners in 1926 and prompted the eight-day General Strike from 4 to 11 May, causing further disruption of tram services. All the tramcar crews joined the strike and no trams operated in Southport except the pier tram, which continued throughout the strike. On 6 May the Tramways Committee chairman asked the strikers to hand in their uniforms but none responded. From 8 May excursion motor charabancs were deployed to operate stage services along the tramways from the Monument to Churchtown, High Park, Scarisbrick New Road and the Crown Hotel, the Ribble bus route to Crossens and the new Corporation bus route to Ainsdale for the last four days of the strike. At the end of the strike all the strikers were reinstated except for the last seven recruits.

Post-war inflation also made its mark as the Corporation raised the minimum fare from 1d to 1¼d on the first day of the amalgamated tram system, 1 March 1918, and issued its 49 conductors with a total of 9,408 farthings in 4-shilling packets to give in change. In September the same year the minimum fare was raised again to 1½d, the intermediate fare became 2d and the 2d fare all the way became 2½d. By the summer of 1919 the minimum fare was 2d. Revenues per car mile for August were: Grand Tour 53.18d, Cemetery 25.94d, Crown Hotel 21.37d, High Park 20.74d, Infirmary 19.49d, Roe Lane 16.92d, Cambridge Road 16.22d, Blowick 16.04d, Smedley 10d and Circle 9.09d. Higher fares marked 1921 as the year of the highest receipts on the Corporation trams: £80,999.

The Corporation needed the extra money to pay for the reconstruction of the cars and tracks but the post-war period saw an appreciable upsurge in patronage of the trams, which also boosted the revenue. In view of the improved financial situation, fares on the Grand Tour were restored to their 1914 level in 1921. Return fares were introduced in 1923 ranging from 2d single/3d return to 5d single/9d return, and pre-paid books of single tickets were sold at concession prices. In 1925 the 1d fare was restored.

The social structure of Southport was reflected in two letters received by the Tramways Committee. The Sunday tram service controversy had been laid to rest in 1918 but in February 1920 the Committee agreed to a request from the North Meols Rural Deanery for tramcars to slow down on passing churches during hours of divine worship, as Company cars had previously done in Birkdale. Twelve months later the Committee ignored a protest from the local branch of the Middle Classes Union against pay rises and bonuses for Corporation tramwaymen!

Reorganisation and reconstruction

The Corporation tramways office moved on 4 November 1918 from the Bank of Bolton Chambers, Parr's Buildings, 44 Chapel Street, to Bank House, 3 Eastbank Street, the back of the West Lancashire Bank. The inquiry office and staff room were opened at 1 Eastbank Street in 1924 and the local bus office is still there today.

Tram routes were reorganised in March 1919 and identified by numbers instead of letters and Maltese crosses. The two ex-Company tram routes became services 1 and 2.

1 Botanic Gardens-Manchester Road-Lord Street-Everton Road-Crown Hotel
2 Botanic Gardens-Hesketh Park-Lord Street-York Road-Smedley
3 High Park-Sussex Road-Eastbank Street Duke Street-Cemetery
4 London Square-Sussex Road-Blowick
5 London Square-Eastbank Street-Infirmary

As a result of the amalgamation, Roe Lane cars were diverted from Queen's Road and Leyland Road to run direct via Manchester Road and exchanged tracks with the Inner Circle, which re-started on 2 June 1919, and

was diverted from Manchester Road to Queen's Road and Leyland Road in both directions. The Inner Circle was also re-routed to run clockwise via Lord Street to Manchester Road and anti-clockwise via Hoghton Street and Chapel Street but, as we have already seen, the service was suspended again on 31 October 1919 for coal rationing. In Birkdale the short spur in Weld Road to the railway station was closed and all York Road cars proceeded to the Smedley.

A Sunday short-working of the Roe Lane route, turning back on the bridge, began early in 1920 as route 6, but was withdrawn after a trial period of one month as it lost more revenue than it saved. Route 5 was extended in March 1922 from the Infirmary to Haig Avenue along the existing track, and routes 4 and 5 were combined in 1923 as a through service, as they had been in the 1914-18 economies. Now only the Grand Tour still used the line from the Cemetery to Ash Street and beyond Haig Avenue to Kew Gardens.

The amalgamation of the tramways opened up the way for improvements and extensions to the infrastructure, cars, services and tours. The first job was to take stock of the mixed and ageing car fleet. Most of the Corporation and ex-Company cars, dating from 1900-02, were overdue for their mid-life overhaul and refit. Their run-down condition was worsened by lack of maintenance during the war owing to staff shortage.

When war ended in November 1918 the Corporation ordered 18 new 7-foot Brill 21E trucks at £180 each, 24 new 30hp motors at £165, and three more 'toastrack' bodies at £480 from the English Electric Company, which was the new name that year of the former Dick, Kerr and United Electric Car works at Preston. In February 1919 the Council appointed a depot superintendent, Ernest Sidgwick, ex-rolling stock superintendent of Rotherham, to supervise the reconstruction of the cars. Over the 10 years from 1919 to 1929 most of the cars were rebuilt and equipped with new or rehabilitated trucks and motors.

All the reconstruction and restoration work on trucks, motors and car bodies was carried out in the Corporation workshops at Crowlands depot, which was extended by 70 feet at the rear in 1919-20 at a cost of £7,000

A decorated private charter car, loaded to the gunwales with women in cloche hats and hangers-on, is ready to leave London Square. This amateur snapshot of one of the last Corporation open-top cars in the early 1920s gives traction buffs a good view of a Southport standard Brill 21E four-wheel truck. *Southport local history collection, Sefton Library Service*

to house the ex-Company cars and enlarge the workshops. The total capacity of the storage roads and workshops was increased from 40 to 50 cars although there were only ever 45 cars in the fleet. As English Electric was overwhelmed with orders for trucks after the war, Southport decided in May 1919 to switch its order for the Brill 21E design of trucks to the Brush Electrical Engineering Company at Loughborough. Some second-hand motors and controllers were bought from Bolton Corporation in 1924.

Now that the Corporation and ex-Company cars were working each other's routes, the Corporation's first eight top-covered cars, even numbers 20 to 34, were banned on route 2. They stood 16ft 4in tall to the roof; the trolley pole was additional and they were too high to pass under the 16ft 6in headroom of Churchtown railway bridge. They were fitted with notices above the motorman's windscreen in red letters on white: 'Caution: This car will not pass under bridges'. The signs were removed in 1931 when the Cambridge Road line closed.

When the next three cars, Nos 8, 12 and 18, went into the workshops in 1919, they were fitted with top covers low enough to pass under the bridge with safe clearance. They were also lightweight covers so as not to cause distortion to the original open-top car bodies. These type B top covers became the standard for future reconstruction from 1919 and these relatively low-bridge cars carried a sign in black letters on the wooden lintel of the windscreen: 'Car for any section'.

With the 'demi-car' gone, the remaining 20 ex-Company cars were all open-top double-deckers. During 1919-21 the first 18 of these cars went through the workshops to be rebuilt with the type B five-bay upper saloons (which were a perfect match to the Brush lower saloons) and canopied balconies. These were mounted on the 18 new trucks. The two remaining Brush cars were top-covered in 1924-25 and placed on reconditioned trucks from redundant California cars.

The last green car disappeared into the paintshops in 1921. These and the rebuilt Corporation cars were turned out in the bright

Above More top-covered tramcars appeared on the streets in the 1920s. Tramcars still dominated the street scene as there was little other vehicular traffic. This is Lord Street in 1921 with two ex-Company cars, viewed from London Square (right). Both cars are plying route 1 between the Botanic Gardens, Churchtown, and the Crown Hotel, Birkdale, via Roe Lane. Both have been rebuilt by the Corporation with Brill trucks and top covers with five-window upper saloons and balconies and are repainted in the Corporation livery of scarlet and cream. The Churchtown-bound car (centre) draws a crowd as it pauses at the stop outside Boots the chemists (left); it is advertising 'Bostock's better boots', of Wesley Street. The child's wooden, folding push-chair in the right foreground was called a 'baby car'. *Geoff Price collection*

Below This is one of the last six Southport tramcars that were still in open-top condition until 1925. It is taking the right-hand curve from Chapel Street (right) into Eastbank Street as it circumnavigates the town centre one-way circuit on route 4, London Square-Blowick, some time between 1921 and 1925. On the right we can see the side of the Congregational Chapel, fronting on to Chapel Street. The tramcar is obscuring the tramway office in the near corner of the three-storey stone building (centre). *James Dean collection*

new Corporation livery of scarlet and primrose. The ex-Company cars now took the odd numbers from 1 to 19 and in sequence from 35 to 44. The Corporation had previously reserved odd numbers for single-deckers but California cars 1 to 11, 15 and 17 were now redundant, the 'Committee Car' No 13 had been sold and the number 19 had never been used before.

The three new toastrack bodies were mounted on reconditioned Brush A trucks from ex-Company cars and numbered 29, 31 and 33, so there were now seven toastrack cars in the fleet with the odd numbers from 21 to 33. The original toastrack car, No 21, retained its ruddy-brown trolley mast and destination box (on the mast) but the rest, Nos 23 to 33, had them painted in dark green like the traction poles.

The 'Committee Car' had been sold in 1916, the 'demi-car' had been scrapped in 1918 and the bodies of the four redundant California cars that had surrendered their trucks to toastracks in 1914 were sold to Barrow in 1920 at £325 each and re-trucked for further service – still in Southport livery – on that 4-foot-gauge system. The remaining four California cars survived in service till 1922-23 and a new single-deck saloon car appeared in 1925. The Tramways Committee minutes record a new one-man single-decker under construction in the workshops in September 1924, and the last four redundant California bodies being sold locally for other uses at £1 each in September 1926. But I beg to differ from the written record here.

I was taken on a tour of the tramsheds and workshops in 1924, when I was only 4 years old, and I remember seeing a California car body on the tram jacks. I believe it was being rebuilt as the new saloon single-decker that appeared later and that only three California bodies remained to be sold in 1926. The new saloon car certainly looked like a converted California car because it retained the outdated clerestory roof with yellow glazing, the two long, segmental-arched windows and the stout bulkhead window pillars in the original positions each end of the original California saloon when the bulkheads were moved to extend the saloon. The extension incorporated matching segmental-arched windows to

enclose the smokers' seats on the former open sections at each end of the car and the driver's platforms were fitted with windscreens. In 1952-53 I found three – not four – California bodies on a farm at Marshside that had been converted to caravans, though that is not conclusive evidence there was not a fourth one somewhere else but it tends to support my theory.

The new saloon car took the number 45, the highest number in the fleet. It was built as a one-man car with four points of access for front-entrance, rear-exit passenger flow in both directions and 30 seats on longitudinal benches. Lattice folding gates protected the two unused offside access points when the car reversed direction. Passengers boarded on the front nearside and paid the driver, who had a cash bag, and alighted at the rear. It saw service on the extended Circle route (see below) but that was short-lived. It was chosen to be the illuminated car to advertise National Electric Week in December 1927, then, after a second spell on the Circle, it was converted to a two-man car and was only used on peak-hour journeys and football specials.

I remember the last six Corporation open-toppers still running in 1925 – cars 2, 4, 6, 10, 14 and 16 – but by 1926 all these had top covers with five-bay upper saloons, were mounted on new 7-foot Brill trucks and carried side rails on the lifeguards.

Then from 1926 to 1929 a total of 26 cars were fully enclosed. Their balconies were glazed-in and the windscreens were extended right around the platforms behind the stairs to the saloon bulkheads. These cars were thus totally enclosed except for the open side entrance on each platform. Ex-Company Brush car No 13 was the first tramcar to be totally enclosed in this way and was the only one with vestibule windows deeper than the saloon windows.

There were other non-standard features. Some Corporation cars retained the original three-bay lower saloons but many, including the last six open-toppers, were rebuilt with five windows each side to give better support to the top covers and match the fenestration of the Corporation's own new upper saloons. In this they were identical to the ex-Company Brush cars. All the upper saloons retained

Fresh out of the paintshop after its rebuilding as a totally enclosed car in 1926, ex-Company car No 13 reposes at Blowick terminus at the end of Norwood Road with the Blowick Hotel in the background. This former open-top car had been rebuilt twice since the take-over by the Corporation, first with a central, upper saloon and balconies. Then in the comprehensive rebuilding programme of 1926-29 it was the first of 26 cars to be totally enclosed with all-round glazing enclosing the balconies and the gap at the foot of the stairs between the windscreens and the saloon bulkheads and streamlined destination boxes built into the coachwork. It was the only one of the 26 with the vestibule windows deeper than the saloon windows, one of the many non-standard features of the four-year rebuilding programme. The summer's evening sunshine picks out the smart scarlet and cream paint scheme, lined out in gold and trimmed with black beading. The silver traction pole, in the middle of the junction with Hart Street, sports the embossed borough coat of arms, a timetable case and a 'Tram Station' flag. The wooden pole beyond the tram has a board warning road users of the unguarded coal tramway crossing. *The late R. Elliott, © A. D. Packer*

bulkheads with sliding doors after enclosure of the balconies. Most cars retained reversed stairs with the original transverse bulkheads and 36 seats upstairs, but seven cars – 24, 28, 30, 36, 37, 38 and 39 – were rebuilt with direct staircases with access through doors in right-angled bulkheads into the upper saloon and had 38 seats on the top deck. Car No 36 was the only car to be rebuilt with rain guttering along the eaves and downpipes inside the bulkhead pillars. There were still 11 cars with balconies in 1930, when the Town Council decided to replace the trams with buses.

The upgrading of the cars did not extend to passenger seating. The wooden seats, which were standard in upper saloons for smokers, were retained throughout. The seat cushions removed from the ex-Company cars in 1918 were never replaced with the leather or moquette upholstery that began to appear in the lower saloons on some of the larger tramway systems about this time – but they were systems with a future; Southport's was about to come to an end.

The changing tramway scene

Probably the biggest transformation of the Southport tramway scene was the construction of the Monument in London Square in 1923. Before that, the square was just a wide open space, paved with wood blocks, in the line of Lord Street gardens with a short range of buildings in the middle comprising a waiting shed for cab and tramcar passengers, a cab drivers' mess room and a public lavatory. The design of the Monument as a war memorial was put out to open competition and the winning design, by Grayson & Barnish of Liverpool, when further refined by modelling, produced a noble town centrepiece of an obelisk flanked by colonnades and water gardens in white Portland stone and this became the splendid setting for the hub of the tramway system.

Above There are six tramcars in this scene at the Monument in 1924 and only one motor car in sight! By this time most of the trams were top-covered cars with central, upper saloons and balconies. The Monument was built in London Square in 1923, and was the hub of the tramway system with trams leaving every few minutes to all parts of town. The nearest car, No 24, is circumnavigating the town centre circuit and is about to turn right into the square to load for route 4 to Blowick. The next two cars are passing each other on route 1 between the Botanic Gardens, Churchtown, and the Crown Hotel, Birkdale. The car on the far left on Lord Street is one of the six remaining open-toppers on the Inner Circle route 7 via Leyland Road, St Luke's station and Scarisbrick New Road. Next to it we can just see a toastrack car approaching the Monument at the end of its Circular Tour. The sixth car, on the north-east side of the square, is loading for High Park on the cross-town route 3 from the Cemetery. *Geoff Price collection*

Below Advertising 'Outram's best bread', ex-Company car No 9, rebuilt with upper saloon and canopied balconies, sails along Lord Street past Nevill Street and the Monument towards the stop outside Boots the chemist (left) on the Roe Lane route 1. In front is totally enclosed car No 36 on the Cambridge Road route 7. Their trolley poles swing wide to the offside because the overhead wires were offset to the bracket arms of the traction poles on the gardens side of the street. A third ex-company car with balconies can be seen approaching in the distance and a fourth car, a toastrack, is loading on the curve into London Square (right). The date is about 1927. © *A. D. Packer*

Halfway up the traction pole at the stop for Blowick, Wennington Road and High Park cars on the north-east side of the square was a notice in white letters on a black board: 'Trams leave the Monument every few minutes'. There was also a clock board showing the departure time of the next car on each route. Several of these small clock boards were fixed to the traction poles at stops around the system; the conductors of the departing cars reset the hands of the clocks to show the times of the next cars. In 1925 the Corporation bought six Bundy time-recording clocks, which were sited at strategic stops on the system for conductors to register the time their cars left the stops. This became common practice on municipal tram and bus systems in the mid-20th century and was designed to prevent services running before time.

From 1923 to 1930 the outdoor work gangs were busy renewing most of the trackwork on the system, with some additional passing loops or short sections of double track, starting in the town centre and working outward. There was some limited, perhaps experimental, thermit welding of rail joints but the effect was negligible as the rhythmic dum-dum sound remained a characteristic feature of tramcar travel in Southport to the end.

Among the improvements carried out in 1923, the track was relaid all the way from Hoghton Street to Sussex Road junction with Tithebarn Road. In the process the Hoghton Street track was doubled as far as the turn into Mornington Road, and the Derby Road track was doubled from the corner of Mornington Road to the corner of Sussex Road with visibility around both corners, so ending the practice of cars waiting at signals at either end of this former single-line section with two blind corners. The single track in Lord Street West was also doubled to link up the double tracks in Lord Street and Lulworth Road. And the single track on the town-side ramp of Eastbank Street bridge was relaid as interlaced double-track, as in Albert Road; this saved pointwork in the track and overhead but could still only be worked as a single line.

All this trackwork resulted in some temporary reorganisation and diversion of routes with cross-town cars terminating short on crossovers in the town centre. For a short time in the winter of 1924-25 Infirmary cars terminated in Eastbank Street Square, instead of looping around the town centre circuit. They reversed where the double track converged to single before the junction with Lord Street and returned along the little-used line from the Square past the tramways office to the trailing points at the junction with Chapel Street.

With the double-tracking of Lord Street West the overhead wires were re-hung from span wires instead of bracket arms. The supporting wires spanned the full width of the street between six or seven pairs of new traction poles planted opposite each other and the running wires were suspended directly above the new double tracks.

Tramway traction poles had multiple uses. Not only did they hold up the running wires but they also doubled as stop poles, lamp posts, mains pylons, sewer ventilators and signposts. As such they carried stop flags, clock boards, Bundy time machines, street lamps, road signs and, at approximately half-mile intervals, mains feeder cables to maintain the pressure of the electric current in the wires. In later years corroded poles and those carrying feeder cables were filled with concrete to fortify them but those that doubled as sewer ventilation shafts were, of course, left hollow. As more motor vehicles came on the road, direction signs were initially attached to tramway traction poles, the first, in 1923, being a sign in Cambridge Road pointing the way to Preston. At that time road signs were called, quaintly, 'destination indicators', which sound more like tramcar equipment.

Automatic trolley reversers, automatic points and automatic signals were also part of the infrastructure renewal programme. The simple but ingenious device of a triangular formation in the overhead wire at the terminus automatically turned the trolley through a Y as the car reversed. This saved the conductor having to walk the trolley pole around the car with a hook on the end of a bamboo pole in the middle of the road among the increasing number of passing motor vehicles. Trolley reversers were installed at Blowick, High Park and the Smedley and perhaps some other terminals in 1923.

Automatic points and signals were innovations towards the end of the tracklaying programme in 1928. Seven of the busiest junctions were so fitted, controlled by tram drivers approaching with the power on or off. Six automatic signals, triggered by approaching trams, were erected on traction poles in Liverpool Road to protect the single-line sections between the loops on the curves on the line to the Crown Hotel.

All these improvements to the cars and infrastructure, combined with revised schedules, helped to speed up Southport's sedate tramcars from an average speed (including stops) of 6½mph to 8½mph over the period from 1919 to 1928.

The extension of the borough into Birkdale meant that the Cemetery Road line could be extended along Eastbourne Road with a branch up Kew Road for Bedford Park. The Eastbourne Road extension, forming a triangular single-track junction with the line along Liverpool Road to the Crown Hotel, opened on 28 June 1924, when the Inner Circle was restored and redesignated as the Circle service No 7, worked by open-top double-deckers instead of Californias. They ran clockwise via Lord Street, Leyland Road, St Luke's Road, Eastbourne Road and Aughton Road. The Kew Road line opened one month later with a through service from High Park.

The new Circle service was a one-way, one-car service, running half-hourly, and was too circuitous to be of any use so it was no wonder

it was withdrawn on 31 March 1925, after being eclipsed earlier that month by a new service, No 10, to the Crown Hotel with cars running through town from 'Wennington Road', an intermediate terminus in Bispham Road on the High Park line. There were now two tram services to the Crown Hotel, the other being on route 2 from Cambridge Road. The Kew Road line extension to the Portland Hotel terminus opened on 17 December 1925. The Southport system was now at its maximum extent with a total of 17.4 miles of tram route, although 11 miles of it was still single track.

Heyday

The services were reorganised in March 1925 and renumbered with headcodes to show which direction the cars were going along each route as all the services were now cross-town. Each headcode corresponded to a specific destination. The single line beyond Haig Avenue terminus was now used only as a siding for parking special cars that carried the Haig Avenue football crowds. This was the final form of the Southport tramways in their heyday from 1925 until 1931 when the system began to disintegrate. The routes are listed in the table below with their headcode numbers coupled with their destination box displays in capitals and the number of cars on each service.

1, ROE LANE	from Crown Hotel via Everton Road and Manchester Road to Botanic Gardens	8 cars
2, CROWN HOTEL	from Botanic Gardens to Crown Hotel	
3, HIGH PARK	from Kew Road via Duke Street and Sussex Road to High Park Place	8 cars
4, BEDFORD PARK	High Park Place to Kew Road	
5, SCARISBRICK RD	from Norwood Road via Sussex Road and Eastbank Street to Haig Avenue	6 cars
6, BLOWICK	from Haig Avenue to Norwood Road	
7, CAMBRIDGE RD	from Smedley via York Road and Cambridge Road to Botanic Gardens	6 cars
8, SMEDLEY	from Botanic Gardens to Smedley	
9, WENNINGTON RD	from Crown Hotel via Duke Street and Sussex Road to Bispham Road	6 cars
10, CROWN HOTEL	Bispham Road to Crown Hotel	

The traffic and timetables for these services required a total of 34 out of a total fleet of 37 double-deckers, leaving three in the depot on stand-by or undergoing maintenance. The toastrack cars were used only on a new Circular Tour from Easter to September although some of these were laid up in the back of the depot after the closure of the Grand Tour in 1924.

The list above does not include the Circle service because it finished at the end of the month and was not re-numbered. The one-man Circle car, No 45, was stored in the depot and in 1927 was prepared as the illuminated car for National Electric Week, 5-10 December, when it was used as a mobile exhibition of electric appliances!

My mother and I visited the exhibition car, outlined in white light bulbs, on the remaining stretch of single track in Hoghton Street; this section was disused following the suspension of the Circle service. The *Southport Visiter*

reported that the car 'was stationed in different parts of the town during the week and visited by large numbers interested in electricity'. I don't know where else it parked but there were by this time quite a few other disused lengths of track where it would not obstruct regular service cars: Eastbank Street Square to Chapel Street junction, Queen's Road, Leyland Road, Park Road and the outer end of Scarisbrick New Road from Haig Avenue to Kew Gardens. As it was winter, the belt line used by the Circular Tour from the Cemetery to Hartwood Road was also seasonally disused.

After National Electric Week No 45 was put back on the Circle route, but this time it ran anti-clockwise, out via Aughton Road and back via Leyland Road. It was interesting to see trams running along St Luke's Road again. But still the service proved unfruitful and did not run for very long. I rode on it in 1928 and by 1929 it was withdrawn.

The sole saloon single-decker of the post-war years was No 45, rebuilt in 1924 from a semi-open California car of 1900 for one-man operation on a short-lived, extended Circle service. It was then converted to two-man operation for peak-time relief services and football specials. It is pictured showing route number 5 (Scarisbrick New Road) and the destination FOOTBALL GROUND and is standing at the end of a line-up of empty tramcars on Scarisbrick New Road outside King George V Grammar School, waiting to

take the crowds home from a match at Haig Avenue stadium. This car retained its four access points as rebuilt for one-man, front-entrance, rear-exit operation in both directions and the lettering PLEASE PAY EXACT FARE AS YOU ENTER on the rocker panel by the front step. The passenger flow was reversed when the car was converted to two-man operation and it now carried a FRONT EXIT CAR plate on the dash panel at each end. *E. N. Osborne, courtesy of Online Transport Archive*

Car No 45 was then converted to a two-man car and used only on relief duties: peak-hour short-workings and football specials to and from Haig Avenue. I saw it working on Saturday peak-hour journeys, usually on a short-working of service 4, Monument to Bedford Park.

I was born in 1920 and was old enough to witness the heyday of Southport tramways in the late 1920s. Then the top-covered trams, both balconied and totally enclosed, dominated the street with their presence. The tree-green traction poles and bracket arms were painted to match the trees from which they projected inconspicuously. The trees themselves, with their multi-coloured fairy light bulbs, represented Southport's brand of illuminations.

In my mind's eye I can see those trams now, rolling majestically along Lord Street, like the tall, stately, Atlantic liners of the day. At the Monument they diverged and proceeded towards their various destinations with a complete absence of obnoxious and acrid exhaust fumes permeating the atmosphere. Along came the Botanic Gardens car, its trolley wheel sliding under the solenoid-operated skate on the wire, a short distance ahead of the automatic road points. The driver shut the power off to go straight ahead and the tram coasted over the points, drumming the rhythm 'dum-di-dum-dum … dum-dum' and dipping gently fore and aft in the characteristic manner of a four-wheeler. It proceeded straight ahead to pick up its waiting passengers just north of the Monument, outside Boots, the 'cash chemists'.

Following behind was a tram to High Park, which had to turn right to reach the Monument loading point for Blowick, Wennington Road and High Park cars. The points were set for straight ahead so the driver had to keep his controller on the lowest series notch. There was a little flash from the overhead skate as the trolley pulled electricity through it and a 'clonk' ahead announced the fact that the points had switched over to the right-hand road. The No 3 for High Park gave a little rock as it swung to the right – 'di-dum-dum … di-dum-dum … dum-dum' – and, with a slight tail-wag, the car cleared the points, crossed over the opposite track and headed for the loading point on the north-east side of the square.

Its trolley pole had actuated the point frog in the overhead wire by means of a purely mechanical, ingeniously simple, gravity-drop lever, hanging down vertically on the right of the point frog so that, as the car commenced its right turn, the trolley pole swung enough to catch and actuate the drop lever. The trolley of the previous car, going straight ahead, had by-passed the lever. I can also recall the 'squis...sh … squis...sh … squis...sh' sound of the trolley wheel as it negotiated the pull-off hangers and ears on the overhead wire above the curve from Lord Street towards the tram stop at the Monument.

Travel by tram

The magic of a ride on the rear balcony of the upper deck is still with me, the trolley wheel above my head singing its little tune – 's...s...s...s...squiss … s...s...s...s...squiss' – as the car makes its way up London Street to the next junction, accompanied by the 'dum-dum … dum-dum … dum-dum' of the two axles on the rails, so different from the rhythm of Manchester's large bogie cars. Ah, happy days! However, we do have trams back in Manchester and very successful they are too.

I was living in Windsor Road at that time and we used to go into town on the tram almost every day. We could either go in on the Roe Lane car, the No 2 on Manchester Road, or we could go to Sussex Road and take a No 4, 5 or 10. All three services came down Sussex Road so that was the better route. I travelled both lines, Sussex Road and Roe Lane, quite regularly with father and mother to and from town.

When we boarded the car, it was two steps up to the platform, one more step up into the lower saloon or eight steps up the stairs, which were quite steep with high risers. I usually rode up top, on the balcony, if the weather was suitable. If we were schoolboys by ourselves the conductor used to come and rush us out and get us back into the saloon in case we caused any trouble; we might fiddle with the destination display or fall over the rail. Some of the conductors were a bit worried about us.

Off the car would go and you would hear

the regular 'dum-dum' beat of the four wheels on the rail joints. They were all four-wheelers in Southport – there were no bogie cars. Generally speaking the track in Southport was well maintained; I don't remember hearing much corrugation. The trams were much quicker in acceleration than the buses that replaced them but they cruised along at a fairly sedate speed in Southport compared with Liverpool. They used to travel no more than 20 miles an hour because the stops were so close together.

I nearly always travelled on the top deck, either on the balcony or sitting in the saloon with the sliding door closed. The front door of the saloon was always shut to keep the draught out and the rear door of the saloon was always open for passengers boarding or alighting at the back of the car. It was the same in the lower saloon, where the front door was always latched so that passengers could not distract the driver. The tramcars also carried bicycles and prams on the front platform with the driver.

There was seating for 22 passengers in the lower saloon, 11 each side on longitudinal seats, and 34, 36 or 38 upstairs, depending on the type of car. In the rush hour the centre aisle of the lower saloon was often so packed with standing passengers that the conductor could hardly get through for his fares. There was none of this 'eight standing' nonsense in those days. Southport had no standing limit painted inside the cars as Liverpool did. On the last car at night they used to pack as many passengers as could get on but they were not allowed to stand on the staircases or platform or on the top deck. Smoking was allowed upstairs only.

I well remember, as a small boy in the late 1920s, being taken by my mother for a ride on a tramcar as a pleasant way of spending part of a morning. We would board the car in Manchester Road and ride up to the Botanic Gardens via Roe Lane. The original ex-Company Brush cars still worked this route but they were now mounted on Brill trucks and had upper saloons with canopied balconies, built by the Corporation at Canning Road workshops and painted in the Corporation's bright new scarlet and cream livery.

As the car entered Roe Lane beyond

Leyland Road Church, the road became narrower and the double-track went into single for about 100 yards then out into a passing loop at the very wide, curving junction with Park Road on our left with its silver-painted traction pole planted in the middle of the junction in line with the rest of the poles along the footpath. In 1923 the Corporation started to repaint all the street furniture, including the lamp posts, seats and shelters, 'tree green', except for any traction poles or lamp posts in the middle of the road, which were painted silver. There were about ten of these at various points in the town.

On we went up Roe Lane bridge over the railway to Preston. There was a passing loop on the summit of the bridge. When sitting on the front balcony seat of a double-deck car as it swung out into the loop towards the side of the bridge, one was quite certain for a fleeting moment that we were all going to end up on the railway far below! As we dropped down the other side of the bridge we had a vista along Roe Lane, straight and wide between the trees, disappearing into the distance and the line regained double track.

We picked up speed again to the far end of Roe Lane, where we passed High Park Place on the right as we turned left into Mill Lane. High Park Place was where Old Park Lane opened out into a sort of square with late-Victorian shops on the far side. Our tram conductor used to call out 'Four Lane Ends' because Roe Lane turned left into Mill Lane, Moss Lane led straight ahead across the moss of Martin Mere and Old Park Lane came in from the right. In the middle of the square was a cabmen's shelter and public lavatories and alongside was the tram terminus of the No 3 High Park service.

The single-line track connection from Mill Lane into High Park Place was a depot working line only for last night cars running light from Botanic Gardens to Canning Road. The connection was not wired so the conductor had to 'jump' the trolley from the Roe Lane wire to the Old Park Lane wire, walking with his bamboo pole aloft. Also the driver had to set the facing points manually with his point iron, then reset them for Roe Lane.

The double track converged to single as we

turned into Mill Lane, which led on to Botanic Road, the narrow main street of Churchtown village. As we wound through the village street we saw a disconnected and dewired branch, a single line for about 100 yards along Manor Road, to the rear entrance and yard of the former Southport Tramways Company depot.

As we emerged from the village street, the line doubled for the trailing junction with the converging double track from Cambridge Road in St Cuthbert's Place and a silver traction pole – the only one in Southport with a bracket arm on each side – stood in the middle of the road just before the junction of the overhead wires.

At Botanic Gardens terminus I would save the conductor the job of reversing the seat backs on the upper deck. If it was a fine day we would sit on the open balcony and, without leaving the car, we would walk through the upper saloon to change ends as the car reversed and the conductor turned the trolley to the trailing end. We would then sample the route all the way to the Crown Hotel in Birkdale, followed by a return to town, probably to have lunch in a restaurant.

We came to recognise many of the drivers and conductors, who became fixed assets, so to speak, at that time in the late 1920s and early '30s when jobs were hard to find and any employment was prized with tenacity. In tramway parlance drivers were known as motormen, as on electric trains, and in south Lancashire conductors were called guards, at least by the older generations in the first half of the 20th century. My mother always called them guards. These appellations distinguished these rail-bound crews from the more mundane bus drivers and conductors – and

Southport tramways enhanced their affinity with railways by flagging stopping places as 'stations'. As I was brought up in the second quarter of the century, I tend to call the platform staff drivers and conductors but where the words motorman and guard creep into quoted texts you will know what they mean.

Many old Sandgrounders who may not have been interested in the trams certainly remembered the characters who worked them. Some of the older drivers pottered along very carefully but there were others who got every ounce out of the car and raced along from one loop to the next.

I remember a 6-foot-tall driver who always wore his hat cocked on one side and crouched over the controls, driving like a demon. I can see him now, flying along Sussex Road, just shutting off power to coast through the loops without applying the handbrake.

Then there was a conductor I used to call the 'Flying Dutchman' because he was tall and fair and he used to race up and down the stairs whistling between his teeth asking for fares and calling out the names of stops but you could never understand what he was saying.

If we were in luck and a rather well-known character, Harry Barlow, was the driver, we would be treated to his rather spectacular act. The passing loop on Liverpool Road at St John's Road was the last stop but one before the terminus at the Crown Hotel. Harry lived on the corner of Liverpool Road and Shaw's Road. Now the loop was a fairly long one and, on entering it and clearing the spring-loaded facing point, Harry would leave the controller on the lowest series notch and, with the motors pulling slowly in series, he would set the handbrake on the ratchet, leap off the front platform, race across the road to his front door and collect his billycan of tea from his wife. He would then leap back on to the front platform in time to pull the car to a standstill opposite the tram stop just before the end of the loop. I thought it was marvellous!

Immediately south of this loop was the junction with the tram siding along Shaftesbury Road to the power station and small depot on Birkdale Common. All the

Southport Corporation Tramways cap badge for drivers and conductors. *Geoff Price collection*

overhead wiring had been removed from the branch in 1919, the points had been taken out and the line had been cut back about 6 feet from its junction with the main line.

My mother used to take me to the Crown Hotel just for the ride; there was nothing to visit – it was just the end of the line on Liverpool Road. I remember that you could not book right through across town; you had to re-book at the Monument. If you were riding from Churchtown to Birkdale the adult fare would be 2½d from Botanic Gardens to town and 2½d from town to the Smedley or 3½d to the Crown Hotel. The conductor would come round again for the fares at the Monument.

The conductors carried a fairly short ticket rack, about 8 inches long with about six bunches of tickets back-to-back. From 1925 to 1931 the fares were 1d, 2½d and 3½d. I also remember the transfer ticket when I went to school. I usually went to school on my bike but when it was cold or drizzly I would go on the tram to town. My fare from Windsor Road to town was 1d and I used to ask for a penny transfer and get a striped ticket, half orange, half white. This was a transfer ticket, which took me to Chapel Street and on a bus to my school in Cambridge Road. I started at University School in September 1930, and I had to use the buses when they took over from the trams along Cambridge Road in March 1931.

Toastrack tours

As at Blackpool there was a post-war boom in riding toastrack tram tours. This peaked in 1920, when the Grand Tour was augmented by a new Circular Tour, hence the need for seven toastracks. In 1921 the fares for both tours were reduced from 9d to 6d for adults and from 6d to 3d for children, the same level as for the period 1914-18. As the toastrack cars were totally open to the weather they did not come out if it was a bad day – when you saw the toastracks out you knew that summer was here.

The Circular Tour ran anti-clockwise from London Square via Scarisbrick New Road, St Luke's Road, Roe Lane, Botanic Gardens, Cambridge Road, Hesketh Park and Lord Street back to London Square. This tour entailed two reversals. In the absence of a curve from Hartwood Road into Roe Lane, the car had to cross the junction into Leyland Road and reverse alongside the Methodist Church to take the curve from Leyland Road into Roe Lane. The second reversal was, of course, at Botanic Gardens terminus. It was obvious that the Circular Tour was the more attractive and interesting of the two and the Grand Tour ceased in 1924, so I could have been no more than 4 years old when I went on the Grand Tour with my mother.

We boarded the car at the Monument in London Square, and it then went up London Street, turned right into Chapel Street, left into Eastbank Street and turned right at the Tabernacle junction into St James Street and Shakespeare Street, where the aroma from White, Hudson's sweets and toffee factory filled the air. We then turned left into Duke Street and crossed the abandoned Sefton Street horse tramway, which had been cut back a few inches each side of the electric tracks, and there was a three-way, single-track junction at Duke Street/Cemetery Road, where we turned left and proceeded to Ash Street.

There was a single-line crossing at Ash Street/Scarisbrick New Road with two single-track curves towards town but no curves towards Kew Gardens. To reach Kew Gardens the tram driver had two options. He could drive straight over the crossing, reverse around the north curve and reverse again without changing ends or disturbing the passengers. Alternatively, he could drive forward around the west curve and reverse once but this would entail the passengers dismounting the car to reverse the seats and the driver, conductor and trolley changing ends. I was not old enough to remember which procedure was adopted at this junction on my trip in 1924, although I think that the double reversal was normal practice. From there we bowled along the single track to Kew Gardens on the rural outer reaches of Scarisbrick New Road and the car reversed again outside the Richmond Hotel.

A single reversal at a stub terminus such as Kew Gardens or the Botanic Gardens was quite a ritual. The driver took his controller handle and reversing key (effectively an ignition key) to the other end of the car and the

Above After the Grand Tour finished in 1924, the Circular Tour still ran till 1932. Here, about 1929-30, toastrack car No 23, one of three built in 1914-15, waits for passengers at the Monument on the single-line curve from Lord Street into London Square while a totally enclosed double-decker, car No 12, loads at the Monument stop on Lord Street, bound for Churchtown. *Cedric Greenwood collection*

Below Another nice picture of toastrack car 23 loading passengers at the Monument about 1929-30 with the Westminster Bank in the background. The slipboard on the fender reads: '45 Minutes Drive around the Town' in blue lettering on white. Below the Circular Tour sign hangs a board that reads: 'Fares: Adults 9d, Children 6d'. *E. N. Osborne, courtesy of Online Transport Archive*

conductor got out the bamboo pole from the hooks on the underside of the car to turn the trolley into the trailing position. Then all the passengers had to get off while the conductor turned over the seat backs; they were quite heavy wooden backs that had to be lifted, but some of the male passengers did their own. When we were all back on board facing the opposite direction, the conductor blew his whistle and we were off again. The passengers had to stay with the car during the ritual; we were not allowed to leave it to visit the gardens and catch the next tour car. It was not free and easy like Blackpool's toastrack tours.

The car reversed again at Ash Street junction – and again this could have been a single or double reversal – into the north-easterly continuation of Ash Street. We then mounted Rose Hill, actually a bridge over the railway, with St Luke's station booking office on our left astride the bridge on the lines to Manchester and Preston. Over the bridge we were in St Luke's Road and swung left into Hartwood Road.

The Grand Tour took the left-hand curve around the corner from Hartwood Road into Manchester Road to return to town. We went down the Manchester Road double track, left into Lord Street and back to London Square.

I think the Grand Tour was withdrawn in 1924 partly because the reversal manœuvres in the middle of Scarisbrick New Road were disrupting the increasing volume of motor traffic and partly because Kew Gardens were in decline following the zoo closure in 1916. The gardens closed about 1930.

I am more familiar with the Circular Tour because that carried on till 1932. I think mother took me on the Circular Tour two or three times. It was altogether a more pleasant afternoon's ride. On the bottom of the dash panel was a slip board in brackets on top of the fender that read: '45 minutes ride around the town'.

We started in London Square and went the same way as the Grand Tour to begin with: London Street, Chapel Street and Eastbank Street. From the Tabernacle junction we carried straight on along Scarisbrick New Road with the trees forming a pleasant canopy over the double-track. We turned left into Ash Street and over St Luke's station to Hartwood Road. At the next junction we headed out of town along Roe Lane to visit the Botanic Gardens.

We crossed the junction to reverse by the church in Leyland Road and take the curve into Roe Lane. We carried on to the top of Roe Lane and turned left into Mill Lane. There were still steam corn mills there then. We wound our way through Botanic Road, the narrow village street of Churchtown with its thatched cottages and small shops. There was also a blacksmith's forge on the corner of Manor Road on the left and at the far end of the street on the right was Madge Brewer's confectionery shop, which, besides its appetising display of cakes and pastries, sold Southport potted shrimps. We converged with the Cambridge Road line in St Cuthbert's Place and ended up at the terminus by the entrance to the Botanic Gardens.

Here, of course, was another reversal and now we followed the Cambridge Road line back to town, passing the old Company tram depot on the left. It was built in 1873 to house the horse trams, converted in 1901 for the electric cars and ceased to be a tramshed in 1920 when the extension to Canning Road depot was opened to accommodate the ex-Company cars. The tracks and overhead wires had since been removed.

At Churchtown station the tram passed under the only railway bridge on the system, which carried the Southport-Preston line. The station was on the embankment on the Preston side of Cambridge Road and you went up steps to the platforms. The bridge had a maximum headroom of 16ft 6in, which effectively barred the use of eight of the Corporation's Dick, Kerr double-deckers on the Cambridge Road route as they were 16ft 4in to the trolley base.

The route was double track under a continuous canopy of trees all the way along Cambridge Road and around Hesketh Park with a very sharp right hairpin bend into Park Crescent. The tramway was laid right against the kerb at the side of the road alongside Hesketh Park as far as the park lodge in Albert Road. The double tracks swung back into the middle of the road as we entered Albert Road, which was not very wide, so after about 25-30 yards the two tracks were interlaced, which took just a few inches more space than a single track but eliminated the need for points at each end and on the two passing loops on that stretch.

The interlaced tracks diverged to double at the town end of Albert Road to make a double-track junction at the corner of Manchester Road and we carried on along double track on Lord Street. The tour terminated on the single-line curve into London Square, where it disgorged its passengers and loaded for the next trip.

In 1925 the owners of the Botanic Gardens asked the Corporation to allow passengers to break their journey there. The Tramways Committee refused but responded by adding slip boards with the name 'Botanic Gardens' on all cars on routes 1 and 7, which only carried the destination 'Churchtown' on their blinds. It may be recalled that the Botanic Gardens, which opened in 1876, were privately owned by a company allied to the Southport Tramways Company. The enterprise foundered financially and the gardens closed in 1932. The Corporation bought the gardens and re-opened them in 1937.

Patronage of the Circular Tour declined in the late 1920s as holidaymakers found other diversions. Two of the seven toastracks considered surplus to requirements were disposed of in 1930.

Hail and farewell

The heyday of the Southport trams reached its zenith in the years 1927 to 1931. Corporation statistics showed the trams clocking up some all-time records in this period. The fiscal year 1927-28 was the year of the heaviest loadings, with 13,489,878 passenger journeys, and 1928-29 was the year of the most car mileage, with 1,297,326 miles in service. Now, when the renewed system was giving its best returns, the Town Council made the momentous decision in 1930 to abandon electric tramways in favour of motor buses. In the last fiscal year of the complete system, 1930-31, the tramways produced a record profit of £10,424. The line-by-line table of revenue per car mile at 31 March 1931 was:

Bedford Park	17.32d
Scarisbrick New Road	15.35d
Roe Lane	13.77d
Crown Hotel (route 2)	13.60d
High Park	13.58d
Blowick	13.16d
Crown Hotel (route 10)	12.45d
Smedley	11.00d
Cambridge Road	10.35d

These figures have to be set against working costs of 10.6d per car mile at that time.

As Southport tramways reached their moment of glory, the tracks were pulled from under them and the bus came marching in.

SOUTHPORT TRAMS IN COLOUR

Including maps and drawings by James Dean

Right Edwardian postcard photo-graphers liked to feature the 'electric cars' prominently in their pictures: they showed that the town was up-to-date and were often the only focal point of interest in the street scene. This well-laden Company car, No 17, is leaving the Botanic Gardens and passing through sunlit St Cuthbert's Place into the shade of tree-lined Cambridge Road on its way to Lord Street and Birkdale. *Picture postcard, Geoff Price collection*

Below Green and white Company cars pass on Lord Street at London Square en route between Churchtown and Birkdale. The lettering on the outside of the upper deck panels reads: 'All the green cars run to Botanic Gardens'. The coloured Maltese crosses for easy route recognition were fitted into slots on the fore and aft upper end panels under the destination boxes. This picture postcard, captioned 'London Square, Southport', also bears the legend: 'Southport, noted for Health and the Springfield Potted Meats'. *Cedric Greenwood collection*

Left This early Edwardian poster published by the Southport Tramways Company was displayed on poster boards at local railway stations. The open-top cars passed the front of Lord Street station and took passengers by two sylvan routes to the Botanic Gardens at Churchtown. The poster is now in the Botanic Gardens Museum. *Courtesy of Sefton Borough Leisure Services*

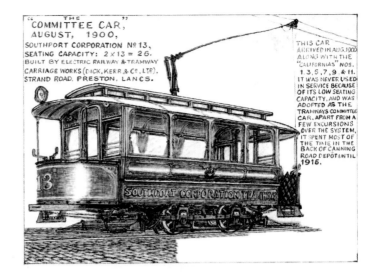

Right No 13, the 'Committee Car' of 1900. *James Dean*

Right A special ticket issued for the opening day of Southport Corporation Tramways, 18 July 1900. *Geoff Price collection*

Below left A ticket of the Birkdale & Southport Tramways Company, found on the surviving car No 7 during restoration. *Geoff Price*

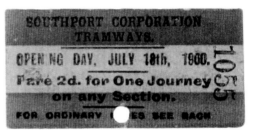

Below right Eight of Southport Corporation's open-top cars were fitted with top covers fabricated by the United Electric Car Company's coachbuilding works at Preston from 1908 to 1910. A full-length roof rested on the bulkheads enclosing the short, central upper saloon and extending over the residual balconies. Car No 24, pictured here, was one of the two prototypes of this design in 1908. The upper saloon was shorter than the lower saloon with three segmental-arched, sash windows on each side. The five windows on each side of the upper deck give the illusion of a longer saloon but the plain end windows on each side were windbreaks on the balconies. Windscreens were added to the platforms in 1910. Some of these cars were distorted by the weight of the top cover resting on unaligned bulkheads and were rebuilt at Canning Road workshops in 1910-13 with extended upper saloons incorporating the outer windows and vertically aligning the bulkheads for better structural support (see the photograph of car No 30 on page 117). *James Dean*

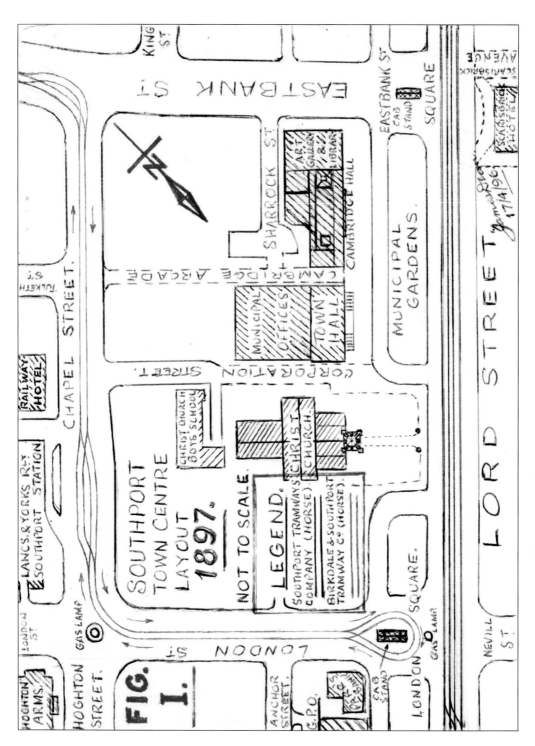

A map of the town centre showing the track layout that existed from 1883 to 1899. *James Dean*

This was the track layout on 18 July 1900, the opening day of Southport Corporation Tramways. The first electric trams in Southport terminated at the town end of Hoghton Street, by the Hoghton Arms public house. The map also shows the traction poles, bracket arms and overhead wires and the anchor poles and pull-off spans on the street corners. *James Dean*

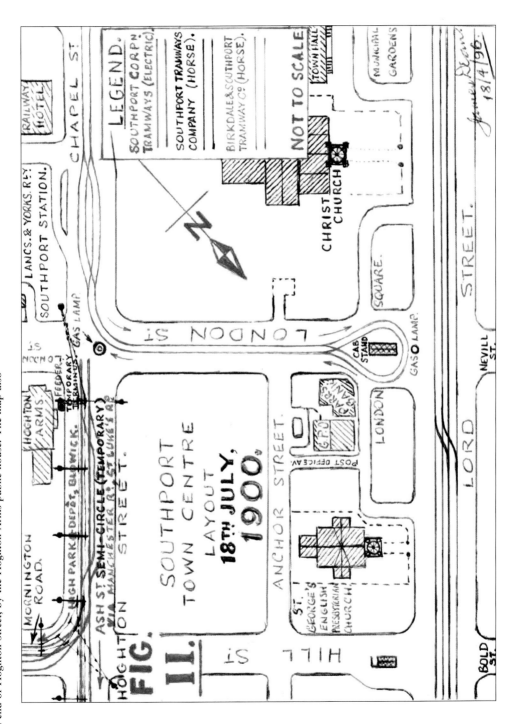

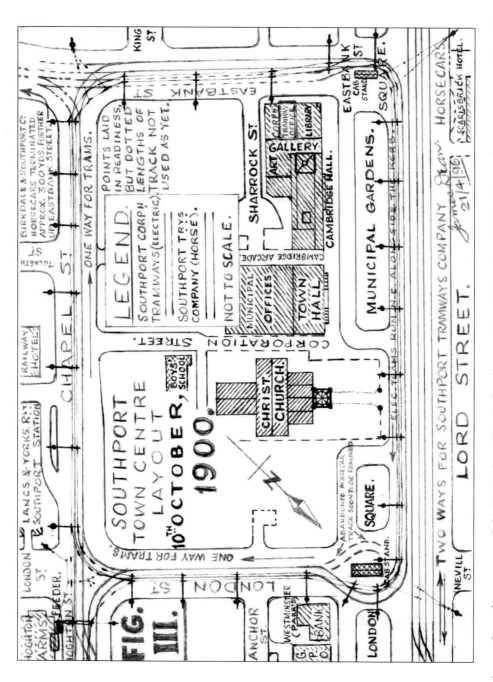

Above This map shows the progress made by 10 October 1900, the day when Corporation trams first used the newly completed, one-way clockwise circuit of the town centre. Again, the map shows both the tracks and overhead wires with their supporting poles and brackets. *James Dean*

Below This track and wiring plan sets the town centre scene from 1 August 1901, when the Southport Tramways Company began electric operation. The footpath on the gardens side of Lord Street was moved back 7 feet to give a margin for other vehicles to pass outside the realigned double tramway offset on that side of the street. Birkdale & Southport horse trams still shared tracks with Corporation electric cars right around the town centre circuit and up Eastbank Street. The south curve from Eastbank Street into Lord Street was used only by the short-lived Opera House service in 1901-02. The broken double lines from Eastbank Street Square to Chapel Street junction mark the track that was laid some time between 1901 and 1909 but was seldom used and only carried a regular service during emergency diversions. The situation shown on this map remained more or less static until about 1913, when Christ Church graveyard was cut back to conform the width of the footpath; the graves were excavated and the coffins re-interred in Southport Cemetery. The building of the Monument in London Square in 1923 altered the townscape but the trackwork remained unaltered. *James Dean*

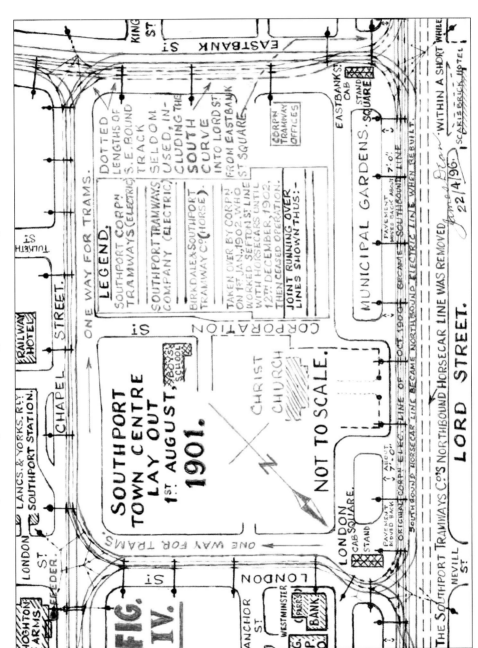

LORD STREET,
SOUTHPORT
© 1924/25.

James Dean
JULY, 1987.

Above There are five tramcars in this view of Lord Street in about 1924-25. On the left-hand track are two Dick, Kerr cars, No 24 on route 3 to High Park and No 6 on the Inner Circle route 7. No 24 was top-covered in 1908 and the upper saloon was lengthened in later years when the bulkheads were moved out above those of the lower saloon. Car No 6 was a three-bay saloon car and one of the last six open-toppers, which mainly worked the Inner Circle. When that route closed in 1925 the six were rebuilt with five-bay saloons on both decks. On the right-hand track is an ex-Company Brush car, top-covered by the Corporation in 1920, on route 2 to the Smedley. This was still the era of enamelled steel advertisements screwed on to the upper deck panels although some of the side advertisements were now painted straight on to the panels by the tramway paintshop staff. In the distance we can see a car turning right into London Square and an oncoming car to the Crown Hotel. *James Dean*

Dn 3035	Wa 2490	Fa 2302	Lb 3264
INNER CIRCLE.			

Above This picture shows the full-length roof and short, upper saloon with which the Corporation first covered its open-top double-deckers in 1908-09. The three centre windows with ruby ventilators mark the short extent of the upper saloon, while the slightly narrower end windows on the top deck partly screened the long balconies. Car No 20 was the only one to retain its 1908 short, upper saloon to the end and the first Southport tram to be scrapped in 1930. The car is advertising Fennell's fish and poultry shop in Eastbank Street; later a Mr Raynor married Miss Fennell and the shop was renamed Raynor's. Posters in the saloon windows advertise shows at the Opera House, the Palladium and the Picture Palace.

Left A selection of tickets from this period, for the Inner Circle, Blowick-Infirmary and High Park-Cemetery routes, with the fare stages named. The reverse side of the tickets carried advertisements for A. Ramsbottom, the draper, of Chapel Street and Eastbank Street, and H. Swarbrick, the pork butcher, of Eastbank Street. The tickets at this period were printed by Williamson, of Ashton-under-Lyne. *Cedric Greenwood collection*

Above This totally enclosed car has advertisement panels sign-written by the paintshop staff at the depot in the Corporation's coordinated paint scheme with red lettering on cream side and end panels and cream lettering on red quarter panels. Advertisements disappeared from the trams after 1930, when contracts were allowed to lapse. *James Dean*

THE OLD CORN MILL
IN MILL LANE, CHURCHTOWN,
FROM HIGH PARK TRAM TERMINUS.
CIRCA 1930.

James Dean
APRIL, 1996

Above Rebuilt ex-Company car No 5 is taking the curve from Mill Lane into Roe Lane on route 2 to the Crown Hotel in Birkdale, closely followed by the corn merchant D. Rimmer's Sentinel steam lorry. The steam corn mills in the background replaced a former windmill, from which the lane originally took its name. The tramcar is negotiating two sets of points in succession, from the single track in Mill Lane to the double track in Roe Lane followed by the junction with the single-line turnout into High Park Place, terminus of the High Park tram route No 3, which came along Old Park Lane. Moss Lane runs off (upper right) across the mossland of Martin Mere, with the result that this crossroads was known as Four Lane Ends. In Company days there was no track connection between the Company tramway in Mill Lane and the Corporation terminus in High Park Place. *James Dean*

Above right The Corporation ceased to use its trams as mobile billboards from 1930 but retained the theatre and cinema posters in the lower saloon windows. The totally enclosed Dick, Kerr car in the foreground is about to swing right from Lord Street into London Square to load for route 6 to Blowick. Acquiring its original top cover in 1908-10, it is too high to pass under Churchtown railway bridge and is confined to the original Corporation routes. An ex-Company Brush car is loading at the Monument on route 3 to High Park. Having acquired its top cover in the post-1918 reconstruction programme, this is a low-bridge car but it still stands taller than the motor buses. A Vulcan Emperor bus circles the Monument to load on the south-west side of the square on the Crossens-Ainsdale route via the Promenade and Nevill Street. *James Dean*

Right The twin towers of Broadbent's department store dominate Chapel Street as one of the last balconied cars passes by on route 8 to Crescent Road (actually Eastbourne Road), a curtailed working of the former route 10 to the Crown Hotel. Motor traffic still used Chapel Street as a two-way street although the tramcars only ever operated one-way around the town centre circuit. A totally enclosed car passes along Eastbank Street in the background. The traction pole on the left also serves as a lamp post and a stop pole. The stop flag bears the words 'Tram Station' and below it is a clock board, on which the hands of the dummy clock were reset by conductors to show the time of the next tram. *James Dean*

THE MONUMENT, SOUTHPORT.
DECEMBER, 1931.

CHAPEL STREET, SOUTHPORT IN 1932.
JAN., 1990.

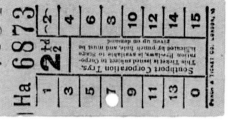

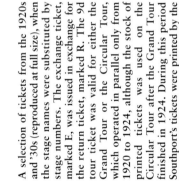

A selection of tickets from the 1920s and '30s (reproduced at full size), when the stage names were substituted by stage numbers. The exchange ticket, marked E, was issued in exchange for the return ticket, marked R. The 9d tour ticket was valid for either the Grand Tour or the Circular Tour, which operated in parallel only from 1920 to 1924, although the stock of printed tickets was used on the Circular Tour after the Grand Tour finished in 1924. During this period Southport's tickets were printed by the Punch & Ticket Company of London. *Online Transport Archive and Geoff Price collection*

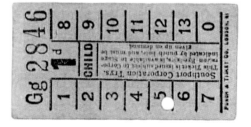

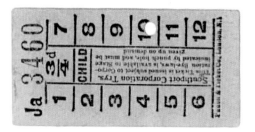

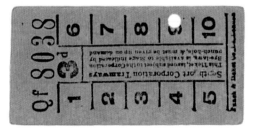

BUSES TAKE OVER

Southport Corporation Tramways
Southport Corporation Transport
1924-1934

Southport began to make legal provision to run motor buses in 1920 when the Corporation amended its 1899 Tramways Order with reference 'to the use of omnibuses' and renewed its 1913 Parliamentary powers to run trolleybuses. The Tramways Committee set up an Omnibus Sub-Committee on 22 December 1921 to investigate the use of motor buses 'as an adjunct to or in whole or part substitution for the existing tramway system'. The Sub-Committee's report to the Tramways Committee on 23 March 1922 concluded:

'Owing to the present high cost of running buses, there are no districts in the borough where it would pay to run buses as an adjunct to the tramways system, taking into account the extra capital and maintenance costs on the roads as compared with the present maintenance of tramway track and the loss to the Electricity Department in revenue for traction current.'

The first Southport Corporation bus was a 26-seat, open-sided, cross-bench Vulcan single-decker on solid rubber tyres, hired from the Vulcan Motor & Engineering Company (1906) Ltd of Bankfield Lane, Crossens. The 'runabout' bus, as it was called, made its debut on 7 February 1924, on a tramway feeder service from Churchtown to Marshside and Crossens with through tickets by tram to and from town. The bus terminated at Kirkham Road, Marshside, and the Plough Inn, Crossens, and ran via Marshside Road, Churchtown station, the Botanic Gardens and the Vulcan works.

This service was withdrawn on 19 March because of low revenue but the bus was deployed to run a seafront summer service from 8 April between Chapel Street station and Pleasureland fairground via the Sea Bathing Lake. This service was more successful and continued to run each year at Easter and from Whit weekend to September. In 1926 it was extended to run from Hesketh Park to Weld Road via the Promenade and Rotten Row. The Vulcan runabout, No 1 in the bus fleet, was suitable for seafront summer service but the Corporation paid Vulcan £452 9s 6d to rebuild it in the autumn of 1926 with a conventional 26-seat saloon and 'balloon' (pneumatic) tyres for general use on a growing suburban bus system. The Corporation returned the bus to Vulcan in 1931 and it was converted to a lorry.

Throughout the 1920s, when Southport was busy rebuilding its tramcars and relaying its tracks, Leyland Motors kept pestering the Tramways Committee with promotional literature to buy Leyland buses, but Southport's second bus was a Willowbrook-bodied AEC Renown in 1925 and the Corporation was more inclined to support the local Vulcan Motor Company, which built the chassis and bodies of the next seven single-deckers between 1925 and 1928. Some of them were hired and some were bought but all Southport's buses were outshopped in the scarlet and cream livery adopted for the tramcars in 1919.

Buses 2 to 9 had two recessed doorways with folding doors on the nearside for rear entrance and front exit passenger flow. The early buses were mounted on a high-clearance chassis but Nos 6 to 9 were on a lower chassis, giving a lower floor height that became standard. All Southport's buses had petrol engines from 1924 till 1932. The electrical engineers at Crowlands depot were not familiar with internal combustion engines and early motor buses were prone to breaking down, so from 1928 Vulcan provided one of its mechanics to repair and maintain them free of charge!

The former Churchtown tram depot, sold to BEV in 1918, came up for sale in 1926 but the

Town Council turned down the idea of using it as a bus garage. It decided instead to stable surplus buses that could not be housed in Crowlands tramshed in an ex-First World War aircraft hangar at the end of Hesketh Road pending an extension of the depot for the buses. This decision was taken with some foresight as the Corporation had only five buses at the time, but it proved to be a useful contingency because, by the time the bus garage opened in Cobden Road in 1932, the bus fleet numbered 23 double-deckers and four single-deckers (the first five single-deckers having been disposed of by then). The hangar was shared with the Corporation Parks, Foreshore & Cemeteries Department, which used it to store equipment. There were two hangars on this old airstrip; the other one housed three biplanes of the Giro Aviation Company used on pleasure flights from Birkdale Sands Aerodrome. Surplus buses were out-stationed on the hangar site again from 1947 to 1963, when the bus garage was extended.

Up to 1930 the buses were not conceived as a replacement for the trams but as feeders and complementary services to outlying suburbs not served by the trams. The tramways, which originally served the whole built-up area in 1900-03, were not extended to the suburbanised villages of Marshside, Crossens or Ainsdale and low-density ribbons of housing of the 1920s.

The first regular, year-round Corporation bus service began in May 1925, from the Monument to Ainsdale village green (or Ainsdale Common as it was then known) via Lord Street, Westcliffe Road, Westbourne Road, Grosvenor Road, Waterloo Road and Liverpool Road, terminating in Station Road by the green. The buses ran Sunday services, like the trams, only from 2pm, which stemmed from post-war coal rationing, and I don't remember the buses running before 2pm on Sundays until the 1950s. The Ainsdale service was extended to Ainsdale station from November 1925, and to Ainsdale beach in the summer from 1926, but every third bus on this service was diverted from Station Road at the green and continued along Liverpool Road to a terminus at Woodvale station, reversing in Dunlop Avenue on the borough boundary.

Here the Corporation buses connected with the Waterloo & Crosby Motor Services running single-deckers between Waterloo station and Woodvale and made a joint arrangement for through tickets between Southport and Waterloo (1s 7d single, 2s 6d return) but the Waterloo service lasted only from April to October 1926.

The service of portable postboxes on evening trams for a later collection of mails and next-morning delivery, begun in 1916, was extended to the buses in November 1926 when the Post Office transferred the little-used postbox on the Bedford Park tram to the 7pm bus from Ainsdale.

The Ainsdale service was coupled with a new bus route to Crossens from 16 July 1927, giving a through run across town from Ainsdale to Crossens. The extension ran from the Monument via Nevill Street, the Promenade, Argyle Road, Hesketh Road, Cambridge Road, Preston New Road, the Plough Inn and Rufford Road to North Road. The Highways Department had to repave Marshside Road and Lytham Road for the buses to serve Marshside on the way and this diversion was incorporated at the end of December 1927.

Next the bus system was extended inland along streets paralleling Scarisbrick New Road. From 16 April 1928 there was a Higher Blowick circular route with buses running both ways from Eastbank Street Square via Virginia Street, Forest Road, Haig Avenue, Everard Road, Cedar Street and Portland Street. Alternate buses ran from Haig Avenue tram terminus outward along Scarisbrick New Road to serve new housing at Kew and turned round at Kew Mill by Kew Gardens station.

Southport saw its first double-deck buses in 1929 – two Leyland Titan TD1s, Nos 10 and 11, with open staircases – and bus conductors were paid an extra 1½d an hour for working them. The TD1s were double-deckers in what was then a field of mainly single-deck buses outside the big cities and in deference to customary low headroom limitations on most country routes in those days, with low trees and low railway bridges, Leyland's first production double-deckers were all of a low-bridge design with a sunken, offside gangway and four-in-a-row seating upstairs. They

The unknown photographer was lucky to catch Southport Corporation's first two double-deck buses, Nos 10 and 11, passing each other in Lord Street in the 1930s. These are Leyland-bodied, Leyland Titan TD1s, built in 1929, with 'piano' fronts and open staircases at the back. Bus No 10 (right) is pulling away from a stop on the corner of Portland Street on route 15, an extension of the Smedley tram route to Burlington Road, Dunkirk Road, Sandon Road and Liverpool Road to Waterloo Road junction. Bus No 11 (left) is stopping at the corner of Coronation Walk on route 9 to Marshside and Crossens. The tramlines and traction poles with their bracket arms are still in place but the electric wires and the tramcars have gone. In the parlance of the former tramways department, the stop flag now reads 'Bus Station'.
Cedric Greenwood collection

worked on the Crossens-Woodvale route and were ideal for the low railway bridge at Woodvale station just 50 yards before the bus terminus. They had upholstered seats and I noticed that they always had a lot of women travelling on them but I stuck by the trams; I was not going to be diverted by these new-fangled machines. I thought they were no use at all. I remember my mother and I had a jolting ride in a Corporation single-decker to Ainsdale in 1927 or '28. And I didn't like the way the double-deckers heeled over on the corners.

The trams were still the mainstay of the town's internal transport system and were heavily used, as we saw from the record figures for the years 1927 to 1931 in the previous chapter. In September 1928 the Tramways Department received an official warning from the Borough Police about overcrowding of tramcars. The system was groaning under the volume of traffic and a month later the Tramways Committee had a letter from the secretary of Southport General Infirmary complaining about the noise of tramcars passing the hospital.

Country bus services

Motor charabancs were the first internal-combustion-engined public transport in Southport, in 1912, plying excursions to

'Lathom and Parbold, Crossens and Banks, Freshfield and Formby, Sefton, Lydiate Abbey, Rufford etc', according to an advertisement in the *Southport Visiter*. They were cross-bench vehicles with open sides, later with individual side doors to the bench seats.

Then the needs of the 1914-18 war honed the development of the motor vehicle and in 1919 Ribble Motor Services, of Preston, was one of the many bus companies spawned in its aftermath, reaping the experience and expertise of the skilled soldiers returning to 'Civvy Street'. This company eventually spread its network of services over the whole of Lancashire, Westmorland and Cumberland from the Mersey to the Solway, becoming one of the largest bus systems in Britain. Ribble operated the first motor buses on scheduled stage services in Southport in 1921, three years before the Corporation's first cautious venture into the mode. This was the year when Ribble buses changed colour from grey to the dark red livery they retained till after nationalisation in 1969.

On 1 August they raised the dust along the country road into town on an 18-mile, summer-only service from Preston via Mere Brow. The Leyland SG7 petrol-engined single-deckers on solid rubber tyres ran five round trips a day, entering and leaving town along Bankfield Lane and the Cambridge Road tramline between the Botanic Gardens and Hesketh Park gates, thence via Park Road West and the Promenade to a terminus on the Esplanade. They were not allowed to pick up and set down passengers within the borough. This condition, set by Southport Watch Committee to protect the Corporation's own services, became standard Ministry of Transport policy for country buses in boroughs with municipal transport systems from 1930 until the deregulation of bus services in 1986.

The Preston service ran again in the summer of 1922 via Hesketh Bank but with only three round trips a day. It was then withdrawn, unable to compete with excursion fares on the parallel railway between the two towns.

The second country bus service to Southport was operated by D. Rimmer from Ormskirk to Blowick tram terminus, where passengers changed to the tramcars to complete the journey into town. The service opened towards the end of 1921 with one solid-tyred single-decker but the bus was often off the road with ignition failures and twice when a locking nut sheared and the body fell on to its rear axle! Mr Rimmer later bought a second bus to augment the service on Ormskirk market days and to operate a second route, from Ormskirk to Aintree tram terminus for passengers to Liverpool. However, he could not afford to buy any more buses and early in 1924 his services succumbed to competition from Ribble.

On 16 May 1923 Ribble began a regular, year-round bus service from Wigan to Southport via Ormskirk. The initial 2-hourly service was augmented to an hourly service in 1925 and half-hourly in 1926. Ribble wanted to run buses into Southport direct along Scarisbrick New Road to the town centre but, while the Corporation had been prepared to offer that facility to the Ormskirk & Southport Light Railway in 1900, it insisted on side-tracking the buses via Meols Cop Road, Sussex Road, Cypress Road, Hawkshead Street, Manchester Road, Leicester Street and the Promenade with the standing ban on picking up and setting down passengers within the borough. This route not only protected the Corporation trams but also provided a better spread of public service. This, too, remained a Ribble route into town from Ormskirk until deregulation.

I remember having to ride with my mother to Ormskirk market in a 1924 Ribble Leyland SG9 on the Wigan service in 1925. It was a single-decker with two arched, recessed doorways on the nearside: rear entrance and front exit. As the chassis and floor were high off the ground, each doorway was reached by three wooden steps. I only went once because it made me feel sick, bumping over the granite setts on hard tyres, rocking from side to side and smelling of petrol. The bus still rocked as the engine ticked over at each stop then off we went again with great roars and shaking windows. It was very slow.

In the mid-to-late-1920s Southport became a honeypot for several country bus operators. Ribble Motor Services came from Liverpool via Halsall from 1 July 1926, with a 2-hourly, summer-only operation serving mainly Walton, Aintree and Maghull. This service did not run the following summer as it was eclipsed by the more profitable service from Liverpool via Crosby and Formby.

Ribble didn't have the road to themselves. Norwest Bus Services, of Liverpool, pioneered the Crosby route in April 1927, Ribble competed from 1 June 1927, and Rymer's Ideal Service, of Liverpool, muscled in on 23 July 1928. Rivalry was so intensive on the Liverpool-Southport services that the fares were reduced to 1s 8d single and 1s 9d return in 1928 and remained so – because of a national fares freeze – until 1950. Rymer's became Ideal Omnibus Services under new management but sold out to Ribble on 5 December 1929. On 19 December Norwest sold out to the Merseyside Touring Company, which, in turn, was sold to Ribble on 1 February 1930. Ribble then had the monopoly of the Crosby route and restored the Halsall route to Liverpool in May as a year-round service. The Crosby route entered town via Liverpool Road, Bedford Road, Kew Road, Eastbourne Road and Duke Street with occasional buses running direct via Waterloo Road.

Ribble re-opened the route from Preston from 1 July 1927 as a year-round service running alternately via Mere Brow and Hesketh Bank, and started new regular services from Chorley via Rufford and Mere Brow on 23 May 1928, and from Warrington via St Helens on 29 June the same year. The Warrington service was a joint operation with

Warrington and St Helens Corporation buses also running into Southport via Hawkshead Street. In the same year Ribble started a twice-daily express coach service between Southport and Blackpool.

Three independents entered the fray to compete in part with Ribble on routes east of Southport. Oliver Hart, of Coppull, started a service from Standish to Southport via Croston, Rufford and Hesketh Bank on 8 July 1929. Rivals on the Wigan run were Webster Brothers, of Wigan, and Cadman's Services, of Orrell. Webster's ran into town along the Ribble route via Hawkshead Street, while Cadman started running between Wigan, Ormskirk, Bescar and Southport in 1930. Refused a licence by Southport Watch Committee, Cadman forced the issue by boldly running into Southport straight along Scarisbrick New Road and getting his licence retrospectively from the Traffic Commissioners in July 1932, albeit with timing conditions.

Hart's buses were mid-green and off-white, lined out in gold, with the initials OHMS on the side: Oliver Hart's Motor Services. Webster's buses were navy blue and white and Cadman's were dark green and yellow with a maroon band under the windows. These were all single-deck buses with the lighter colours on the roof and windows and the darker colours on the panels.

Ribble bought out its rivals on the Wigan service, Webster Brothers, in 1927 and Cadman's in 1935. Webster Brothers' business was bought jointly by Ribble and Lancashire United and from 1927 the Wigan-Southport service was run jointly by the two companies. Hart's Standish-Hesketh Bank-Southport service survived joint operation with Ribble until 1953, when the Preston giant bought up the Coppull independent.

All country bus services to Southport terminated at the town end of the Esplanade atop the bank overlooking the Cheshire Lines goods yard. There was space to make a U-turn across the road to turn the buses round but, with the growth of motor transport, this was considered unsatisfactory and the Corporation provided a small, off-street terminal yard for country bus services in Coronation Walk, which opened on 1 January 1933, although excursion coaches still used the Esplanade.

Congestion prevailed in this area until Ribble acquired the former Cheshire Lines terminus on Lord Street; the railway closed in 1952 and the bus station opened in 1954.

To round off the story of the country buses up to the end of the tramway era, Ribble's acquisition of Cadman's services on 11 August 1935 gave it the direct entry into Southport along Scarisbrick New Road that it had previously been denied, but Ribble could only use this route for the service from Wigan via Bescar. Even then the Traffic Commissioners denied Ribble access to the town centre as the buses were diverted from Eastbank Street along Talbot Street and Duke Street to the bus station. It is interesting to reflect that the obscure routes by which Ribble and other country bus operators entered Southport right up to deregulation in 1986 were dictated by Southport Watch Committee, the Ministry of Transport and, from 1930, by the North-west Traffic Commissioners to protect Southport's own municipal transport system in the period 1923 to 1935.

The run-down begins

In December 1928 the Roe Lane tram route was cut back from the Botanic Gardens to High Park Place, cars reversing on the single track in Mill Lane. This appears to have been done in the context of economies in service running costs at the end of the 1920s. The curtailment lasted at least into the following summer and long enough for MILL LANE to be added to the destination blinds about that time as this was not previously a short-working. Meanwhile the Cambridge Road cars maintained a service to the Botanic Gardens and the very profitable Circular Tour continued to go through Botanic Road in the summer. It is possible that this short-working of the Roe Lane route continued until the closure of the worn-out Cambridge Road line on 31 March 1931, and the service was then restored through to the gardens from 1 April because we know that Roe Lane cars were the last to go to the gardens on 1 August 1932.

The year 1930 was a landmark and turning point in the history of the tram and the bus. It was the year when the first oil-engined bus went to work (a Mercedes-Benz in Sheffield) and began a revolution in bus economics. It was the year of the Road Traffic Act, which sought to bring order to bus services with licences issued by Area Traffic Commissioners. And it was the year when Southport Tramways Committee and the Town Council agreed to replace its trams with buses.

In 1931 a Royal Commission on Transport signed the death knell of tramways nationally in one brief paragraph of its report. No reasons were given but the Commission considered that tramways were obsolescent and caused congestion and danger to the public. It recommended that trams should 'gradually disappear and give place to other forms of transport' and that no more tramways should be constructed.

Liverpool responded contrarily in 1932 by deciding to retain, modernise and extend its tramways, and over the next 10 years new fleets of cars were built and new lines were opened along radial routes to new inter-war housing developments. Leeds, Birmingham and Glasgow followed suit. This time Southport did not follow Liverpool's lead, as it had done in 1900, because it had already embarked on a policy of replacing trams with buses, like many other smaller municipal systems, including Preston, Wallasey and Birkenhead.

It seems that there was traffic congestion on Scarisbrick New Road as early as 1927, when the Tramways Committee, mooting parallel routes for the new bus service to Higher Blowick and Kew, blamed the congestion on the tramcars running along the single line in the middle of the road from St Philip's Church to Haig Avenue. The Committee thought the situation could be eased by running buses instead.

In December 1929 the Committee asked the Manager to prepare a report on the tramway system and the option for its replacement with buses. Mr Kendrew obtained estimates from the Borough Engineer and the Borough Treasurer on the cost of relaying the lines with new rails and the cost of removing the track, reinstating the road surface and buying new buses. On 24 July 1930 the Committee made the historic decision to start the conversion programme but members felt that the Tramways Department had insufficient experience of motor buses to justify wholesale replacement of the tramways with motor buses and that they should proceed step by step and get more experience and advice.

It was reported that the Crown Hotel line was in a very bad state of repair and the Cambridge Road trams were running at a loss – as we saw in the figures at the end of the previous chapter – because of the competing buses, which could be re-routed. The Committee decided on a provisional 10-year conversion programme starting with the replacement of the Cambridge Road line together with the two lines in Birkdale but not to plan any further amputations to the system for the time being.

The first part of the system to disappear was the disused tracks in Queen's Road, Leyland Road and Park Road, which were removed in 1930 to replace worn-out track elsewhere on the system. Balcony car No 20, the only car to retain its short upper saloon of 1908, was the first double-decker to be scrapped, in 1930, and car No 40 was the first ex-Company Brush car to go, some time in 1930-31. Three toastrack cars, surplus stock since the closure of the Grand Tour in 1924, were disposed of in

A letter from Thomas Kendrew, General Manager of the Corporation Tramways, to the Borough Engineer, A. E. Jackson, on 2 January 1930, during the period of transition from trams to buses. Six months before the decision on replacing trams with buses, Mr Kendrew is investigating the comparative costs of renewing the tram tracks and removing them and reinstating the roads for buses. *Graham Fairhurst collection*

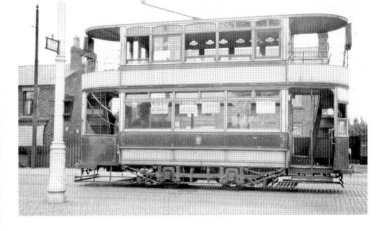

Top It is the end of the line for car No 30, looking rather forlorn at Blowick terminus in Norwood Road on 9 July 1932. The balconied cars were the first to be scrapped in the run-down of the system and all had disappeared by the end of 1932. This was one of the minority of 11 double-deckers (in a fleet of 37) on which the balconies and the offsides of the platforms by the reversed staircases remained unglazed to the end. The route number and destination boxes are mounted between the balcony rails and the canopies. Advertising contracts had been stopped in 1930 but posters in the car windows still advertised shows at local theatres and cinemas. The 'Tram Station' stop flag is attached to the silver traction pole in the middle of the junction with Hart Street. *The late Dr Hugh Nicol, © National Tramway Museum*

Middle Leaving behind the shops along Eastbank Street, rebuilt ex-Company car 9 enters the interlaced track section up the ramp on the town side of Eastbank Street bridge, outbound on route 8 to 'Crescent Road' (Eastbourne Road), Birkdale, in the summer of 1932. This route was renumbered after the closure of the Cambridge Road, Crown Hotel and Smedley lines the previous year. *The late Dr Hugh Nicol, © National Tramway Museum*

Bottom The first tramcar replacement buses were 14 Vulcan Emperors with Short Brothers bodies, delivered in 1931 to replace trams on the Cambridge Road, Crown Hotel and Smedley routes with extensions into the growing suburbs. These buses seated only 51 passengers compared with 58 or 60 seats on the trams. This one is loading on the south-west side of the Monument on the service between Crossens and Ainsdale. On the other side of the Monument a 1902-vintage tramcar with an early, arched-window upper saloon is loading for one of the remaining lines to Blowick, Wennington Road or High Park. *Cedric Greenwood collection*

1931, leaving four toastracks to continue the Circular Tour.

At the end of 1930 the Committee stopped taking new advertising contracts on the trams but advertising cards, usually for cinema and theatre shows, were displayed in the lower saloon windows. External advertisements gradually disappeared from the trams and they looked much smarter without them. The buses never carried advertising.

The closure of the tram services came in three stages:

31 March 1931	Cambridge Road, Smedley and Crown Hotel
1 August 1932	Roe Lane
31 December 1934	High Park, Blowick, Scarisbrick New Road, Bedford Park and Crescent Road

In 1930 Southport had its first double-deck bus with enclosed staircases, a Vulcan Emperor demonstrator with a Vulcan body, bought by the Corporation as No 12, and 1931 saw the first specific tramcar replacement buses: 14 Vulcan Emperors with Short Brothers' bodies. They had the usual 26 seats downstairs but only 25 seats upstairs instead of the usual 30, giving them a total of 51 seats compared with the normal 52 or 54 seats on double-deck buses of that period and 58 or 60 seats on the trams. The sheet metal roofs on these buses were suspended from outside ribs and made a noise like thunder. On 31 March 1931 they replaced trams on the York Road route to the Smedley, the Everton Road route to the Crown Hotel and the Cambridge Road route to the Botanic Gardens. The buses extended these routes at both ends to serve the growing suburbs.

The closure of the tramways was quite sad for me. The rot started in 1931 with a general run-down in maintenance, and by 1932-33 we began to notice the deterioration in the track, cars and overhead. Many people only remember the tramcars in their latter days, when woodwork creaked, traction motors groaned, the cars jolted and rocked over dropped rail joints and steel wheels rang and ground along the worn-out tracks. The

overhead wiring was in such a bad state by 1933 that a trolley could jump off the running wire and bring down a section of overhead with a spectacular fireworks display! Wide junctions with span-wire suspension were vulnerable because of the risk of a trolley jumping a frog and the total weight of the rigging. These accidents also happened in an earlier period of neglect, in the First World War (see Appendix 3, 'Memories of Southport tramwaymen').

The closure of the Everton Road and Liverpool Road line to the Crown Hotel (route 1/2) also curtailed route 9/10 at Eastbourne Road/Liverpool Road junction and this became '7, Wennington Road'/'8, Crescent Road', taking the route numbers of the abandoned Cambridge Road-Smedley service and using the destination 'Crescent Road' for the name of the terminus at the end of Eastbourne Road.

Trams continued to operate the Roe Lane end of the Crown Hotel route between the Monument and the Botanic Gardens as '1, Roe Lane'/'2, Monument', terminating in Lord Street on a crossover by Boots' chemist shop. The tracks and wires along Cambridge Road and Albert Road were retained for the Circular Tour till June 1932, when the tour returned to town via Roe Lane for its last three months of operation.

The Crown Hotel and Smedley lines were replaced by buses running (a) from Eastbank Street Square via Lulworth Road, Weld Road and Liverpool Road to the junction with Waterloo Road and (b) from Eastbank Street Square via York Road, Smedley, Burlington Road, Dunkirk Road and Sandon Road to Liverpool Road/Waterloo Road. When the Cambridge Road line closed, the Ainsdale-Crossens bus route was diverted to return via Bankfield Lane and Cambridge Road and the Liverpool Road buses operated the reverse of that route around Churchtown, Crossens and Marshside. There were diversions and variations of these bus routes over the years before they settled down to the pattern we know today.

Last trams from Churchtown

A casualty of the great depression of 1929-32, the Vulcan Motor & Engineering Company was in financial difficulties in 1931 and went into receivership, so Southport's next order for

Above The Roe Lane service had only three weeks left to run when this photograph was taken of ex-Company car 1 on route 1 outbound up Manchester Road to the Botanic Gardens in the summer of 1932. *The late Dr Hugh Nicol, © National Tramway Museum*

Below During the last weeks of the trams to Churchtown, ex-Company car 1 is seen again at the Botanic Gardens terminus of route 1 together with a toastrack car on the Circular Tour. Both tram crews are wearing their summer white-topped caps and the conductor of the toastrack car is turning the trolley with his bamboo pole. This picture was taken on 9 July 1932; route 1 closed on 1 August and the Circular Tour last ran at the end of that summer season in September. *The late Dr Hugh Nicol, © National Tramway Museum*

buses went to Leyland Motors. The Corporation Rolling Stock Engineer was not enthusiastic about Vulcan engines, which were inclined to be defective, but he preferred Vulcan bodies to Leyland's. In receivership the Vulcan Works continued to produce bus bodies and complete four-wheel lorries, including two bus bodies for Southport in 1936 to the English Electric design.

The ailing firm was taken over by Tilling, Stevens Ltd of Maidstone, and moved to the Kent works in 1938. The Vulcan name continued with the production of light lorries for the home and overseas markets and buses for Malaya till the late 1950s. Southport's 1931 batch of Vulcan buses survived in service there till 1945.

The Vulcan works at Crossens was taken over by the Brockhouse Engineering Company, which produced parts for buses and other road vehicles, including torque converters for gearless transmission, popular in the late 1930s for tram drivers switching to motor buses. When I worked there in 1938-39 Brockhouse had turned its hand to war production and was making parts for bombers. After the war it reverted to bus work, rebuilding wartime bus bodies, and made torque converters for diesel railcars.

In August 1931 the Corporation decided to get expert advice about the future of its buses and trams and engaged as consultant Arthur Fearnley, manager of Sheffield tramways and a founder, former president and currently treasurer of the Municipal Tramways Association. He was once manager of the Bradford & Shelf steam tramway and the Birkenhead electric tramways. He was a leading authority on tramway management, much in demand as a consultant, and foresaw the role of the motor bus.

Mr Fearnley reported to the Tramways Committee on 17 March 1932. He recorded the average speed of the trams as 7.2mph, probably because of the initial run-down of the trackwork and cars. He found no attempt to modernise the system with new cars and high-speed motors as in many other towns at that time nor had any serious attempt been made to recondition the old cars to make them more attractive. He did not think the speed of the cars could be appreciably improved with

one-third of the system being single track, on which cars had to wait at passing loops.

He complimented the undertaking on its efficiency and said that, of the 55 tramway systems for which he had the figures, only four systems were operating at less that Southport's expenditure and the net surplus for 1931 (£10,424) was the highest in the history of the Department with operating costs of 10.6d per car mile the lowest since 1918. Ordinary return fares were slightly under 1d a mile and workmen's returns 0.6d. The tramway system had repaid its total capital outlay (£255,509) within the last two months and was now free from capital liability.

He concluded that the Corporation would attract more passengers and more revenue by speeding up the services and making them more comfortable by abandoning the tramways and providing modern buses and he recommended that the provisional 10-year replacement programme should be halved with conversion to buses by March 1936. He also recommended a swift conclusion to the protracted dispute with Ribble over coordination of services within the borough for the benefit of both undertakings and the travelling public.

On 5 April the Council stopped all further track renewals and limited track maintenance to minor repairs only where necessary. The writing was on the wall for the deliberate run-down of the rest of the system.

From 1 November 1932 the Corporation withdrew its bus services between Ainsdale Green and Woodvale and between Haig Avenue and Kew, and allowed Ribble to pick up and set down passengers over those stretches of route and between Blowick laundry and Kew Gardens station on payment of one-third of the revenue to the Corporation. Fares were not to undercut Corporation bus fares. Ribble provided the only bus services in Southport on Sundays before 2pm and was then allowed to pick up and set down passengers at designated stops along its routes anywhere in the borough. In fact, the Company offered to operate all the town bus services but the Corporation declined, intent on developing its own bus system as the natural successor to the trams.

The Corporation stock engineer had been impressed by Leyland engines and chassis since the advent of buses 10 and 11 in 1929. In May-June 1932 I remember seeing a demonstration Leyland TD2 low-bridge bus with enclosed stairs in blue and white livery substituting for one of the trams on the Roe Lane service. Bank holiday, 1 August 1932, was the last day of the Roe Lane tram service and six of these Leyland TD2s took over on the 2nd. One, No 23, was Southport's first oil-engined bus – the rest had petrol engines. They were of normal (high-bridge) double-deck arrangement inside but the ceilings were low and everything was squashed down so that they could get under low bridges. Again they had only 51 seats. The Roe Lane tram tracks and overhead wires were retained for the Circular Tour, which continued to the end of the 1932 summer season, in September, when it finished.

The end of the line

There was one section of track in the town centre that was hardly ever used because it ran counter to the clockwise one-way circuit forming a double track from Eastbank Street Square to a trailing junction with Chapel Street and was rusty with disuse. The Eastbank Street double track converged to single track in the square and could be used to reverse cars in emergency or during track relaying. During the track renewal programme, the Tramways Committee approved it as the terminus and starting point for cars to the Infirmary for three months from December 1924, although that route became part of a cross-town operation from March 1925. The line ran past the Tramways Office in Eastbank Street (opposite King Street) and might also have been used by cars on departmental duty.

Only once did I ever see a car using this track. I was at the junction of Lord Street and Eastbank Street at lunchtime one day in 1932-33 when I saw car No 28 coming down Eastbank Street. I thought it was going around the circuit to the Monument but it stopped on the single track in Eastbank Street Square. The conductor jumped off, turned the trolley and put it on the outbound wire, which was green with weathering of the copper. The driver walked to the other end and the tram rocked over the points and headed back up Eastbank Street. It made lots of sparks and flashes on the wire and ploughed an accumulation of dirt and dust out of the grooves!

An extension of the Scarisbrick New Road tram route in January 1933 was a paradox in the context of the general run-down and abandonment of the tramway system. The Corporation decided to lop the Kew branch off the Higher Blowick circular bus route and to re-extend the Scarisbrick New Road trams from Haig Avenue over the extant tracks to the loop outside King George V Grammar School

In the Indian summer of the Southport trams, car No 28 stands at the Monument in London Square on route 7 from Crescent Road to Wennington Road in the summer of 1934. The last tram ran on 31 December that year. This was the third car to be top-covered, in 1909, with a short upper saloon. It was rebuilt in 1926 with a longer upper saloon and direct stairs and was back in the workshops in 1928 when the balconies were enclosed. It was one of only seven Southport cars rebuilt with direct stairs. Southport trams were unusual in that the end windows on both decks were not full-height up to the ceilings as on most British tramways; they were shortened by valance panels level with the transoms on the sides of the car. *J. A. Pendlebury, Cedric Greenwood collection*

Above Two balconied trams, now clean of advertisements, are heading out of town along Eastbank Street on route 4 to Bedford Park and route 8 to Crescent Road (actually Eastbourne Road) on 20 September 1931. Car No 26, nearer the camera, was the last balcony car to be scrapped, in 1932. A Vulcan Emperor bus appears at the end of the street, symbolically following the trams as they eke out their last few years in service. The Volunteer Arms is on the right and a J. E. Webb patent sewer gas ventilator lamp stands on the corner of Talbot Street (left). *S. L. Smith, courtesy of Paul Fox collection*

Left The end of the line: totally enclosed ex-Company car No 32 is standing at Crescent Road in Birkdale, the terminus of the curtailed route to the Crown Hotel from 1931. The conductor has changed the route number and destination blinds to '7, Wennington Road' for the return journey but he has not yet turned the trolley pole. No tracks were ever laid in Crescent Road or Wennington Road – the terminals of this route were actually in Eastbourne Road and Bispham Road. © *A. D. Packer*

to serve the post-war housing. The remaining 200 yards of the line beyond there to Kew Gardens was never re-opened but this extended tram service continued until the last day of the system.

In 1933, on one of my many cycle excursions over the tram routes during the school holidays, I rode my bicycle between two tramcars passing on the loop in Mornington Road. I was overtaking a car that had stopped for an oncoming car to clear the single track. The inbound track was offset to one side of the road so there was no room for me to pass the stationary car on the nearside. There was just room for me to cycle between them as I knew the cars would not deviate from their tracks. The driver of the oncoming car thought I was going into his car and dropped his lifeguard on the road. My brake levers stuck out from the handlebars and actually touched the sides of the cars. Having cleared both cars, I looked back to see the conductor of the down car leaning out of the rear platform shouting words at me that cast doubt on my sanity and my parentage. It was a stupid act on my part but it showed how safe the tramcars were in their predestinate grooves. I would not have dared to do the same thing with two passing buses.

One day in 1933 I cycled to Birkdale to have a look at the situation there. Trams were still running along Kew Road to the Portland Hotel showing the route number 4 and the destination 'Bedford Park'. The line along Eastbourne Road was still being operated to a terminus just before the junction with the abandoned tram route along Liverpool Road. This was the cut-back terminus of the former route 10 to the Crown Hotel. Cars terminating in Eastbourne Road now showed '8, Crescent Road', although this was stretching it a bit because Crescent Road was the continuation of Eastbourne Road on the other side of the junction and never carried trams. Conversely, the signal box at Crescent Road railway crossing was named Eastbourne Road!

The tracks along Liverpool Road were already covered with tarmacadam and the route was being worked by 51-seat Vulcan Emperor buses. I wondered about the wisdom of replacing larger-capacity tramcars with smaller-capacity buses when the volume of traffic on the roads was increasing.

On returning to the scene around Shaftesbury Road and the view across Birkdale Common, I could see the power station still working with its smoking 60-foot chimney stack on the boiler house and the steam rising from the rectangular, wooden cooling tower of about the same height. This power station, built for the Southport Tramways Company in 1902, still supplied dc power to Birkdale but no longer supplied traction current to the tramways. The Corporation power station at Crowlands had been expanded after amalgamation of the tramway undertakings and supplied all the current for the enlarged system from 3 October 1921. Some 1930s semi-detached council houses were encroaching on parts of

the common and building had started on the still unmade Grantham Road.

Rusty tramlines ran along Shaftesbury Road and disappeared through an iron gate into long grass in the field where the power station stood. I found that the tram shed was still there and a line of rusty traction poles with bracket arms, bereft of wires, emerged from its shadow, crossing the common like a parade of forlorn witnesses to better days. There was no decorative wrought ironwork on the brackets here but the poles still sported their British Electric Traction 'flower-pot' finials. A cast iron feeder box and a cable on a traction pole at the junction of Liverpool Road and Shaftesbury Road was the point at which the underground supply from the power station had once fed the Birkdale tramway system.

From 1 January 1934 the Westcliffe Road bus route (from Crossens) to Ainsdale was cut back to the junction of Liverpool Road and Waterloo Road while the Weld Road route (from Crossens) to Liverpool Road/Waterloo Road was extended to Ainsdale. Three months later the two routes reverted to what they were before but the Westcliffe Road service was extended from Ainsdale to Woodvale and the Weld Road route from Liverpool Road/Waterloo Road was coupled with the Roe Lane bus route to Botanic Gardens.

The changing times were reflected in the change of title of the Tramways Department to the Transport Department during 1934. The Committee chairman, Cllr T. Ball, read a paper to Southport Rotary Club on 21 February 1934 explaining why Southport was switching from trams to buses. He said trams were still paramount in shifting large numbers of passengers in the shortest time on high-density routes but on low-density lines with single track and passing loops, like Southport, it was more economic to abandon tramways as soon as the tracks were in need of reconstruction. By that stage Southport had 25 miles of bus routes and 7 miles of tramway, half of it in need of renewal at a cost of £34,000.

He said the tramways would have to be renewed and extended to serve the whole borough with 33 miles of double track and overhead wires and 50 modern cars at a total cost of £983,000 plus the cost of road widening. The conversion to motor buses, he said, would cost only £16,300. He said that both trams and trolleybuses were inflexible for emergency route diversions and vulnerable to power failures and he contended that motor buses were faster and more profitable.

The doom of the trams was sealed by Southport Town Council on 6 March 1934 when a large majority of members backed a Tramways Committee recommendation to replace all the remaining tramways with buses as soon as possible. The *Southport Visiter* of 8 March reported that Cllr Billington, a former Tramways Committee chairman, moved an amendment to retain the High Park line, on which he said the Council had spent £20,000 in the last 12 years. He said this line should not be closed until the Council knew the financial result of closing the other lines. He suspected that the arithmetic of the financial figures in the Manager's report was misleading. The cost of compensating and superannuating 20 redundant tramwaymen should be included in the debit against the buses.

Speaking against the amendment, Cllr Geldard referred to three danger traps for motorists on the High Park line and reported that lessons at the Girls Secondary School on

Scarisbrick New Road were interrupted every time a tramcar went by because of the terrible noise. Cllr Scholes said residents of Scarisbrick New Road could not get to sleep until the trams stopped running at night because of the state of the track. Cllr Hodge said a ride on a Blowick tram was like a vibro-massage: 'One gets a jolt on entering a loop and another jolt on leaving it.'

Cllr Barker said it would be uneconomical to operate and maintain one tramline. The amendment was lost and the Council agreed with Cllr Barker to make a 'clean sweep of the tramway system' and decided to borrow £33,000 to buy motor buses – twice the figure quoted by the Committee chairman a month before.

This debate sparked letters to the *Visiter* arguing for the retention and redevelopment of the tramways and the case for trolleybuses instead of motor buses. They said trams and trolleybuses consumed home-produced electricity instead of imported oil, which was taxed, and modern electric vehicles were more economical to run, more reliable, quicker in acceleration, quieter running and more comfortable than motor buses.

The Council, however, was already committed to replacing trams with motor buses and as a result of the decision on 6 March the Corporation placed an order for 20 Leyland TD3 oil-engined buses with bodies from the English Electric Company – which was then building modern tramcars for Blackpool. The new buses arrived in October and November 1934 and were numbered 29 to 48. They were not immediately put on the tram routes because the destination blinds had

A passenger boards a tram in the middle of High Park Place on its arrival at High Park terminus. The conductor has turned the destination blind but not the trolley pole for the return journey on route 4 to Bedford Park. This is ex-Company car No 7 as rebuilt by the Corporation with its original five-bay lower saloon matched by a five-bay upper saloon and enclosed balconies. The full-drop sash windows of the upper saloon are wide open as it is a warm summer's day. In the background is the road junction known as Four Lane Ends, where the single track from Old Park Lane converges with the Roe Lane tram route coming in from the left and turning into Mill Lane. Moss Lane is off to the right. The wires are still up in Roe Lane and Mill Lane, indicating that this photograph was taken before the closure of the Roe Lane line. *The late Dr Hugh Nicol, © National Tramway Museum*

not been ordered. They replaced petrol buses on existing bus services until the scheduled replacement of the trams on 1 January 1935.

The remaining tramlines, to High Park, Blowick, Scarisbrick New Road, Bedford Park and Crescent Road, closed on the last day of 1934. The last car ran from Bedford Park to High Park and then along Canning Road to the depot. Ex-Company Brush car No 35, which had previously been stripped of reusable materials, was ritually cremated on a ceremonial funeral pyre on a patch of wasteland at Crowlands in the early hours of 1935. I did not attend the final ceremony. I don't like last-day tram ceremonies – it's like going to a funeral.

I remember when the buses took over they said they were faster and more comfortable than the trams. Their average speed, including stops, was given as 9¾mph. No wonder. The bus stops were spaced further apart than the tram stops. I used to count the stops and there were only three bus stops to every five tram stops. The buses came with upholstered seats, which were certainly more comfortable than the wooden tramcar seats that dated from the turn of the century. Trams built for the Blackpool and the big city systems in the 1930s had upholstered seats too and they gave a much smoother and quieter ride than the buses.

The *Southport Visiter* reported on 1 January 1935:

'Trams in Southport are now a thing of the past and today buses will operate on all routes. The passing of the trams was celebrated last night by the members of the Transport Committee, who, accompanied by the Mayor and Mayoress, visited the Garrick Theatre and had supper at Woodhead's Café. Later they boarded a special tramcar, which ran to the depot behind the last ordinary tram of the day. The car was driven by Insp J. T. Brennan, who drove the last horse tram to the sheds 32 years ago and, including his services with the late Southport Tramways Company, has seen 44 years' tram service. He was accompanied by motorman Ainscough, the oldest Corporation tramway employee, who last year completed 43 years' service. After the arrival of the party at the depot an old tramcar was set alight as a conclusion to the celebrations.'

Statistics given at the close of the system showed that the Corporation trams had run a total of 23,416,000 miles and carried 249,730,000 passengers, an average payload of 10.66 passengers a mile, day and night. In 35 years they had operated at a profit for 24 years and incurred losses during 11 years – nine of those before the 1914-18 war. They had made a gross profit of £411,000, contributed £36,000 to the relief of the rates, repaid their capital outlay (£255,509) by 1932, and made a net profit of £59,000.

Tramway vestiges

Only one tramcar was burned, some were sold locally as shanties, sheds and summerhouses, and the rest were sold for scrap to Grahamsley's Ltd, at South Gosforth, Newcastle-upon-Tyne. The overhead wires were removed within days of closure on each line but the rails remained in place longer. The rails from the closures of 1931 and 1932 were lifted within those years and stored in the Corporation yards at Canning Road and Weld Road for sale. Much of this rail was sold to A. Devey & Co of Birmingham. The tracks of the last five lines, closed in 1934, remained in the streets of Southport for a few years after the last trams had gone and were lifted in 1938-39 for the pre-war scrap metal drive. All the steel, copper and brass from the track and overhead ended up in scrapyards at St Helens, Manchester and Birmingham, and was probably melted down to be remade into munitions for the 1939-45 war.

There remained one Corporation electric tramway that was still in operation, if only occasionally, and that was the extended railway siding along Butts Lane and Crowland Street bringing trucks of coal from the nearest railway goods yards to the town's gas works and power station at Crowlands and taking coke and chemicals out (see Appendix 4, 'The Blowick coal tramway').

Crowlands power station also supplied the pier tramway throughout its electric era from

The lower saloon of a retired Corporation tramcar made a nice summerhouse in the back garden at 38 Norwood Avenue, Southport. It retained its longitudinal seating but the central bay of the three windows on one side had been cut away for French doors and a canopy had been added when this photograph was taken in the early 1970s. When the summerhouse was dismantled in the 1980s parts of the body were used in the restoration of a Stockport tram, now running at Blackpool. *Cedric Greenwood collection*

1905 to 1950. Up to 1936 the pier had been owned by Southport Pier Company but in that year it was bought by Southport Corporation, which thus found itself of the owner of another electric tramway less than a year after the closure its 35-year-old street tramway system. Three years before that closure, Blackpool had begun the renewal of its tramcar fleet and in 1937 Southport Corporation modernised its pier trams with streamlined coachwork similar to Blackpool's new trams (see Appendix 5, 'The Southport pier tramway').

The bodies of several Southport tramcars survived locally as garden sheds and summerhouses. In about 1953-54 my son Geoffrey and I discovered three California car bodies and some double-deck bodies on an Irishman's farm at Marshside. The Californias could have been there since they were disposed of by the Corporation in about 1922-23. These trams had been converted into shanties for homeless people; there were curtains in the windows. In the post-war period people bombed out of their homes lived in old buses, trams and railway carriages around the edges of the fields.

The last surviving traction pole in Southport was the unusually stout terminal anchor pole on the corner of London Street and Chapel Street that dated from the opening of the first electric tramway in Southport in July 1900, when the trams terminated outside the Hoghton Arms. It remained there, with an upper extension, as a street lighting column until it was replaced in 1994.

The former Churchtown depot of the Southport Tramways Company, fronting on to Cambridge Road and backing on to Manor Road, survived until demolition in 1994-95. It had been used as a factory since 1918, latterly by Frank Wilson's Railex office filing systems. The former tramsheds, workshops, offices, outbuildings and stables, dating from 1873, were abandoned in a tumbledown state by the early 1990s and the architectural façade, with its archways, roundels and ornate gables, was propped up by scaffolding for the last three years. The buildings were sold in 1994 and demolished to make way for a large complex of terraced houses with the old yard gateways leading to an inner courtyard. The Cambridge Road frontage of the new houses features faithful replicas of the tramshed gables in new pressed brick, with the stone roundel in the main gable and capped by the original yellow stone copings and finials, to remind us that there was once a tram depot in this part of Cambridge Road.

The only surviving Southport tramcar is, in fact, the second oldest preserved streetcar in Britain. It is the 1876 horse tram that was found in a coalyard in Banastre Road, Southport, in 1970. It had been used as a hay and lamp store for the horse-drawn coal wagons and latterly as a coalmen's tea hut. The knifeboard seat was still largely preserved under the slate roof and the builder's

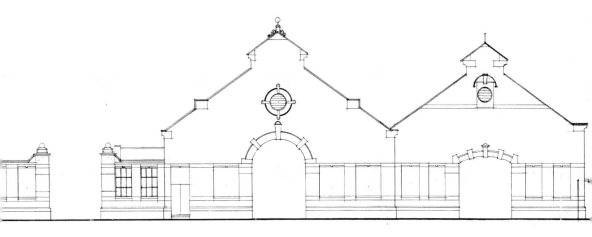

The former depot of the Southport Tramways Company still looked like a tramshed in 1989 after 71 years as a factory, as shown in this architect's outline drawing of the Cambridge Road elevation. The old buildings were structurally defective and demolished in 1995 for residential redevelopment but the gables have been rebuilt on the façade of the new terraced houses, complete with the stone roundel in the main gable and the original stone cappings and finials, as seen in the 2007 photograph. © *Martin Perry Associates/Graham Fairhurst*

nameplate, 'The Starbuck Car & Wagon Co Ltd, Tramway & Light Railway Rolling Stock Builders, Birkenhead', was still screwed to a bulkhead in the saloon.

The coalyard was only a stone's throw from the former Birkdale & Southport Tramways Company's depot in Boundary Street. The body was removed to Steamport museum, where restorers found Birkdale & Southport tickets down the backs of the seats and a programme for a variety show at the Kew Gardens Pavilion in the 1890s. When they rubbed down the paintwork they found the oval red garter sign 'Birkdale & Southport Ty. Co.' around the fleet number 7 on the waist panels. Along the letterboard above the saloon windows were the names 'London Sq., Scarisbrick Rd. & Richmond Hotel'.

Most of the Birkdale & Southport horsecars were bought second-hand. As the paintwork was rubbed down further, the words 'Oxton, Claughton & Woodside Ferry' appeared on the letterboards and the oval garter sign of the Birkenhead Street Railway Company on the waist panels. This was George Train's pioneer British tramway company of 1860 but it had

This old horse tram body found in use as a tea hut in a coal merchant's yard in Banastre Road, Southport, in 1970, turned out to be the body of the second oldest surviving street tramcar in Britain. It was Birkdale & Southport Tramways Company car No 7, a Starbuck car built in 1876 and bought second-hand from Birkenhead in 1883. It has been restored as a Birkenhead Street Railway car and is back in its native town on display in Woodside Ferry tollhouse. *Southport Visiter, Rob Jones collection*

no Act of Parliament so the Birkenhead Tramways Company was formed in 1877 as a legally constituted successor. The car had worked in Birkenhead for its first seven years before being sold to Southport in 1883 and still carried its original paintwork beneath that of the later owners.

The restored horse tram is now on display at Woodside Ferry, Birkenhead, as a Birkenhead Street Railway car. It is antedated only by a Ryde pier tram of 1871, by the same builder, in Hull Transport Museum and an 1874 Sheffield horse tram at the National Tramway Museum, Crich. It is of interest in featuring access steps on both sides of each platform so that passengers could board and alight on the offside as well as the nearside. This was a standard feature of the early tramcars built by Starbuck of Birkenhead for both Southport companies and elsewhere but the offside access under the arch of the staircase was discontinued in the late 1880s.

Southport's own memorial to its tramways is the elegant, Dutch-gabled, pressed-brick and stone façade of the former tramcar depot in Canning Road, still used as the bus garage and the base for bus operations over the same routes as the tramways. This is a rare case of the tramshed/bus garage being one of the most handsome buildings in a town of fine buildings for this was one of the most lavishly architectural tramsheds ever built and demonstrates the pride the Corporation had in its tramcars at the inauguration of the electric era.

The Corporation trams carried 12.6 million passengers in 1930-31, the last full year of the system. By 1940-41 the Corporation buses were carrying 17.5 million passengers and this figure rose to 29.6 million by 1950-51, the peak year for public transport in Southport and in Britain as a whole. Southport Corporation ran its own public transport from 1900 till 1974, when municipal bus operations

The old Corporation tram depot in Canning Road, photographed in April 2007, is a monument to Southport tramways. It was built in 1899-1900 in the style of the period in pressed brick with stone trim and the building has been used by motor buses since they took over service from the tramcars. The bold trinity of gables with scrolls, cupolas and finials over the portals are the most lavish examples of curved Dutch gables in Southport and show how much more proud the Victorians were of their 'electric cars' than we are of our diesel buses when you compare it with the plain extensions of 1932 and 1963 in Cobden Road. In tramway days a single track entered each portal and the electric wires were hung under the keystones of the arches. In recent times the wooden doors have been replaced with metal roller shutters, the arches above have been tastefully filled in with matching brickwork and the stone capitals of the pilasters have been extended as lintels over the doors in matching, reconstituted stone. The ground floor office windows have been blocked up with inset plywood panels painted turquoise, the livery of Arriva buses. The side elevation of the tramshed in Cobden Road is in similar style with brick pilasters, dummy windows, arches and roundels (portholes), all trimmed with stone string courses, copings and finials. The old tramshed is a superlative piece of industrial architecture and the front and side elevations should be listed. *Graham Fairhurst*

were taken over by Merseyside Transport as a result of local government reorganisation.

Over the next 20 years Southport buses lost their identity under a succession of strange, corporate liveries, but from 1994 to 2000 they reappeared in the former, distinctive scarlet and cream with the old borough coat of arms on the side and the legend 'Southport & District', under the aegis of Merseyside Transport. This local identity was lost again under the turquoise and cream livery of the present operator, Arriva, which took over Merseyside Transport in 2000. The Southport livery and coat of arms appeared again on a private beach bus, on a Burnley-registered Magirus army lorry chassis, running along the sands from the pier to Ainsdale beach in the summers of 2004 and 2005.

APPENDIX 1
THE ORMSKIRK &
SOUTHPORT LIGHT
RAILWAY

by Graham Fairhurst

The light railway or rural tramway to Ormskirk only ever existed on paper but it was an example of the philosophy behind the Light Railways Act of 1896. The Act was intended to spread the benefits of railways to less populous rural areas, where other railways could not afford to go, by easing the authorisation procedures, construction standards and conditions previously applied to main-line railways and street tramways. Many urban and rural tramway promoters took advantage of this Act where the line served more than one local authority. But the Act did not define what a light railway was. The Ormskirk & Southport Light Railway was proposed in 1899 as a single-track, standard-gauge light railway a little over 5 miles long. The line was to be laid in or alongside the road that now forms the A570.

The choice of route had the advantage of reducing land purchase and potential opposition from those who might not wish to part with their land. It did, however, incur the obligation to provide a proper road surface in the vicinity of the railway tracks. Most roads at this period had very poor surfaces and this particular road was sometimes impassable in winter. The engineer was R. H. Scotter and the line would have been in effect a rural extension of the Southport tramway system from Kew Gardens, rather in the style of the North American electric interurban railways.

The turn of the 20th century was the period when a great number of British towns converted their horse or steam tramways to electric traction or built completely new electric systems. The year 1898 saw the opening of the Blackpool & Fleetwood

Tramroad, one of the best examples of a British interurban line, through a similarly rural area, and perhaps the promoters of the Ormskirk project were inspired by that venture.

As a light railway, the Ormskirk line was planned for a 10-ton axle load, a 25mph speed limit and minimal signalling. Passing loops were to be provided with home signals only, and distant signals would only have been set up where the home signals could not be seen from a distance of a quarter of a mile. Halts or stopping places would not necessarily be provided with shelters or any other facilities. The proposals included regulations for the use of steam traction but also sought powers to use electric traction as an alternative. In the event, with the electrification of the Southport line to Kew Gardens there is no doubt that electric traction would have been adopted with overhead trolley wires.

Starting from a terminus in Church Fields, just below and to the south-west of Ormskirk's famous parish church, the line would have run through what were then open fields to join the main road about half a mile west of the town centre. It would then have followed the main road all the way through Scarisbrick to the Richmond Hotel outside Kew Gardens, where it would have joined up with the Southport tramway system. The light railway promoters had agreement in principle for running powers over Southport tracks along Scarisbrick New Road and Eastbank Street to the town centre circuit and the cars would have terminated in London Square.

The only diversion away from the main road was a short cut-off through a field at Carr

Cross to avoid a sharp bend in the road. The canal bridge at Pinfold was much more hump-backed in those days than it is now and as part of the railway works it was proposed to widen and regrade the approaches to this bridge so that the gradient on the Southport side would be 1 in 50 and on the Ormskirk side 1 in 33. No other major civil engineering works were proposed but the provision of a better surface to the highway was a major item in the estimated cost of the project. The steepest gradient would have been between Diglake and Pinfold, rising at 1 in 28 towards Southport.

A freight branch was proposed around the north side of Ormskirk town centre to link up with the Lancashire & Yorkshire Railway goods yard by the station on the other side of town. This branch would have formed a junction at the point where the tramway left the Southport road on the western outskirts of the town. The promoters hoped for traffic in agricultural produce from the rich mossland area it served. Taking farmers' produce to markets was one of the objects of the Light Railways Act and one of the benefits of the North American interurban. This traffic would, of necessity, be directed towards Ormskirk as Southport Town Council was not likely to sanction wagon-loads of cabbages, potatoes and turnips trundling through the streets of its fair town. However, the light railway would have passed under the bridge of the erstwhile Liverpool, Southport & Preston Junction Railway at Kew Gardens station and a spur could have been put in to connect these two lines to direct the produce of the mossland to Southport and Preston as well.

The capital sought for the project was £60,000, comprising an estimated £46,400 for the construction and highway works and £13,600 for the rolling stock. The Southport Tramways Committee agreed to give the promoters running powers over Corporation metals from Kew Gardens to London Square subject to agreement on car mileage payable to the Corporation and the local press was favourable to this and all other local, interurban tramway schemes of that period. The Company filed its plans with the Light Railway Commissioners – then inundated with schemes – but failed to raise the cash and the project was never heard of again.

It is hardly surprising that the Ormskirk & Southport Light Railway never left the drawing-board. This sparsely populated rural area was an unlikely route for an electric tramway. The Lancashire & Yorkshire Railway, which ran trains between Ormskirk and Southport via Burscough Bridge and had taken over the LS&PJ line through Kew Gardens, would probably have opposed the scheme, having already noticed a downturn in passengers on its lines in Liverpool and elsewhere in south Lancashire following the electrification of tramways. Mossland farmers were already carting their produce to stations on the line between Burscough Bridge and Southport. No point on the tram route was more than 2 miles from an existing LYR station. The population of the settlements along the route and the freight prospects were relatively small. Had the line been built, it is difficult to visualise it surviving the growth of road motor traffic after the 1914-18 war.

The Blackpool and Fleetwood line survives, however, serving two much larger towns and a populous seaside suburban belt that has grown up alongside its tracks.

APPENDIX 2
THE SOUTHPORT &
LYTHAM TRAMROAD

by T. B. Maund

Across the Ribble estuary, Lytham is clearly visible from Southport as, on a clear day, is the famous Blackpool Tower, a few miles to the north. The distance as the crow flies is only 7 miles across marsh, sandbanks and tidal waters but the road journey by way of the first bridge across the river at Preston measures 31 miles. During the late 19th century and throughout the 20th century there were many proposals for bridging the river below Preston but it is still not bridged today. None of these schemes was more fantastic than the tramways mooted around the turn of the century.

In 1896 a Southport architect, S. Speedy, suggested a tramway between Southport and Lytham, crossing the river by a swing bridge. A committee was appointed to evaluate this scheme but it was abandoned after a few months.

Two years later a Liverpool engineer, J. T. Wood, announced a three-stage plan for electric tramcars of traditional design to run through between the two towns. Commencing at a junction with the street tramways at the corner of Albert Road and Park Road, the 4ft 8½in-gauge line would have followed Park Road West then turned on to a private right of way across the marshes, following a route similar to the present-day Marine Drive. The line would have been carried over Crossens Sluice on a 350-foot-long viaduct before turning towards the coast.

It was proposed to lay two parallel tracks about 2½ miles long on the sea bed, terminating at the navigable channel of the Ribble. A moving platform mounted on four long iron shafts was to run on these tracks, which would probably have been of 2ft 8½in gauge and about 18 feet apart. Standard gauge track laid in the deck of the platform would enable a tramcar to travel across the deep

water on this contraption, which would take its power by trolley pole from a continuation of the tramway overhead wire. It would have been similar to the vehicle dubbed 'Daddy Longlegs' that operated the Brighton & Rottingdean Seashore Electric Tramroad somewhat erratically between 1896 and 1901. The platform would travel at 6mph and would be able to cope with 15-foot tides.

At the edge of the navigable channel the tramcar would pass on to a transporter bridge platform suspended from an electromotive bogie on a track along the underside of a 980-foot-long span across the shipping lanes. The span would give a headroom of 103 feet above high spring tides and the platform would skim 8 feet above high water. The line would be completed by a pier running out from the East Beach at Lytham to the landing at the north end of the bridge.

At the time these proposals were published, Southport trams were still powered by horses and Lytham trams by gas, so no through service would have been possible. However, both systems were soon electrified and an extension was built from Lytham's Market Square to the East Beach. If the cross-Ribble scheme had come to fruition there would have been 36 miles of tramways extending from Southport to Fleetwood.

A company originally named the Southport District Tramroad Company was formed and a Bill was presented to Parliament in the 1899 session. Southport Corporation supported the scheme but opposition came from Preston, which for several years had been intent on establishing itself as a seaport, building a dock and spending a great deal of money on dredging the approaches. Preston demanded that the bridge span should be at least 200 feet high over the channel but, as the Tramroad

Map of the proposed tramways across the Ribble estuary linking Southport with Lytham. *Reproduced from Modern Tramway magazine, July 1969, by courtesy of the Light Rail Transit Association*

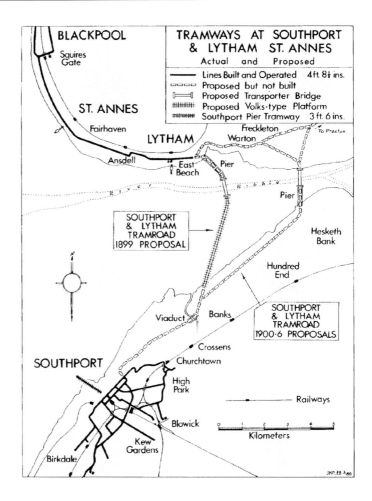

Company could offer only a 150-foot clearance, the scheme was rejected – except for the tramway to the edge of the marsh, to which there was no opposition.

Undaunted, the Company presented another Bill for the 1900 session. This changed its name to the Southport & Lytham Tramroad Company, abandoned the sea-going platform tramway and extended the tramway on the south bank north-east for a further 3½ miles to a point near Hesketh Bank, whence a 328-foot-long pier would reach the edge of the navigable channel. The transporter bridge would have been erected at that point, approximately 2 miles up-river from the original site. From the north end of the transporter bridge a double-track tramway would link up with a proposed Preston-Lytham tramway. Junctions would have been sited at Walton for Lytham and at Freckleton for Preston. The pier and its carriage would have catered for road vehicles, goods and livestock as well as the tramcars and supported a load of up to 25 tons. Crossing the channel would take 1½ minutes and the danger of collision was virtually negligible as it was recorded that shipping to and from Preston averaged only 1¾ vessels per tide.

The transporter platform was redesigned with an electric tramcar type controller on a small, upper deck for the motorman to take it across the channel. The platform would be suspended from 130-foot-long rods and it was said that there would be no 'pendulum motion'. Despite Preston's opposition, the Bill was passed. The cost of the whole scheme was estimated at £183,500, of which £53,154 was for the transporter bridge. J. T. Wood was later

An artist's impression of a Southport-Lytham car crossing the Ribble shipping lanes on the proposed transporter bridge. *Illustration by Mark Pearson in Modern Tramway magazine, July 1969, reproduced by courtesy of the Light Rail Transit Association*

prominent in the scheme for the Widnes-Runcorn transporter bridge, which opened in 1905 and was the first such structure in Britain; when it opened there were high hopes for the Southport-Lytham scheme.

Talks with the Preston-Lytham tramroad promoters cleared the way for a Southport-Preston through service via the proposed Ribble transporter bridge. Sir Hiram Maxim was an enthusiastic supporter and when his company, Vickers, Sons & Maxim, was awarded the contract in 1904, it agreed to take 25% of the contract price in shares. However, nothing was done and the Company obtained an Extension of Time Act in 1902 and again in 1906.

Southport Corporation considered opposing the 1906 Bill on the grounds that the Company's inactivity was damaging the development of the resort. The Company claimed to have spent £40,000, which would be lost if the Bill failed, so the Corporation demurred on the undertaking that the embankment should be finished by December 1907, and that part of the tramway on Corporation land by July 1908.

However, the Widnes-Runcorn bridge was suffering a great deal of technical trouble and was suspended twice in 1905. One of the problems was that the 1,000-foot span tended to sag, causing four of the 32 driving wheels to lose traction. Poor braking was another problem and, despite assurances, high winds did cause pendulum motion, which caused distortion of the decking on the platform. These problems at Widnes discouraged investors in the Ribble scheme and the Southport & Lytham Company was unable to raise the necessary capital. Under powers granted by the Southport & Lytham Tramroad (Abandonment) Act of 1909 the Company was dissolved, J. T. Wood being appointed liquidator.

APPENDIX 3
MEMORIES OF
SOUTHPORT
TRAMWAYMEN

The following texts are extracts from articles by Cedric Greenwood published in the *Southport Visiter* under the following headings.

A TOUGH LIFE FOR THE CLIPPIES
(*Southport Visiter*, 30 June 1973)

The tramcar crews were as tough as the conditions they worked in, according to Mrs Millicent Robinson, of 4 Warwick Close, one of Southport's last surviving 'conductorettes' from the dark days of World War I.

'The women conductors had to swing the trolley at the terminus the same as the men. The trolley was very heavy – there was a strong upward pull from the springs – but very few drivers would help us. The tramcars seemed to carry a lot more people than the buses do. Passengers crowded on and standing passengers sometimes filled the rear platform and the top deck, even in the rain.'

The driver, or motorman, was the skipper of his car and meted out swift justice to any troublemakers on board, literally throwing off drunks into the street if they refused to pay their fare and whisking off misbehaving children by the scruff of the neck. Trolleys brought down the overhead wires at Tabernacle junction on many occasions during her wartime service by jumping off the wire when the driver took the corner into St James Street too fast. She also had a driver who apparently appreciated the fact that nearly every tram terminus was at a public house and even abandoned his car en route in Albert Road for a quick beer in the Imperial Hotel!

BILL (91) HAD TO LEARN TRAM DRIVING – UNPAID – IN HIS FREE TIME
(*Southport Visiter*, 4 September 1981)

Bill Jaeger, the oldest surviving Southport tram driver, is 91 today. The sprightly five-footer still hops on the bus to town (sporting a Merseyside Transport tie the Director General sent him on his 90th birthday) and walks home to Poulton Road if the time invalidates his pensioner's pass. He still goes old-time dancing and goes away for an annual holiday.

Old Bill was in the first bunch of 10 men to receive a tram conductor's cash bag and ticket punch and take over from the wartime 'conductorettes' (women conductors) in 1919. He had been a stretcher bearer on the war front with the King's Liverpool Regiment from 1914. He had to learn a tram conductor's duties, the routes, stages and fares in his own time, unpaid, two hours a day for a fortnight while on leave from his regiment at the end of the war. He also had to learn to drive a tramcar and, later, a motor bus in his own time, unpaid, when he became a tramcar motorman in 1921 and a bus driver in 1924. Thus he was in the cab at the start of the motor bus era in Southport and from 1924 till the end of the tramways in 1934 he was driving tramcars and motor buses alternately.

Through the 1920s the remaining open-top tramcars were enclosed. Bill said:

'Passengers had no option but to sit on the open top deck in the rain if the car was full inside but it was very popular up there on a fine summer's day. As a conductor I was always handy with a duster to wipe the seats on the top deck for tips from the ladies. It was common in those days to go home on Christmas Eve with at least £5 in Christmas bonuses from the wealthier passengers.'

Bill remembers the time his de-wired trolley-pole brought down the network of overhead rigging at Tabernacle junction. If the car had to turn out to the left or the right the conductor had to jump off the car as it approached the junction and pull a handle on a traction pole at the side of the road to work a spring-loaded switch in the overhead wire but sometimes the trolley wheel took the wrong route. 'I came down Eastbank Street bridge,' said Bill, 'and the car turned right into St James's Street but the trolley carried straight on for Scarisbrick New Road.' When the trolley came off the wire, the spring-loaded trolley-pole erected itself and collected up the web of wires spanning the junction. 'There were live wires spitting and sparking on the pavement,' said Bill, 'and cars on this section came to a standstill. This kind of thing occurred a few times. Trolley wheels used to fly off the end of the poles and were found later sometimes 100 yards away in somebody's front garden.'

While the conductor had to leap out at junctions to switch the frog in the overhead wire, the motorman had to pull up and step off his platform with an iron lever to change the points in the track. In 1923, however, some of the points were automated, being set by the power being drawn by the approaching car. A car would cruise, power off, through the points for the line straight ahead or put power on to turn out to the left or right.

Bill also recalls that the motorman had to step off the car to switch primitive signal lights on the traction poles in Mornington Road and Sussex Road governing the single-line section around two corners in between. 'The driver who got there first, whether from Mornington Road or Sussex Road, switched the light on and he got the road. Any oncoming tramcar had to wait.'

The tramcar motorman had to stand up at his controls all his eight-hour shift, whirling the big, brass handbrake handle at each stop, jumping off to change the manual points at junctions and again to switch the single-line

signals. Being rather short in stature (five feet), Bill found driving a tramcar, particularly the handbrake, 'like hard labour'. He felt quite tired at the end of a day's duty.

Bus driving was easier. He was sitting down and his service brake was a footbrake. But bus driving between the wars was still not easy by today's standards. There was no self-starter, no power-assisted steering, no semi-automatic gear change, no indicators.

'We had to swing a crank handle to start the bus after the lay-over at the terminus. I got my job bus driving through a driver having his wrist broken by a kicking crank handle. When the oil-engined buses came in we had a whiffle at the depot to start the buses in the morning. It was a kind of battery-powered starter motor on a truck and it was connected up to the crank handle. We had to keep the engines running at the terminus or we'd never get them started again.

All the buses had crash gearboxes and we had to double de-clutch through each gear shift up and down. The petrol-engined buses were not very powerful and we had to climb Eastbank Street bridge in first gear. And while you were changing down the gears with your left hand for a corner you had to give a hand signal with your right hand. Somehow you had to steer as well!

When the buses took over the tram routes we found that the tram stops were too close together. We'd only just got into third gear when we had to stop again. So the Corporation spaced out the stops; there were about two bus stops to every three tram stops.'

Driving a pre-war bus was made more difficult during World War II with blackout conditions, unlit streets and navigation sidelights 'about the size of a shilling'. There was compulsory overtime to transport round-the-clock shift workers to Brockhouse Engineering Works at Crossens and Woodvale airfield construction and to provide substitute services for railways and tramways in Liverpool where the tracks had been bombed in the blitz.

Bill retired from the buses in 1955.

BIRKDALE TRAMS RESPECT SUNDAY AND DRIVE PAST CHURCHES SLOWLY

(from Part II of an article about Southport tramways, *Southport Visiter*, 9 June 1973)

Mr Norman Hamer, of 88 Liverpool Road, tells the story of motorman Harry Barlow, who lived in a house by the loop at St John's Road on the Crown Hotel line. As the outbound car entered the loop, he would whirl around the big brass handle, leap off the platform, dash across the road 'like a scalded cat', collect a can of tea left at his garden gate and rejoin his car just as it was coming to a stop in the middle of the loop. 'I would say Harry Barlow was the fastest tram driver in Southport,' says Mr Hamer. 'He really used to drive a tram; he could really go. He was a wonderful driver – very alert and very quick in his actions. He should have been driving jets, that chap. He was no mug. A lot of people remember Harry Barlow.'

APPENDIX 4
THE BLOWICK COAL TRAMWAY

by Cedric Greenwood

The Cinderella of the Southport tramways was the line along Butts Lane and Crowland Street. It was a municipal heavy railway system hauling trucks and tank cars from the nearby railway goods yard. The line brought coal to the Corporation gas works and power station and carried away the by-products of coal gas production, namely coke, benzol and other chemicals.

At a cursory glance it looked like another tramway, paved in granite setts, with an overhead electric wire, but this was a single line offset along the north side of the road, laid alongside the kerb in railway standard heavy rail with check rails like a dock railway, the traction poles were timber, like telegraph poles, with plain wrought-iron brackets (no scrollwork) and the overhead wire was lower than for double-deck tramcars. The line was worked by two box-cab electric locomotives that looked rather like railway goods brake-vans with an unglazed driving platform at each end and a trolley pole on the roof with a horizontal, outside spring.

The line from Blowick station sidings crossed Norwood Road on an ungated level crossing at the corner of Butts Lane about 50 yards beyond the tram terminus and continued straight along Butts Lane and Crowland Street. At the corner of Wennington Road it was joined by another single line from Meols Cop station sidings, which left the main-line embankment after Cobden Road and descended through a 90-degree curve to join the street railway. At Crowlands the line passed over a weighbridge and branched out into a maze of short spurs around the coal store, the gas works and the power station. These sidings totalled 1¾ miles of single track. One siding extended across Canning Road to the piles of coal and coke stored between Canning Road and Wennington Road, known as 'the Blowick Alps'.

These Corporation sidings were laid from Blowick station by the Lancashire & Yorkshire Railway in 1871 and from Meols Cop station by the Liverpool, Southport & Preston Junction Railway in 1891. They were worked by draught horses from the opening of the gas works in 1872 and the power station in 1894. The Gas Department wanted to buy a steam locomotive in 1915 but the Electricity Department won the day and the system was electrified in 1916.

To save the cost of buying a new electric locomotive, quoted as £480, the Electricity Department bought a second-hand Dick, Kerr tramcar, the little-used 'Committee Car' No 13 of 1900, from the Tramways Department for £379 17s 5d and converted it, using the old truck, motors, control equipment and trolley pole. This unit, however, with only two 25hp motors, proved to be underpowered for hauling coal trains and was prone to breaking down.

The coal tramway was operated initially by the Gas Department but with electrification the operations passed to the Electricity Department, which provided the traction poles, the overhead, the haulage, the driver and brakeman while the Gas Department retained responsibility for the trackwork. During the 1920 coal strike, however, the Gas Department was dissatisfied with the breakdowns and torpid shipment of coal from the railway yards and took over operation from the Electricity Department, buying the locomotive, the traction poles and overhead.

The Gas Department bought a new traction unit with four 25hp motors on two heavy railway bogies and electric equipment, supplied new from Dick, Kerr & Company of

The 100hp bogie, box-cab, electric trolley locomotive that was the staple power unit on the Blowick coal tramway from 1920 to 1940. It is pictured outside the one-road loco-shed in the gasworks yard. *Graham Fairhurst collection*

Preston in 1920, although the four-wheeler was kept as a relief and yard shunter at the gas works and power station. Both locomotives were assembled at Crowlands with functional, home-made, wooden bodies housing the cabs and control equipment and supporting the overhead trolley pick-up. They looked grim and shabby but carried a maroon paint scheme under the grime of their coal-dusty working environment.

Electric traction was superseded, oddly enough, by steam with two industrial 0-4-0 saddle-tank engines: first a new Peckett in 1940, augmented in 1947 by a second-hand, rebuilt Manning, Wardle as a relief engine. They also carried the maroon paint scheme and the Peckett, whose driver proudly kept it in a clean, smart condition, was lined-out and adorned with the borough coat of arms on the cab sides

plus tank-side nameplates that read *County Borough of Southport Gas Department*.

Following nationalisation of the electricity supply in 1948 and of gas in 1949, the Peckett was deployed to Darwen gas works in 1952 and is now preserved, carrying *North Western Gas Board* nameplates. It was stabled for a time at Steamport museum in Southport's former Derby Road loco-shed and is now on the Ribble Steam Railway at Preston. Both electric locomotives were retained for emergencies until the wire came down with the end of dc electric supply from Crowlands power station in 1950. A new Ruston & Hornsby 0-4-0 diesel shunter took over the job from the steam engines in 1952 and worked all traffic on the Corporation sidings until they closed in 1961. The coal tramway was removed directly and Butts Lane and Crowland Street were repaved.

APPENDIX 5
THE SOUTHPORT
PIER TRAMWAY

by Cedric Greenwood

Southport has Britain's oldest promenade pier and it is still the second longest public pier in these isles (ie excluding oil jetties). Such a long pier requires a railway or tramway and the line along Southport Pier was the first of its kind. It is now in its sixth reincarnation and one of the few remaining pier railways in Britain.

It has had four forms of traction – manual, cable, electric and diesel – or seven forms if you sub-divide the electric and diesel traction into third-rail electric, diesel-mechanical, diesel-electric, diesel-hydraulic and battery-electric. It has had three different gauges, although it has standardised on 3ft 6in for all but the last 50 years of the 20th century, when it was a miniature diesel railway. For most of its history it was a railway laid on sleeper track, fenced off along one side of the pier, but now, as at the beginning, it is a tramway laid flush with the timber deck along the middle of the pier.

The pier was built in 1859-60 by the Southport Pier Company primarily as a promenade pier but also as a landing pier to save steamer passengers being ferried in boats between ship and shore. To reach the steamers in the South Channel of the Ribble estuary across the flat sands, the pier was an incredible 1,200 yards (1 kilometre) long but only 5 yards wide. The first tramway was laid along the middle of the pier deck and opened on 7 May 1863, worked by one hand-pushed car, which could hardly have coped with all the passengers of a paddle steamer and was probably used mainly as a luggage trolley.

As the channel shifted, the pier was lengthened in 1865 and again in 1868 to an ultimate 1,465 yards to reach the steamers at the channel's edge. In the 1865 extension the deck was widened to 8 yards, with the tramway rebuilt as a railway realigned along the south-west side, railed off from the pedestrian walkway. The railway was now 1,188 yards long and was converted to cable traction with an endless cable (1¼ inches thick and 2,400 yards long) running both ways and an 8hp steam engine in a winding house halfway along the pier, connected by electric telegraph to the two terminals. This was an adaptation of the system used in mines and quarries and on the London & Blackwall Railway from 1840 to 1848. Part of the wooden engine house on the pier is still there today.

The North of England Carriage Company of Preston built the two-car, cable-hauled train. They were wooden, open, centre-entrance cars with back-to-back 'knifeboard' seating for a total of 100 passengers and the train made the trip along the pier in 5 minutes. There was a fatal accident on 1 August 1865 when one of the cars derailed and two passengers were severely injured; one died.

Recent research into the accident reports discloses conclusively that the driving car was equipped with cable gripper apparatus and brake levers to start and stop the tram instead of being fixed to the cable. In this the Southport pier train was nine years in advance of San Francisco's famous cable cars and 20 years before the tramway over Highgate Hill, London. San Francisco has always been regarded as the pioneer of gripped cable technology but the idea was patented in Britain in 1838 so we don't know if Southport was the pioneer but it was certainly one of the first.

After repairs and inspection, the line reopened on 5 March 1866 and in the ensuing period achieved brief fame on 9 October 1872 when the train was elegantly fitted out to convey Princess Mary of Cambridge (the Duchess of Teck), the Duke of Teck and their entourage during a Royal visit to Southport.

The railway was rebuilt in 1892-93 with new track, cable and winding engine and new, covered cars. It was previously believed that this was the time when the pier train ceased to be fixed to the cable and was fitted with cable grippers and brakes for driver control but this was evidently a complete renewal of an existing cable-gripping system.

Southport's 1,465-yard pier was the second longest in Britain after Southend pier (2,346 yards). Fires in the pier head pavilion in 1897, 1933 and 1959 reduced it to 1,211 yards, although by that time the steamers had gone. As rebuilt the pier is 1,154 yards long today. The railway or tramway has generally been a bit shorter than the pier, ranging between 1,188 and 900 yards.

Southport pier was busy around the turn of the 20th century with a fleet of more than 100 sailing trawlers moored off the pier head, many of them giving pleasure trips in the holiday season, and paddle steamers also plied to 15 ports and resorts from Beaumaris to Barrow. The last steamer left for Blackpool in August 1923 because of the silting-up of the channel.

After the 1897 pier head fire the railway was shortened by 109 yards and in 1905 the line, still railed-off on one side of the pier deck, was electrified by the British Westinghouse Company with a live third rail on the seaward side fed at 500 volts dc taken from the town supply from Crowlands power station. The new train entered service on 3 April and cut the running time to 3 minutes. It consisted of three long, bogie cars: an arched-roofed, saloon traction car, with two 30hp Westinghouse motors, marshalled between two open, high-sided driving trailers. From about 1912 the driver was confined to the traction car in the middle of the train. It could run as a one-, two- or three-car train, as traffic warranted. Each car could carry 60 seated and 28 standing passengers so the three-car set could carry up to 264 passengers and this was just what was wanted to meet the paddle steamers. The enclosed traction car ran the winter service on its own.

The Corporation bought the pier from the ailing Pier Company in 1936 and the line was closed for renewal, re-opening in 1937. At the same time the electric cars were rebuilt by Hill Brothers, coachbuilders, of Southport, with new bodies on the old running gear with extended underframes. The streamlined coachwork was specifically modelled on the tramcars built by English Electric and Brush for Blackpool Corporation in 1934-37, the two open trailers resembling the famous Blackpool 'boat' cars. The cars were even painted in Blackpool cream and green livery instead of Southport cream and scarlet – but not until two years of salty air had proved the Corporation's idea of unpainted 'silver' steel panels to be impractical. They were painted in 1939 when they were re-equipped with new bogies by the Central Wagon Company of Wigan and new motors and controllers by Metropolitan, Vickers of Manchester.

These relatively modern cars were prematurely scrapped when Crowlands power station replaced dc with ac supply in 1950 and the line was scaled down to a miniature railway on the 1ft 11½in gauge with diesel locomotives: diesel-mechanical (1950-53), the diesel-electric *Silver Belle* (1954-73) and the diesel-hydraulic *English Rose* (1973-2000) on the same track.

The pier and its railway passed from the ownership of Southport Corporation to Sefton Borough Council with the reorganisation of local government in 1974. In 2000 the pier closed in a dangerous condition after decades of decay from lack of maintenance. Forty of the 400 cast-iron piles, or columns, needed replacing and everything on top – the steel girders and trusses and the timber deck – had to be replaced. The pier no longer serves sea trips and is only an elevated promenade that runs most of the way over land, sand and mud, spanning only the Marine Lake, although high spring tides creep in halfway along its length, when it also becomes an angling platform.

This looked like the end of the pier story but Southport Pier Trust was formed and rallied public opinion to save the pier. The Borough Council agreed by the margin of one vote. Financial assistance came from the European Objective One Fund and the Heritage Lottery Fund, which diverted money from a Lord Street restoration scheme to save the pier.

Southport still has one tramline today, serving the long promenade pier. The battery-electric two-car unit was pictured at the pier head terminus when new in August 2005. *Ron Phillips*

As rebuilding work proceeded the cost rocketed from £4.1 million to £7.2 million, to which the Borough Council contributed a massive £3.5 million. The new pier, now 1,154 yards long, re-opened in 2003 with an ultra-modern pier head pavilion and a new 3ft 6in-gauge tramway, with running rails salvaged from the previous miniature railway plus new checkrails, stretching for 1,114 yards along the centre of the pier deck – but no tram.

As the project was overspent, extra funding for a tramcar was found by the Mersey Waterfront Regional Park with assistance from the Borough Council and the Pier Trust. The car was built by UK Loco at Cropthorne, Worcestershire, with aluminium coachwork on mild steel frames and motors and control equipment supplied by Electric Vehicle Systems of Gateshead. The tramcar entered service on the pier on 1 August 2005.

It is a battery-electric, double-ended, close-coupled, two-car unit on four bogies, totally enclosed, of modern design with one-piece windscreens. The original wavy blue and yellow livery with the legend 'Mersey Waterfront' was superseded in 2007 by an overall advertising livery of dark blue with a light blue trim under the windows and the legend 'Ocean Plaza', a retail complex on the seafront. It runs half-hourly in winter and quarter-hourly in summer on its 5-minute trundle along the length of the pier, the same journey time as the cable tram of 1865-1905. The car's maximum speed is 16mph but the normal operating speed along the pier with pedestrians is 10-12mph. The 96 volt dc battery, which is said to last 10 hours in service, is recharged overnight from an electric point at the pier head buffer stops.

The unit is 71ft 6in long, 7ft 10½in wide and stands 9ft 6in above the rails with doors at each end on the south-west side only. The floor is 2ft 3½in high, with two steps up from the pier deck and wheelchair access. The two saloons have 6ft 4in headroom and fixed, transverse, double seats each side of the gangway for a total of 74 passengers plus two wheelchair spaces and no standing. The total weight of the unit with batteries is 18 tons.

The modern tram is a pleasant way to view

the seafront from this windswept pier, especially in winter. As the pier tram is owned and operated by Sefton Borough Council, it would not look amiss to see the borough coat of arms, a gold cross on a blue shield, on the car in the tradition of municipal tramways. As the 15-minute headway is inadequate for the summer crowds and the pier restoration was a heritage project, it would be nice to see the service augmented with a replica of one of Southport's semi-open California cars or open toastrack cars for visitors to enjoy the salty air along the pier in summer. Again as a heritage project, it would seem more appropriate for a Victorian or Edwardian-style pavilion to house the café and the interesting working museum of old penny-in-the-slot machines at the pier head terminus.

INDEX